Conch Salad

Page - 75

Conch Fritters

Page - 60

Avocado Half with Crab Salad

Page - 141

Appetizers

Page - 53 - 66

Beer Corn Cheese Bread

Goombay Fruit Salad

Page - 70

Jerk Chicken Wings

Page - 192

Conch Emerging From
Its Shell

Broiled Crawfish

Page - 171

Corn Beef Mounds

Page - 129

Chicken Souse & Johnny Cake

Page - 122 - 88

African Beef Stew

Page - 119

Curried Chicken

Page - 121

Samana Baked Red Snapper

With Conch Stuffing

Page - 156

Andros Stuffed Crabs

Page - 200

Vegetable Fried Rice

Page - 211

Pigeon Peas 'n Rice

Page - 206

Stuffed Baked Breadfruit

Page - 249

Fried Plantains

Page - 244

Plantain Santa Maria

Page - 225

Dillie Dinner Rolls

Page - 97

Barbecue Turkey Roll

Page -188

Ginger Shrimp

Page - 177

Guinep Royale
Juice & Roasted Seeds
Pages - 63 - 26 - 354

Coconut Tart

Page - 277

Mango Salsa with Breadfruit Chips

Page - 66 - 56

Avocado Dessert

Page - 324

Guava Duff

Page - 337

Seagrape Jam

Page - 362

Confections

Page - 351 - 367

Solar Rum Punch

Page - 375

Many Tastes Of The Bahamas

& Culinary Influences of the Caribbean

This cookbook is spiced with historical facts and great tips.
It is also flavoured with delightful information
about exotic fruits, vegetables, spices, dishes
and other interesting things
about the Caribbean.

By Lady Darling

Many Tastes Of The Bahamas
and Culinary Influences of the Caribbean
by
Lady Darling

First Printing - December 2001

ISBN 976-8108-60-6

Layout, design and photography by:
Azaleta Ishmael-Newry
Nassau, The Bahamas

Cover Dish: Mango Salsa with Breadfruit Chips

Bon Appétit!

Formal Dinners at Government House

were an elegant affair.

The recipes in this cookbook reflect those that were

prepared for Heads of State...

as well as for everyday living.

They are yours to enjoy!

This book is dedicated
to my mother Olga Merdina
who was a great cook and
who took the time to write out
any new recipe she found
and shared them with me
all of my life.

To my son George for requesting that I write this book

To my sons Philip & Timothy for always eating whatever I cooked

To my husband Sir Clifford for supplying the fruits and vegetables
from his garden and being my taste-tester

Special Thanks

Azaleta Ishmael-Newry
Kelli-Anne Sands
Pyramid Marketing
Patricia Beardsley Roker
Lynn Anne Martin
Tonya C. Collier
Chargrega D. McPhee
Winifred L. Murphy
Olive Rolle
Melvenia A. Cash
Derek W. Smith
Alain Torchon-Newry
Laverne Sula
Nibia Souza
Timothy Allan Collier

✺

Acknowledgements

Endorsement

The Bahamas Ministry of Tourism

✺

Sponsors
Burns House Limited
Allied Domecq Spirits & Wines
Commonwealth Brewery Limited
P. W. Albury & Sons Limited

✺

Their Excellencies

Sir Clifford Darling
and Lady Darling

Photo by Franklyn Ferguson

A Formal Dinner at Government House

*Menu for Government House Formal Dinner
honouring Mr. Nelson Mandela*

❋❋❋❋❋❋❋❋❋❋❋❋❋❋❋❋❋❋❋❋❋❋❋❋❋❋❋

*Minced lobster in puff pastry
Served with crab claws
A colourful
explosion -
Array of garden
greens
Balsamic vinai-
grette dressing
Bahamian
grouper
"Macadamia"
covered with a nut
crust laced with
vanilla bean
sauce
Bouquetere of
fresh vegetables
Mushroom potato
Fresh guava
mousse
Petite fours*

❋❋❋

GOVERNMENT HOUSE

*Menu For Dinner Function
December 20, 1993*

*Minced Lobster in puffed pastry
Served with crab claws*
* * * * * *
*A colorful explosion
Array of garden greens
Balsamic vinaigrette dressing*
* * * * * *
*Bahamian grouper "Macademia"
covered with a nut crust
laced with vanilla bean sauce*

*Bouquetere of fresh vegetables
Mushroom potato*
* * * * * *
Fresh guava mousse

The Bahamas and Caribbean

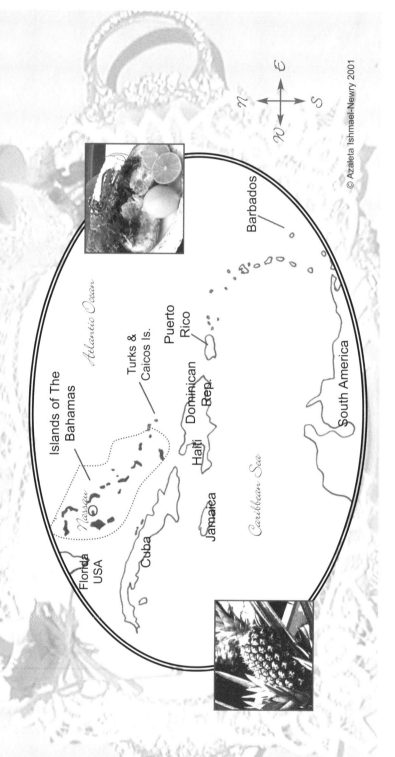

Florida USA

Cuba

Islands of The Bahamas

Nassau

Atlantic Ocean

Turks & Caicos Is.

Jamaica

Haiti

Dominican Rep.

Puerto Rico

Caribbean Sea

Barbados

South America

N W E S

Contents

List of Helpful Tips - 12

List of Historical Facts - 13

About the Author - 14

History of Government House - 18

How To Use This Cookbook - 22

Food Preparations - 24

List of History of Fruits, Vegetables & Spices - 33

Beverages - 41

Appetizers & Dips - 53

Salads & Dressings - 67

Breads & Rolls - 83

Soups & Curries - 101

Breakfast & Lunches - 125

Fish & Seafood - 153

Meat & Poultry - 181

Dinner Side Dishes - 203

Vegetables - 237

Meat Sauces & Gravies - 255

Pastries, Pies & Tarts - 267

Cakes, Cookies, Dessert Sauces & Icings - 293

Duffs, Puddings & Cheesecakes - 319

Confections, Jams, Jellies & Chutneys - 351

Party Drinks & Punches - 369

Index - 383

Bibliography - 408

Helpful Tips

A garlic secret - 34

Chinese secret for hot towels - 37

Clean-up operation - 35

Colorful "bowl" for dip - 40

Crisper fried foods - 36

Decorative ice cubes for drinks - 34

Freeze pastry crust during holiday "rush" - 39

Fresh lime or lemon juice year-round - 40

Gravy secret - 38

Have a clean cake platter - 39

How to handle roast meats - 36

How to keep fresh ginger fresh - 37

How to keep red cabbage red - 38

How to keep the mush out of a mushroom - 35

To keep stuffed green peppers from collapsing - 38

How to thicken a fruit sauce - 40

If you don't have a rolling pin - 39

If you don't have a gravy browner - 39

My family tip when cooking rice - 40

No more dark mushrooms - 35

No-lump gravy - 38

No-stick rolling pin - 39

Patio Punch - 34

Perfect baked potato - 36

Quick mashed potatoes - 37

Rest in peace - 35

Rum flavoured ice cubes - 34

Save on paper towels - 36

Sweet "secret-less sugar" - 35

Tamarind as a marinate - 36

Tasty way to save cooking time - 37

Thicken a sauce at the last minute - 38

To avoid eggs cracking while boiling - 35

To avoid "the pot boiling over" - 37

To hasten chilling - 39

To keep a moist cake moist - 40

To keep butter from burning - 34

Too much bacon - 36

Warm plates for a crowd...easily - 37

Where to store herbs - 34

Historical Facts

First in the Americas - 52

Pre-Columbian Cultures - 106

The Arawaks - 263

Oldest Influences - 135

Barbecue & Jerk - 192

East Indies / West Indies - 210

Global Exchange - 95

Tabaca / Tobacco - 217

The Potato - 82

Seeds of Change - 241

New World Crops - 143

From Africa to the Americas - 219

African Culinary Influences - 185

Sugar & Spice - 286

Legacy of Christopher Columbus - 382

About the Author

Lady Darling with 3 of her 4 brothers
and her mum in 1949.

When I think back to my childhood, the preparation of food has always been a central focus of my life. I was born and grew up in the quaint village of Fox Hill, on the island of New Providence, a village that was known for its early nineteenth century settlers who were liberated Africans mainly from the Yoruba tribe. I was a middle child, the only girl surrounded by four boys. "Mummy," a single mother, had to work outside of the home in order to make ends meet. In spite of the traditional belief that food preparation was "woman's work," my brothers had to learn to cook and help out around the kitchen because Mummy depended upon us to keep the house in her absence.

However, even though my brothers could cook, my chores included meal preparation and baking the bread. It seemed that I was always baking bread because our diet consisted of two meals where bread was usually the main component: breakfast and lunch. For breakfast we sometimes ate porridge but, more often, we ate bread with guava jam. For lunch, we ate bread and butter with avocado, when it was in season, or the fruit that Fox Hill is famous for, the sapodilla.

I was about ten years old when I embarked upon my career as a baker. Always a tiny person, I can remember that my chin was barely above the tabletop, so my mother stood me on a wooden box, which became an essential part of my kitchen accessories. Our oven was a large chest constructed of wood, tin-lined with metal rods that served as shelves. Looking very much like a refrigerator, the oven was painted green and sat in a corner of our kitchen.

After the "first rising" of the bread, the dough was put into the six loaf pans that we owned. My brothers were responsible for "starting the fire" in the coal stove that looked very much like a modern day hibachi. I can remember them fanning and fanning the flames because the coals had to be just right when the stove was placed into the oven for about ten minutes to heat it up. Since we did not possess such a thing as a thermometer or gauge of any kind to determine the temperature in the oven, my mother had taught me how to guess when the oven was the right temperature to place the loaves on the shelves. While they were cooking, I had to be careful not to open the door too wide so as to let the heat out when I checked on the bread, shifting the pans around so they would cook evenly, until they were nice and brown. To test whether or not the bread was done, I would thump each loaf with my thumb and forefinger until I heard that perfect hollow sound. By the time I was fifteen years old, it was said that I was the best "baker" in the neighbourhood.

Occasionally we were allowed a very special treat of a slice of warm bread and newly made guava jam. Otherwise, when the bread was done, it would go straight into the breadbox after cooling.

When we ran out of bread, which was very often, I was always informed before I went to sleep so that I could get up earlier than usual in the morning in order to make a Johnny Cake for that day's breakfast and lunch. After I had prepared it, the Johnny Cake would be placed into an iron skillet and, on rainy mornings, baked on top of the stove. If the weather was good and the boys had time or during school vacations, they would light up the coal stove outside and the Johnny Cake would be baked in the skillet there.

Cooking really took up a lot of my time, growing up. For example, when I cooked Bahamian Peas and Rice, I would have to boil the peas in rain water on the coal stove outside for about two hours. That meant I could not leave the yard for the entire time because the fire had to be tended constantly and the peas checked regularly. The "kitchen stove" inside the house was a tricky 3-burner affair that necessitated I became an expert at regulating its flame. The rice could also be cooked there. Especially when cooking rice, I also learned the value of a "damper" or heat diffuser under the pot so that the rice would not stick to the bottom. I did this with mixed emotions because the burned-on rice, which we called the "pot cake," was "ever so tasty!"

We had an icebox in our kitchen, which kept perishable foods fairly fresh for a few days. Frozen foods or meats were not available to us in those days, so we ate a lot of tinned meats, especially corned beef. I became very creative in cooking corned beef. I have included in this book some of those wonderful dishes that I created during my childhood.

Living on a small island surrounded by the waters of the North Atlantic Ocean, whenever my brothers had time they would go fishing so, from time to time, we would augment our diet with fresh fish. Sometimes we would buy fresh fish from the "fish man" that used to come around the neighbourhood with a wooden box fastened to the handlebars of his bicycle.

On Sundays, Mummy took over the kitchen to cook the sumptuous traditional Bahamian Sunday dinner of fried chicken, peas & rice, macaroni and cheese, potato salad and fried plantain, guava duff for dessert washed down with a pitcher of homemade switcher. The boys were responsible for killing and dressing the chicken before we went to church every Sunday.

During our school vacations, while Mummy was at work, the boys would scout around our neighbourhood doing odd jobs and "locating" anything that we could cook. One day they brought home a live turkey in a crocus sack, which they attempted to kill and dress like the traditional Sunday chicken. The exercise got a little out of hand because the turkey was so big, but they got it done and brought it to me, the resident cook, to prepare. So I did, using the only method I knew for cooking poultry: I fried it in the iron skillet on the coal stove outside!

We grew all of our fruits and vegetables, which I would then find creative ways to prepare. We had pigeon peas, split peas, okra, cassava and pumpkin soups. I also used my imagination with the cabbage and beet leaves.

August was the month devoted to preserving the summer harvest. Jam making was a family affair with Mummy supervising the whole project. The boys would pick the guavas, gooseberries, sorrel and plums to make jams and jellies. Guava jam was definitely our overwhelming favorite. We would be sure to cook several batches of that, filling every available jar of all sizes. As children, like children all over The Bahamas, we would eat our fill of plums, guineps, tamarinds and sea grapes as they came into season. Most of us seemed to lose our taste for these tart tropical delights when we became adults. I, however, have never lost my taste or fascination for this

The model of Lady Darling's childhood home above was made by her from Balata, a rubber-like substance which is great for sculpting and is from Guyana.

summer bounty, finding more and more creative ways to include them in the dishes I learned to cook over the years.

My mother, Olga Merdina, was a truly great cook whose influence inspired that little ten-year-old girl back in Fox Hill to constantly use her imagination when preparing food. She introduced me to the magic of combining different tastes and the joy that comes from putting a delicious meal on the table, preparing me for my role in which I supervised meal-planning during my tenure as The Bahamas' First Lady. My mother was also an adventurous cook, constantly creating new dishes and trying new recipes. She always took the time to write out new recipes and she generously shared them with me all of my life. It is to her that I dedicate this book. ❖

History Of Government House

Photo by Azaleta Ishmael-Newry

Government House, known as Mount Fitzwilliam after Governor Richard Fitzwilliam who followed Woods Rogers in 1733, is located at the top of George Street. The Governors of The Bahamas from Fitzwilliam to Lord Dunmore lived in the house until 1802. The building of the new Government House was begun in 1803 and completed in 1806.

American naval forces "invaded" Nassau on March 4th 1776, capturing the city without firing a shot. United States marines quickly occupied Nassau's two forts and established head-quarters at Government House. The Americans stayed in Nassau for two weeks. They received royal hospitality from the natives, a custom familiar even to today's visitors.

When they sailed away on March 17th - loaded with ammunition and foodstuffs - they went en masse, thereby forfeiting their prize. Many historians believe that had they chosen to maintain control, Nassau and The Bahamas would today be a part of the United States.

In front of the house - midway up a flight of 15 steps - stands a statue of Christopher Columbus. It was modeled in London by an aide of Washington Irving for Governor Sir James Carmichael Smythe. The Governor presented it to the Colony in 1831.

The eastern wings were built early in the twentieth century, but the structure was so badly damaged in the 1929 hurricane that it had to be demolished. The new building was ready to receive Sir Bede and Lady Clifford in 1932.

The mansion, built of wood and stone, is 250 feet long and has 32 rooms. Ten acres of grounds surround Government House in which are planted hundreds of tropical plants and a variety of vegetables.

Members of the Royal family have held the office of Governor General in several Dominions but it was a unique and pleasant experience for a small, though very ancient, colony to have a former King in the office of the Sovereign's representative. His Royal Highness the Duke of Windsor accepted the appointment as Governor of The Bahamas in the early part of the second world war. He served from 1940-1945.

In 1992, Sir Clifford Darling was appointed Governor General of The Bahamas. He and his wife, Lady Darling, established residence in Government House as the Queen's Representatives. To continue the preservation of Mount Fitzwilliam, Lady Darling invited members of the local Garden Clubs to assist in the beautification of the gardens as well as to create floral arrangements for special occasions.

In 1992, Their Excellencies hosted dignitaries from around the world for the Quincentennial, the commemoration of the meeting of the Old and New Worlds.

❖

Introduction

Why would you need an introduction to a cookbook? Will cooks who buy this book, intent upon trying the recipes, actually read an introduction? I believe they will if it tells a story. The history of the world and its peoples can be told by the food each region produces. This cookbook, with recipes calling for ingredients familiar to Caribbean cooks, tells the story of the tropical islands of the Caribbean region - in the very special language of food.

The historic "Encounter" of the Old World and the New took place on a tiny island in The Bahamas that the native peoples called Guanahani. As you turn the pages of this book, you will step back in time, preparing dishes using indigenous foods cultivated by the Taino people who occupied these islands in pre-Columbian times. You will cook with vegetables like cassava or manioc, as they called it, sweet potatoes, maize and peanuts and fruits like guava and soursop, as well as plentiful seafood.

As time passed and others arrived to live in the islands, the cuisine changed, including distinct African, European, Asian and American, as well as the native Arawak influences. Although these cultures merge from one generation to the next, in kitchens in the islands, just as those around the world, people take pride in preserving the culinary traditions of the past. The impact of the sublime blend of all of these cultures will become clearer as you use the cookbook to prepare the feasts described within its pages.

In recent years, there has been a migration of peoples and their foods from the Caribbean to other parts of the world. The fruits and vegetables that are commonplace in the islands are now appearing on the shelves of neighbourhood grocery stores all over the globe. Inhabitants of Europe and North America are becoming more and more familiar with fruits such as plantains, avocados and mangoes. This trend is likely to continue as population shifts and the demand for "food from home" grows. Sadly, the finest specimens of some of the exotic fruits and vegetables are not found in the supermarkets of North America and Europe because some of these delicious treats are not good travelers. Therefore, I would encourage those interested in tasting this food at its best to visit the exotic destinations where they grow in abundance, seeing them in their natural surroundings while you enjoy the incomparable Caribbean sunshine. Until you can visit, however, the recipes in this book will tantalize you with a delicious idea of what is in store for you in the islands. ❖

How To Use This Cookbook

 Equipment

For easy reference, equipment used in recipes is displayed in bold print in the method of recipe preparation and alternative equipment is displayed in Italics

 Liquid measurements

Dry ingredients such as rice, grits or polenta are not washed first; liquids are measured to cook dry ingredients.

 Food Preparation

Methods of preparing and preserving unfamiliar fruits, vegetables and meats can be found in the Food Preparation Section beginning on page 24.

 Bake at

Oven temperature and baking times are set for the oven to be pre-heated for 10 minutes.

 Tips

Tips which may come in handy in the preparation of recipes can be found at the beginning on page 34.

 Reference to other recipes

In preparing some recipes, you will be referred to other recipes in the book.

 Menus

After preparing dishes, you may want to include them in your family's meal planning. Menus can be found at beginning of chapters.

 Seasonings

The secret to Caribbean cooking, especially seafood and rice dishes, is the use of fresh herbs, fresh spices, hot peppers, limes and lemons. When these ingredients are not available, you may substitute, for example, red pepper flakes or ground cayenne pepper and frozen or bottled lime or lemon juices.

Lady Darling Island Sesonings is a special mixture of seasonings blended to enhance the flavour of salads, soups, stews, rice and vegetable dishes and is available on my Caribbean web site: caribbean-productions.com

 ## Where to buy foods

If you live in a neighbourhood that has ethnic grocers who supply Caribbean, Latino, Asian or Indian food products, many of the foods used in this book will be available at these stores, specialty shops or supermarkets. If fresh products are unavailable, canned or frozen products may be substituted.

 ## Beer substitute

Any recipes using Kalik Beer, the beer of The Bahamas, can also be made using regular beer or non-alcoholic beer.

Food Preparation

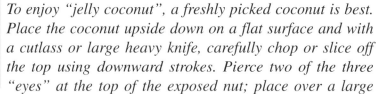

Coconut

"Jelly" Coconut

To enjoy "jelly coconut", a freshly picked coconut is best. Place the coconut upside down on a flat surface and with a cutlass or large heavy knife, carefully chop or slice off the top using downward strokes. Pierce two of the three "eyes" at the top of the exposed nut; place over a large glass or pitcher and drain out the water completely. This water is a healthy, natural drink. With the knife, make an opening in the nut large enough for a spoon and scoop out the soft "jelly" and add to the water; chill and serve as a delicious dessert. A special tropical treat when you visit the islands is a mixed drink served from a coconut fresh off the tree (page 376). A little "Gin 'n coconut water is good for ya"!

"Dry" Coconut

"Shucking" or removing the smooth outer bark of a fresh coconut requires a bit of practice with a cutlass or large heavy knife. Place the coconut on a flat surface and, with firm downward slashes, carefully cut away the bark. (However, fresh coconuts are usually sold after the bark is removed and husk covers the shell). Using the knife, pull the husk away from the nut. Pierce two of the three small "eyes" at the top of the shell, place over a large glass or pitcher and drain out the water.

After the water is drained out, place the coconut on a flat surface and with a heavy blunt tool (hammer), crack the nut in half or into large pieces. To remove the meat from the shell, use a knife with a rounded tip and pry loose. Peel off the brown skin from the white meat. Now you are ready to grate or process coconut for baking or cooking.

Grated Coconut

Place chunks of peeled dry coconut into a food processor fitted with the knife blade and process until coconut is finely grated. You can also grate chunks with the fine side of a hand held grater.

Shredded Coconut

Fit the food processor with the disc for shredding and shred the peeled dry coconut. Or shred using the coarse side of a hand held grater.

Coconut Milk
Prepare one dry coconut and cut into chunks. Place the chunks into a food processor; add about 2 cups of water and process for about 2 minutes. Pour into a muslin cloth placed over a bowl and squeeze to extract all of the juice or "milk" or extract using a food mill. The process may be repeated before the coconut is discarded.

Freezing
For "fresh" coconut year-round, measure grated or shredded coconut; place into freezer bags, label and freeze.

If fresh coconuts are not available, packaged or canned shredded coconut may be substituted in some recipes.

Ackee
The Ackee is used as a vegetable and should be eaten only when it has fully ripened and opened naturally. For preparation, the shell, seed and pink or reddish membrane are discarded. The whitish or creamed coloured "meats" are usually soaked or simmered in salted water then fried in butter, dipped in batter and cooked as fritters or prepared with salt fish (page 159). Canned ackee can be used in place of fresh ackee and it will not be necessary to boil.

Pineapple
To check for freshness when buying a pineapple, thump the side of the fruit with the leafy fringes, a dull solid sound will indicate good quality, and a hollow thud would indicate poor quality. Choose one with a nice bright yellow colour; avoid a really hard fruit, one with soft spots or an under-sized pineapple. Keep at room temperature until it is slightly soft to the touch.

Place the pineapple on a cutting board; with a sharp knife, cut a thick slice from the top and bottom. Stand the pineapple on its bottom and remove the skin using wide downward strokes. Remove and discard the "eyes"; cut into 1/2" slices, then into chunks or chop finely, preserving the juices. Or cut the pineapple lengthwise and remove the core. Cut the pineapple into slices and the core can then be cut into spears.

Guava

Wash the guavas; peel, using a potato peeler, and cut into halves. Using a teaspoon, scoop out the seeds with surrounding pulp leaving a "shell". Cut the shells into strips called "slips" or chop finely.

• *Purée*

Place the seeds and pulp into a food mill or sieve and strain out the pulp to produce purée (discard the seeds).

• *Freezing*

Wash and peel the guavas; place whole fruit into freezer bags and freeze. Prepare shells, slips, finely chopped guava or purée; measure, place into freezer bags and freeze.

• If fresh guavas are not available, substitute canned shells in recipes.

Tamarind

Remove tamarind meats from the pods; break into small pieces and using a paring knife, carefully remove the seeds.

• *Boiling for juice*

Place the meats into a stockpot with water to cover and boil for about 20 minutes. Drain off liquid and reserve for juice, punch or jelly.

• *Purée*

Cool the boiled, drained tamarind pulp; place into the bowl a food processor fitted with the knife blade or blender and purée (if necessary, add liquid while puréeing).

• *Freezing*

Place tamarind meats, boiled meats or purée in freezer bags and freeze.

Guinep

Although guineps can be "as tart as limes," they are usually eaten "out of hand" or can be boiled to make a delicious tasting juice or jelly. Using a paring knife, remove the skin of guineps and drop flesh covered seeds into a saucepan, with water to cover and boil for about twenty minutes. Drain, preserving liquid for juice or jelly.

• *Freezing*

Remove skins; place guineps in freezer bags and freeze.

• *Roasting Seeds*

"Eat" the flesh from the seeds; place into a heavy iron skillet or a pan. Bake in the oven or place directly into hot coals and roast.

Soursop

Although soursop has a tart taste, it is a delicious fruit and can be "eaten out of hand." For desserts, peel the soursop; remove the centre membrane and carefully remove all seeds. Mix with condensed (sweet) milk and a dash of nutmeg and enjoy.
• Purée
Place the "seeded" pulp into the bowl of a food processor fitted with the knife blade or blender and purée.
• Freezing
Place peeled, seeded or puréed pulp into freezer bags and freeze.

Sugar Apple

Delicious, sugar apple usually eaten "out of hand" and no sugar is needed.
• Purée
Break open sugar apples; remove centre membrane and carefully remove the seeds; place the pulp into the bowl a food processor fitted with the knife blade or blender and purée.
• Freezing
Place seeded pulp or purée into freezer bags and freeze.

Sapodilla (Dillie)

Sapodilla is a delicious tropical treat, usually eaten "right off the tree, skin and all." To prepare fruit for recipes, wash the dillies; peel and break into halves. Remove the seeds and centre membrane; slice or cut into chunks.
• Purée
Place the slices or chunks into the bowl of a food processor fitted with the knife blade or a blender and purée.
• Freezing
Peel dillies; remove centre membrane and seeds, or process to make purée. Place into freezer bags and freeze.

Mango (ripe)

Sweet and juicy, mango is the ultimate tropical treat, usually eaten as soon as they are soft to the touch. Peel and slice the flesh from the seeds; cut into chunks or slices or finely chop.

• *Purée*
Place the chunks or slices into the bowl of a food processor fitted with the knife blade or into a blender and purée.
• *Freezing*
Place peeled whole mangoes, slices, chunks or purée into freezer bags and freeze.

• *Mango (green)*
The firm meat of green mangoes can be compared to apples and makes a delicious filling for pies and tarts. Wash and peel green mangoes and cut the meat from the seeds. Cut into thin slices or chunks.
• *Freezing*
Place slices or chunks into freezer bags and freeze.

Papaya
Papaya is a delicate fruit and is delicious eaten as soon as it is ripe and soft to the touch. Cut papaya in half, scoop out seeds and slice, or cut into chunks and place into a blender and purée. Serve in fruit salads, over ice cream or use purée in punches or juice.
• *Freezing*
Place purée into freezer bags and freeze.

Tropical plums, cherries and sea grapes
Scarlet plumbs, hog plumbs, Surinam cherries and sea grapes are usually eaten "right off the tree" but can be used to make juices and punches or jams and jellies. Wash, place into a saucepan, with water to cover, and boil for about 20 minutes. Cool, squeeze, and, using fingers, remove skins and pulp to make purée for jam. Drain and strain reserving liquid for juice or jelly.
• *Freezing*
Wash fruit, place into freezer bags and freeze.

Sugarcane
Sugarcane is usually available in 3 to 6 foot lengths, peeled and eaten "out of hand" or squeezed to produce "cane juice." Cut into lengths of shorter pieces having about three "joints" and, using a sharp knife, peel off the hard skin. Cut the joints around at the hard membrane and

then cut into strips. Prepare to do a lot of chewing to suck the juice from the cane but it is "ummm-delicious!"

• Cane juice
Place lengths of cane into a specially designed machine and squeeze out the juice; chill and serve immediately.

Avocado pears
There are many varieties of avocados and the fruit is ripe when soft to the touch. Caribbean avocados are large, sweet and moist with smooth bright green skins.
• Cut ripe avocado into sections and serve as a vegetable.
• Cut in half and remove seed; fill cavity with salad and serve.
• Cut into sections; peel and cut into slices or chunks and add to salads.
• Mash or purée
Cut, remove seed and mash with a fork; for guacamole or dips, place into the bowl a food processor fitted with the knife blade or into a blender and purée.
Avocados will discolour when cut unless sprinkled with lime juice. To avoid discolouration of dips or mashed avocado, place the seed into the mixture until ready to serve.

Breadfruit
Breadfruit, described as "bread growing on trees" is a very delicate fruit and can be substituted for potatoes in many recipes. Avoid buying fruit with dark or soft spots; when ripe it is soft to the touch and should be used right away. Wash, cut in half and remove centre membrane. Peel; cut into large chunks, place into a saucepan with water to cover and boil until soft, 15 to 20 minutes.
• Freezing
Peel fruit and remove centre membrane; cut into slices or chunks, place into freezer bags and freeze.

Plantain
Plantain, cousin of the banana, is cooked before eating and can be used in all forms from green to over-ripe and is usually served as a vegetable.
• Fried ripe plantain
Choose plantain soft to the touch; peel, slice and fry in vegetable oil until golden brown.

• *Bake or microwave*
Wash ripe plantains; place into baking pan and oven bake at 350°F for about 20 minutes or wrap in wax paper and microwave for 6 to 8 minutes.
• *Boiled green plantain*
The skin clings tightly to the green fruit and has to be carefully peeled away using a paring knife. Cut into halves; place into a saucepan with water to cover and boil until soft.
• *Freezing*
Peel ripe plantains; slice, place into freezer bags and freeze.

Cassava
A tapered cylindrical root, cassava has a thick, almost bark-like brown skin and starchy white flesh and can be used as a substitute for potatoes in some recipes or grated for bread. To prepare, cut around into 2-inch pieces and peel off the skin. Cut pieces in half and remove the centre membrane.

• *Grated for bread*
Place chunks into the bowl of a food processor fitted with the knife blade and process until finely grated.
• *Boiled*
Place into a saucepan with water to cover, salt and whole allspice and boil for about 15 minutes or until soft. Or place chunks into soups and stews, cooking until soft.
• *Purée for soup*
Place cooled boiled cassava with liquid into bowl of food processor and process making a smooth purée.
• *Freezing*
Place cassava chunks into freezer bags and freeze.

Hot Peppers
Peppers grow in abundance throughout the Caribbean and are an important ingredient in many of our recipes. Growing on small bushes, mature fruits are picked when they are green or red. Familiar names of peppers are cayenne, chili and pimento, but in the islands, you will find names like bird peppers and scotch bonnet or goat peppers. If you are an adventurer, when you visit the Caribbean, you would eat native dishes like the natives do – with lots of pepper. However, I would suggest a "mild" approach especially with scotch bonnet or goat pepper.

Pigeon Peas

Green or dry peas can be used in recipes calling for pigeon peas.

• Dried peas

Pick through the peas; place into pressure cooker with water to cover and cook (15 lb. pressure) for about 30-minutes. Or place in a stockpot with water to cover and boil for about 1-hour until peas are soft (adding hot water during cooking).

• Green peas

It is not necessary to boil green pigeon peas before adding to recipe. Shuck the peas; pick and wash.

• Freezing - dried peas; place boiled dried peas with stock into freezer bags and freeze. Green peas - pick peas and wash; place into freezer bags and freeze.

Conch

Conch is a mussel and tenderizing by pounding, is very essential, especially for dishes like cracked conch.

Method One - "Bruising" or tenderizing

Lay the conch flat on a hard surface and, using a sharp knife, cut in half horizontally. Place the sections, one or two at a time into a heavy plastic food storage bag and using a meat hammer, pound the conch thoroughly. But at last! Tenderized conch is now available at some wholesale seafood outlets.

• Method Two - Pressure Cooking (for soups, curries and stews)

Place conchs into a pressure cooker; add water to cover, salt and about 1-teaspoon of vegetable oil (to avoid "boiling over"). Following manufacturer's instructions, (15 lb. pressure), cook for 15 to 20 minutes. Drain (preserve liquid if needed), cut the conch into chunks.

• If you do not use a pressure cooker, bruise the conch (above); place into a large pot with water to cover and boil over medium-high heat for about one hour or until the conch is tender.

• Method Three - Ground Conch

For Conch Fritters or Burgers the conch must be coarsely ground. Wash the conch thoroughly in cold water and cut into large chunks. Place into the bowl of a food processor fitted with the knife blade, along with the vegetables, and pulse speed, or, using a meat grinder, coarsely grind the conch.

For Rissoles the conch must be finely ground. Place the chunks into the bowl of a food processor fitted with the knife blade and process.

•*Sliced & Shredded Conch*
Wash the conch in cold water and cut into chunks. Fit a food processor with the disc for slicing; reverse disc for shredding. Or thinly slice using a large sharp knife. Partially frozen conch is best.

• *Method Four - Dried Conch (Hurricane Ham)*
Dried conch or "hurricane ham" is good in soups. It is the result of preserving the conch through the drying process, exposure to the sun. The dried conch is hard to the touch much like beef jerky. Begin by soaking the conch overnight with water to cover. Pour off soaking water; place into a large heavy saucepan with water to cover and cook until tender, 45 minutes to 1 hour.
• *Quick cook method: place into a pressure cooker and following manufacturer's instructions (with 15 lb. pressure) cook for 15 to 20 minutes. Drain (preserve liquid if needed) and cut into desired sized chunks.*

Crawfish

Wash the crawfish tails in cold water; place into a saucepan with water to cover. Add salt and oil; over high heat bring to a boil, reduce the heat and cook uncovered for about 5 minutes. Remove, drain and allow to cool. Place the tails on a cutting board with the soft side of shell on the board. With a large sharp knife, firmly cut through the top of the shell but do not completely separate the tail while spreading flat.

Crabs

During the rainy season, land crabs abound on the islands of The Bahamas and are considered a delicacy, cooked in a variety of ways including soups, rice, grits and the traditional "crab & dough".

To prepare - remove the legs (discard) and remove the biters. Wash and scrub the bodies and biters thoroughly. Pry open the bodies and scrape the fat from the backs; and the lower bodies reserving in a small dish. Discard the backs and break the bodies into halves.

History & Description of Fruits, Vegetables, & Spices

Citrus Fruit - 44

Papaya - 48

Guinep - 64

Avocado - 72

Journey Bread - 88

Sapodilla - 96

Cassava - 107

Pepperpot - 115

Hurricane Ham - 118

Banana - 132

Ackee - 158

Hot Peppers - 165

Pigeon Peas - 207

Plantain - 224

Breadfruit - 248

Akara - 253

Nutmeg - 269

Coconut - 276

Soursop - 284

Sugar Apple - 287

Sugarcane - 303

Guava - 336

Mango - 340

Sesame Seeds - 356

Pineapple - 360

Tamarind - 365

Coconut Water - 376

Helpful Tips

 ### Where to Store Herbs

Store dried herbs and spices in a cool, dark place or they will rapidly lose both flavour and colour. The absolutely worst place to keep them is on a shelf over the kitchen stove where they get heated and cooled whenever you use the stove.

 ### Frying With Butter

To keep butter from burning when frying foods, use equal amount of olive oil.

 ### A Garlic Secret

Before chopping garlic, sprinkle the cloves with salt. The salt will pick up the juice that is otherwise left on the chopping board.

Beverages & Party Drinks

 ### Ice Ball for Patio Punch

Make grapefruit-sized ice balls for your summer punch bowl by filling balloons with water until the desired size and then freeze. To serve, peel off the balloon. It's a conversation starter.

 ### Decorative Ice Cubes

Fill ice trays with water, place in each section one of the following before freezing: mint leaves, pineapple chunks, pieces of lime or pieces of lemon.

 ### Flavoured Ice Cubes

Flavour cubes with Ole Nassau Pineapple, Coconut or Banana Rums by mixing 1 tablespoon of rum to the water before pouring into trays. Freeze and serve the cubes with lemonade or other cold drinks.

Sweet Secret-less Sugar

You will need less sugar in iced tea if you add the sugar while the tea is still hot.

Salads & Dressings

 Clean-up Operation

The tail end of the catsup might not shake out of the bottle, but there's still enough there to put to good use. Add a little water, give a good shake and use in meat loaf, baked beans or in place of tomato sauce. Or add a little oil and vinegar for a quickie French dressing.

 No-cracked Boiled Eggs

To avoid eggs cracking while boiling, use a sharp pick or long needle to make a small hole in the large end of the egg. With a long slotted spoon, lower into boiling water and boil until eggs are done. Crack shells slightly and place the eggs into ice cold water to avoid the yolks darkening.

Soups & Curries

 Keep the Mush out of a Mushroom

Don't soak mushrooms in water, as they absorb it. Just wipe the mushrooms with a damp cloth. Cook them rapidly over high heat.

 No more Dark Mushrooms

To keep the natural white colour of fresh mushrooms, add a little lemon juice to the butter or margarine in the frying pan.

 Rest in Peace

The best spoon rest you can buy is a small sponge! It rinses out in a jiffy and is always handy to wipe up spills and drips.

Breakfast & Lunches

 ### Too Much Bacon

When you are cooking more bacon than the pan will hold, criss-cross the slices and turn all at once with a pancake turner or a wide spatula.

 ### Perfect Baked Potato

If you want a flakier potato, prick it with a fork halfway through baking.

 ### Save on Paper Towels

At today's prices, paper towels cost as much as steak did in the good old days. But there is at least one way to economize. Instead of using several thicknesses of paper toweling to drain bacon or other fried food, use only one towel layer placed on top of several layers of newspaper. This works well.

 ### Fried Foods

Some fried foods will remain crisper if placed on a wire rack to drain instead of placing directly on paper towels to catch drippings.

Fish & Seafood

 ### Tamarind - Lime Juice Substitute on Fish

After cleaning and scoring whole fish; cut into filets, cutlets, chunks or strips, sprinkle with salt and red pepper, rub in seeded, boiled or puréed tamarind instead of lime juice and marinate. Bake, broil, grill or fry the fish as usual.

Meat & Poultry

 ### How to Handle Roast Meats

When you remove a roast from the oven, let it stand for 15 minutes. This will make carving easier and the meat will be moist and flavorful. Do not attempt to cook a roast weighing less than three pounds. It becomes dry before it is fully cooked.

Tasty Way to Save Cooking Time

Marinating meat overnight reduces cooking time by almost half. You will not only save time and energy but also have a more flavourful dish.

Dinner Side Dishes

 ### Chinese Secret for Hot Towels

It is always a delight to eat in a Chinese or Japanese restaurant and be offered hot towels before you eat or between courses. You, too, can charm your guest with this Oriental custom by dampening towels and wrapping them in foil. Put the towels in a hot oven for a few minutes. Hot towels are very welcome freshners after fried chicken or ribs.

 ### Keep Fresh Ginger Fresh

Cut leftover fresh gingerroot into small pieces and put into a small jar. Add a little dry sherry, cover the jar and store it in the refrigerator. Fresh gingerroot can also be sliced, wrapped in aluminum foil, and frozen for up to two weeks.

 ### Quick Mashed Potatoes

In just a few minutes you can boil potatoes soft enough for mashing if you cut the raw potatoes with a French-fry cutter into small, even-sized pieces.

 ### Warm Plates for a Crowd...Easily

Put the plates in your dishwasher and turn the dial to the drying cycle. Your plates will be piping hot.

 ### Avoid "The Pot Boiling Over"

When cooking starchy foods such as pasta, potatoes or sea foods such as conch or crawfish, add about a teaspoon of butter or vegetable oil to the water.

Vegetables

Keep Stuffed Green Peppers From Collapsing

Bake stuffed peppers in greased muffin tins. The tins will give them some support as they cook. The same trick can be used when making stuffed onions or tomatoes.

Keep Red Cabbage Red

To brighten the colour of red cabbage, cook the cabbage uncovered and add a little lemon juice or vinegar to the salted water.

Meat Sauces & Gravies

Thicken a Sauce at the Last Minute

To thicken a sauce at the last minute, blend together equal amounts of butter and flour. You can do this in the palm of your hand. Start with two teaspoons of softened butter and use your thumb to work in two teaspoons of flour. Add a speck of the mixture at a time to the hot sauce and stir it with a wire whisk. Sauces can also be thickened by stirring in cornstarch dissolved in cold water. Start with one tablespoon of cornstarch stirred into two tablespoons of cold water.

Gravy Secret

This secret is a great time saver. Freeze leftover gravy in an ice-cube tray. Transfer solid frozen gravy cubes into freezer bags and when you need some gravy, reheat a cube or two.

No-lump Gravy

The trick is to use flour that has been browned. It not only makes gravy taste better and gives it a richer colour, but also helps to keep lumps from forming. The easy way to brown your flour is to put a little in a heat-proof dish when you're using the oven and leave in oven until the flour has turned a nice brown colour. Store it in the refrigerator in a jar until you are ready to use it.

If You Don't Have a Gravy Browner

Use a little of that coffee left over from breakfast. Add just enough to give the gravy the rich brown colour everyone likes. Two or three tablespoons of coffee will probably be sufficient. Surprisingly, the gravy will not taste of coffee.

Pastries, Pies & Tarts

No Rolling Pin?

If you do not have a rolling pin, use a round, tightly capped bottle filled with ice water.

Hasten Chilling

To hasten chilling, place the bowl of filling or mixture into a large bowl of ice and water; stir until the mixture is cold then place in refrigerator if necessary.

Holiday "Rush"

During holiday "rush" season, prepare pastry crust ahead of time and cut into 5-inch circles. Prick with a fork; stack with wax paper between the circles and freeze in zip lock bags until ready to make tarts, turnovers or tartlets. To make tartlets, line muffin cups, fill and bake as usual.

No-stick Rolling Pin

Pastry dough will not stick to your rolling pin if you put the dough in the freezer or refrigerator until chilled. This way you can avoid having to use additional flour. Too much flour toughens pastry.

Cakes, Cookies & Dessert Sauces

Have a Clean Cake Platter

To protect the cake platter from spills while you are frosting a cake; slip strips of waxed paper beneath the edge of the cake. Any spills will fall onto the paper instead of the plate. Remove the paper carefully.

Keep a Moist Cake Moist

To prevent a partially eaten cake from becoming dry, slip half an apple or lemon alongside the exposed sides of the cut wedge. Cover the cake with a cover or transparent wrap. If the cake is frosted, insert several toothpicks into the frosting so the wrap won't touch the frosting and "tear" when it is lifted off.

 ## *Thicken a Fruit Sauce*

Purée soft fruit or berries in a food processor. Heat the purée and stir in one tablespoon of cornstarch or arrowroot dissolved in two tablespoons of cold water. Add this mixture a little at a time until correct thickness is achieved. Sauce will be shiny and clear, not opaque.

 ## *Colourful Bowl for Dip*

Serve your favourite dip in a hollowed-out artichoke or red cabbage. The dip will look marvelous in any one of these vegetables. Remove a thin slice from the bottom so that it will stand upright.

 ## *Fresh Lime, Lemon, or "Big Sour" juice... year round*

When limes, lemons and "big sours" are in season and there is more than enough juice, squeeze, strain and pour into ice trays and freeze. Remove frozen cubes to freezer bags and when ready to use for seasoning o r m i x i n g drinks, just pop out a cube or two.

 ## *My Family's Tip for Fluffly Rice*

If you prefer fluffier rice, add about 1/4 cup of water during the last 10 minutes of cooking time when a placing heat diffuser under the pot.

Beverages

Recipes

❋ **Thirst Quenchers**

Bahamian "Switcher" (Limeade)

Lemonade

Tropical Solar Iced Tea

Ginger Limeade

Ginger Iced Tea

Ginger Beer

Tamarind Cooler

Mock Pink Champagne

❋ **Juices**

Papaya, Papaya Orange

❋ **Shakes**

Banana, Mango

❋ **Daiquiris**

Banana, Banana Guava, Papaya,

Pineapple, Sugar Apple,

Soursop

❋ **Punches**

Tropical Plum, Tropical Fruit,

Mango, Scarlet Plum, Hog Plum,

Sea Grape, Soursop, Tamarind,

Sea Grape

Bahamian "Switcher" Limeade

3 or 4 big sours or sour oranges
1/2 gallon water
Sugar to taste
Orange slices for garnish

Roll the big sours, squeeze and strain the juice into a **large pitcher**. Add water and sugar to taste and chill. Pour into **tall glasses**, add ice cubes and garnish with the orange slice just before serving.

Lemonade

2 to 3 tbsp. Lemon Syrup for Lemonade page 317
1 glass ice water
Sugar to taste
Mint leaves

Stir the syrup and sugar in the glass of ice water. Add ice and garnish with mint leaves.

Tropical Solar Ice Tea

1/2 gallon water
4 Tropical flavoured tea bags, Mango, Pineapple or Orange
Sugar to taste
Freshly squeezed lime juice
Lime slices
Mint leaves, frozen

Pour the water into a **large glass jar** *or pitcher* with a **cover**. Place the tea bags in the water with labels hanging over the edge. Cover and put the container outside in direct sunlight.

Let stand until the tea is drawn to desired strength 30 to 40-minutes. Squeeze the bags and remove. Sweeten to taste.

Chill thoroughly and when ready to serve, pour into **tall chilled glasses**. Stir in lime juice; add ice and garnish with lime slices or frozen mint leaves.

Citrus Fruits

Citrus trees originated in southeast Asia and the first citrus fruit appeared in Europe when Alexander the Great conquered western Asia.

Bahamian Key Limes

Europeans enjoyed eating and cooking with citrus, using it to season meat and fish. It is believed that Columbus brought orange seeds to Hispanola in 1493. Citrus seeds were first brought to the United States in 1518 by Spanish and Portuguese traders.

The Portuguese also planted lemon, lime and orange groves along the Atlantic coast. Resourceful captains then provisioned their ships with citrus fruits for their crew and human cargo to inhibit scurvy, a vitiman C deficiency disease common to seamen without fresh fruits or vegetables in their diet.

English sailors became known as "limeys" because they were required to eat or drink the juice of lemons or limes as a way to prevent scurvy.

Grapefruit was developed in Barbados in the 1750's and got its present-day name after a Jamaican farmer noted how the fruits clustered together on the tree, "just like a bunch of grapes". ✺

Ginger Limeade

3-1/2 cups water
3/4 cup sugar
2 tbsp. minced fresh gingerroot
1 cup freshly squeezed lime juice
Slices of limes for garnish

In a **small saucepan**, stir together 2-cups of the water, sugar and the ginger. Bring to a boil, stirring until the sugar has dissolved. Simmer for 3-minutes.

Strain the syrup through a **fine sieve** set over a **bowl** and allow to cool.

In a **pitcher**, combine the cooled syrup, remaining 1-1/2-cups of water and the lime juice stirring well. Divide the *Limeade* among **glasses** and garnish with slices of lime.

Ginger Iced Tea

1 qt. *Tropical Solar Iced Tea, page 43*
Freshly squeezed juice of 3 lemons
Sugar to taste
1 qt. chilled ginger ale
Sprigs of mint

Combine the *Tropical Solar Iced Tea*, lemon juice and sugar in a **large serving pitcher** mixing well.

Chill, and when ready to serve, stir in the chilled ginger ale. Pour into **glasses** filled with ice. Garnish with sprigs of mint.

Tamarind Cooler

4 tall glasses
2-1/2 cups boiling water
1/4 cup light brown sugar
2 tbsp. minced ginger
1 tbsp. *Tamarind Purée, page 26*
1 tbsp. freshly squeezed lemon juice
Lemon slices for garnish

In a **bowl**, using a **wire whisk**, whisk together the boiling water, brown sugar, ginger and the *Tamarind Purée* mixing thoroughly. After cooling, strain through a **sieve** set over a **pitcher**.

Stir in the lemon juice and chill for at least 1-hour. Divide the Cooler among **tall glasses** filled with ice. Garnish with lemon slices.

Ginger Beer

2 lbs. fresh gingerroot
1/2 gal. (8 cups) bottled water
3 cups sugar, or to taste
(White sugar for light beer or brown sugar for dark beer)

Peel the ginger, cut into chunks and place into the bowl of a **food processor** fitted with the knife blade. Add 1-cup of the water and process for about 1-minute.

Scrape into a **large glass container** with remaining water. Cover loosely and store in a cool place for 24 to 48-hours.

Using a clean **linen cloth**, strain the beer carefully into a **large bowl**. Sweeten to taste return to the glass container, cover and refrigerate.

When ready to serve, carefully pour into **tall glasses** filled with crushed ice. (Avoid pouring in the sedimentation if any).

Mock Pink Champagne

2 cups Scarlet Plum Punch, page 51
1/2 cup sugar
Few drops red food colouring
2 cups chilled ginger ale

Combine the strained *Scarlet Plum Punch*, sugar and food colouring in a **serving pitcher** and chill. Just before serving, stir in the chilled ginger ale.

Papaya Juice

Large slice of ripe papaya, peeled and chopped for 1-cup purée
3-cups water.

Place the papaya slice into the bowl of a **blender** and purée. Mix together the purée and water in a serving pitcher, chill and serve.

Papaya Orange Juice

Large slice of ripe papaya, peeled and chopped for 1-cup purée
3-cups orange juice

Place the papaya slice into the bowl of a **blender** and purée. Mix together the purée and orange juice in a **serving pitcher**, chill and serve.

Banana Shake

1 soft-ripe banana, mashed
1 cup chilled milk
1/3 cup orange juice
1 tsp. sugar
Dash of salt

Combine the mashed banana and remaining ingredients in the bowl of a **blender**; blend thoroughly and serve immediately in a **tall glass**.

Mango Shake

1/2 cup *Mango Syrup*, page 318
1/3 cup chilled milk
Dash of salt
1 large scoop of *Vanilla Ice Cream*, page 345

Combine the syrup and remaining ingredients in the bowl of a **blender**; blend thoroughly and serve in a **tall glass**.

Banana Daiquiri

1 ripe banana
1 cup *Lemonade*, page 43
1 tbsp. canned coconut milk
1/2 glass crushed ice

Combine ingredients in the bowl of a **blender**, blend and pour into a **tall glass**.

Banana Guava Daiquiri

1 ripe banana
2 ripe guavas
Juice of 1 orange
Sugar to taste
1-1/2 cups crushed ice
Guava slices

Peel and chop the banana. Peel the guavas; remove the seeds and slice.

In the bowl of a **blender**, combine the banana, guava slices and orange juice with ice. Blend; pour into a **tall glass** and garnish with a guava slice.

Papaya

Long esteemed through-
out the Tropics of both
hemispheres, Papaya is
becoming more and
more valued for the
ripe fruit which is both
delicious and healthful.
The unripe fruit and plant
are also of interest, for they both
contain a milky latex that is rich in
papain which is used medicinally as a digestive and in beauty
preparations and soap.

Indeed, the leaves of the plant have been used in Mexico as a soap
substitute for washing clothes. The papain content is such that, if
leaves are first bruised to release it and then wrapped around
tough meat, they will tenderize meat overnight. Papin is the main
ingredient in commercial meat-tendizer.

When ripe, the papaya is slightly soft like a ripe melon and turns
entirely to a bright yellow or orange. Chilled, it is a popular
breakfast fruit and used in desserts and salads. Chilled papaya
juice is a popular beverage in the tropics. ❀

Papaya Daiquiri

Large slice of ripe papaya, peeled and chopped for 1 cup purée
Juice of 1 orange, freshly squeezed
1 tbsp. fresh lime juice
Sugar to taste
1-1/2 cups crushed ice

In the bowl of a **blender**, combine the papaya, orange juice, sugar and ice. Blend; pour into a **tall glass** and garnish with an orange slice.

Pineapple Daiquiri

1/4 fresh pineapple, chopped for 1 cup
1/2 cup coconut milk, fresh or canned
1-1/2 cups crushed ice
Orange slice for garnish

In the bowl of a **blender**, combine the pineapple, coconut milk and ice. Blend; pour into a **tall glass** and garnish with an orange slice.

Sugar Apple Daiquiri

1 large sugar apple for 1 cup pulp page 27
1/2 cup milk
1 cup crushed ice
Mint leaves for garnish

Open the sugar apple, scoop out the pulp and remove the seeds. In the bowl of a **blender**, combine the pulp, milk and ice. Blend, pour into a **tall glass** and serve with mint leaves garnish.

Soursop Daiquiri

1/2 cup soursop pulp (seedless) page 27
2 oz. sweetened condensed milk
2 tbsp. canned coconut milk
1/2 glass crushed ice
Dash of nutmeg

Combine ingredients in the bowl of a **blender**, blend and pour into a **tall glass**.

Tropical Plum Punch

6 cups Hog Plum Juice page 28
6 cups Scarlet Plum Juice page 28
Orange slices
Ice Ball page 52

Combine the juices in a **large punch bowl**; stir in the sugar and chill. Just before serving, add the orange slices and *Ice Balls*.

Tropical Fruit Punch

1 - 46 ounce can Hawaiian Punch
1 - 46 ounce can Orange juice
1 - 46 ounce can Pineapple juice
1 orange, thinly sliced
1 lemon, thinly sliced
l liter bottle Ginger Ale
Mint leaves
Ice Ball page 52

In a **large punch bowl**, combine the punch, orange and pineapple juices and chill. Just before serving, stir in the chilled ginger ale and float the orange and lemon slices, mint leaves and a large *Ice Ball* in the punch. Serve in **punch cups**.

Mango Punch

1 large ripe mango
Juice of 1 orange
Sugar to taste
Water

Peel the mango, chop the meat and place into the bowl of a **blender** adding the orange juice and purée. Pour into a **pitcher**; add water and sugar to taste and chill. Stir just before serving in **tall glasses**.

Sea Grape Punch

1 pound ripe sea grapes
6 cups water
Sugar to taste

Prepare same as *Hog Plum Punch page 51* except substitute sea grapes for the hog plums.

Hog Plum Punch

1 lb. ripe hog plums
6 cups water
Sugar to taste

Wash the plums, place into a **4-quart sized saucepan** with water to cover and bring to a boil. Simmer for 15 to 20-minutes, remove from the heat and let cool.

Using your fingers, slip off the skins from the seeds, removing as much of the pulp as possible. Discard the skins and seeds and mix the pulp into the liquid.

Strain and pour into a **pitcher**. Add the sugar, chill and stir just before serving.

Scarlet Plum Punch

1 lb. ripe scarlet plums
6 cups water
Sugar to taste

Prepare same as *Hog Plum Punch* (above) except substitute scarlet plums for the hog plums.

Soursop Punch

1/2 large soursop for 2 cups pulp page 27
Sweetened condensed milk to taste
Canned coconut milk or whole milk
1/4 to 1/2 tsp. freshly grated nutmeg

Scoop out the pulp and remove the seeds. In the bowl of a **blender**, combine the pulp, half of desired sweet milk and half the canned coconut milk and purée.

Pour into a **large pitcher**; add additional sweet milk or whole milk to taste and chill. Serve in **tall glasses** with dashes of nutmeg on top.

Tamarind Punch

Liquid from boiled tamarinds page 26
Sugar to taste

Pour the liquid into a **pitcher** or *individual glasses* adding sugar to taste. Chill and serve with a slice of lemon or mint leaves.

Guinep Punch

Prepare same as *Tamarind Punch* (above) substituting liquid from boiled guineps page 26 for the tamarind.

Ice Balls

Fill balloons of various sizes with water and freeze. Prepare punches and when ready to serve, peel off balloons and float balls into the punch.

First in the Americas

The first inhabitants of the Americas appeared about 50,000 years ago. At that time the Bearing Strait between Asia and North America was not covered by water. Scientists believed that over a period of several thousand years people from Asia traveled east over this passage in their search for food, they probably followed herds of animals to what is now the Americas. These newcomers from Asia were the ancestors of the indigenous people of the Americas. Their descendants slowly traveled south, making homes all over the continent. After thousands of years they adapted to their different environments, learned new skills, created new traditions and developed diverse cultures. By the time the Europeans came, various peoples occupied different areas of the Americas.

Appetizers & Dips

Recipes

Summer Fruit Kabobs

Avocado Stuffed Celery

Plantain Chips

Plantain Crisps

Breadfruit Chips

Tia Maria Cheese Straws

❉ Canâpés

Conch Nips

Shrimp & Avocado

Zippy Cheese

Sardine

Smoked Fish Roe

Corned Beef

Tuna Pinwheels

Avocado Bacon Rings

Pizza Bites

❉ Canâpés continued

Seafood Canapes

Conch Fritters

Sardine Stuffed Eggs

Fish Roe Stuffed Eggs

Sherry Beef Bites

Fried Chicken Rissoles

Party Drummetts

Barbeque Party Drummetts

Rum Balls

Tamarind Guava Rum Balls

Guinep Royalé

❉ Dips

Guacamole, Clam,

Cream Cheese,

Avocado Bacon,

Mango

❉ Salsa

Mango

Summer Fruit Kabobs

Cut 1-inch cubes of the following fresh fruits, preserving the juices.

Pineapple
Mango
Papaya
Avocado
Banana slices
Maraschino cherries

Chop the fruit into chunks, preserving the juices in a **small bowl**. Dip the avocado chunks and banana slices into the pineapple and mango juices.

Alternate the fruit chunks with the banana slices on **7-inch skewers**. Place a cherry on the end of each skewer and arrange on a **serving platter**.

Avocado Stuffed Celery

1 medium-sized ripe avocado
1 tbsp. French Dressing
1/2 tsp. salt
1/2 tsp. black pepper
1/2 tsp. chili sauce
Celery stalks for stuffing

Peel the avocado; mash with a fork and place into a **small bowl**. Mix together with remaining ingredients until smooth.

Stuff the celery stalks with the mixture, cut and arrange on a **platter** around a **small serving bowl** of the mix.

Plantain Chips

3 half-ripe plantains
3 limes
Vegetable oil for deep-fat frying

Carefully remove the plantain skin with a **sharp knife**. Slice into very thin rounds.

Squeeze the lime juice into a **medium-sized bowl** and soak the slices in the juice for 15-minutes. Remove and dry thoroughly on paper towels.

Heat the oil in a **deep-fat fryer** or *deep pot* and fry the plantain chips until golden brown. Drain on a **wire rack** placed over **paper towels** and serve hot.

Plantain Crisps

2 ripe plantains
2 tbsp. all purpose flour
1/4 tsp. ground cinnamon
2 oz. vegetable oil

Peel the plantains and cut into 1/4-inch rounds.

Blend the flour and cinnamon in a **shallow pan** *or plate*. Place the plantain pieces into the flour mix, coating lightly.

Heat the oil in a **medium-sized non-stick skillet**, and fry the crisps until golden brown, about 5 to 6-minutes. Serve immediately.

Breadfruit Chips

1 firm-ripe breadfruit
3 cups water (approximately)
Salt to taste
Lady Darling's Island Seasoning to taste
3 oz. vegetable oil

Peel and core the breadfruit, *page 29* and cut into wedges.

In a **large stockpot**, bring the water to a boil, adding the salt. Drop the wedges into the boiling water and boil for about 15-minutes. Drain and allow to cool. Pat dry and cut wedges into very thin slices. Allow to dry completely.

Heat the oil in a **medium-sized skillet** and fry the slices until golden brown. Sprinkle lightly with the Island Seasoning and serve immediately.

Shrimp Avocado Cânapés

1/2 lb. small shrimps, cleaned
1/2 tsp. salt
Clam Dip page 65
Crackers

Place the shrimps into a **small saucepan** with the salt and water to cover and bring to a boil. Cook for about 5-minutes.

Prepare the Clam Dip.

Spread a teaspoon of the dip on each cracker, top each with a shrimp and arrange on a **serving platter**.

Tia Maria Cheese Straws

4 oz. Sharp Cheddar cheese, shredded
6 tbsp. butter, softened
3 tbsp. Tia Maria
1/2 tsp. Tamarind Paste page 366
1/4 tsp. salt
1 cup all purpose flour
1 egg yolk
Finely chopped almonds or sesame seeds

Bake at 375ºF

In a **large bowl**, combine the cheese and butter; stir in 2-tablespoons of Tia Maria, *Tamarind Paste* and the salt. Blend in the flour mixing well.

Turn onto a floured **board**, and with a floured **rolling pin**, roll out into a 12x15-inch rectangle. Cut into 5x3/4-inch strips.

In a **small bowl**, beat the egg yolk with remaining Tia Maria and brush over the straws. Sprinkle with the chopped almonds *or sesame seeds* Place on ungreased **cookie sheets** and bake for 7-minutes or until golden. Cool on **wire racks**.

To store, refrigerate in **airtight containers**.

Conch Nips

Thin slices of conch, 2" long
Freshly squeezed lime juice
Salt to taste
Clam Dip page 65
Crackers

Roll up the thin slices of conch; place into a **flat dish**, seam side down and sprinkle with lime juice and salt. Marinate for about 15-minutes.

Prepare the *Clam Dip* and spread a teaspoon on each of the crackers. Place the rolls of conch on the dip, arrange on a **serving platter** and serve.

Zippy Cheese Cânapés

Zippy Cheese **Spread**, *page 140*
Crackers

Spread 1-teaspoon of the cheese spread on each cracker and arrange on a **serving platter**.

Sardine Cânapés

Pâté
2 tins (4 oz. ea.) sardines
1 tbsp. chopped onion
2 tbsp. mayonnaise
2 tbsp. freshly squeezed lime juice
Hot peppers to taste
Crackers

Drain the sardines and place into the bowl of a **blender**. Add the onions, mayonnaise, lime juice and hot peppers and purée.

Place a teaspoon of pâté on cracker and arrange on a **serving platter**.

Smoked Fish Roe Cânapés

Smoked fish roe
Freshly squeezed lemon juice
Hot peppers to taste
Fresh garlic, minced
Butter
Light cream
Crackers

Remove the skin from the smoked roe and discard. Place the roe into a **shallow dish** and mash thoroughly with a fork. Lightly season with lemon juice, pepper and garlic.

Blend in the butter and just enough cream for consistency of soft pâté. Spread a teaspoon of pâté on each cracker and arrange on a **serving platter**.

Corned Beef Cânapés

Corned Beef Salad page 79
Party crackers

Prepare the salad. Just before serving, place one teaspoon of the salad mixture on each cracker and arrange on a **serving platter**.

Zippy Cheese Pinwheels

Prepare same as *Tuna Pinwheels* (below except) substitute *Zippy Cheese Spread, page 140* for *Spicy Tuna Salad*.

Tuna Pinwheels

Spicy Tuna Salad page 78
Slices of square sandwich bread

Prepare the tuna salad; carefully remove the crust from the bread slices and spread the salad thinly over each slice. Roll up, cut each slice into 3 pinwheels and arrange on a **serving platter**.

Seafood Cânapés

Sauce

1 tsp. curry powder
2 tbsp. mayonnaise
1/2 clove minced garlic
1/2 tsp. minced onion
Hot peppers to taste

1 cup of the following cooked chopped seafood

Shrimp
Crawfish
Conch

Sauce

In a **small bowl**, mix together the ingredients with pepper to taste.

Chop the seafood of your choice into small chunks. Toss gently with the sauce and chill.

Spoon onto chips or crackers and serve.

Avocado & Bacon Rings

1 medium-sized ripe avocado
4 slices bacon
1 tsp. freshly squeezed lemon juice
1/2 tsp. salt
1 tsp. onion juice
1/2 tsp. paprika, for garnish
Chopped parsley for garnish

Fry the bacon in a **large skillet** (not crisp); drain and while hot, form into rings, secure with **toothpicks** and place onto a **serving dish**.

Peel the avocado; mash with a fork and season with the lemon juice, salt and onion juice. Mix together and spoon into the bacon rings. Garnish with the paprika and parsley and arrange on a **serving platter**.

Pizza Bites

Pizza Sauce page 260
1/4 lb. Sharp Cheddar cheese
1/4 lb. salami or pepperoni
Oregano
Melba toast or crackers

Bake at 400°F

Cut the cheese and salami into tiny cubes. Spread small amounts of *Pizza Sauce* on the Melba toast; top with the cheese and meat cubes.

Place on **cookie sheets**, sprinkle with oregano and bake for 4 or 5-minutes or until the cheese melts. Serve hot.

Conch Fritters

2 large conchs
1 medium-sized onion
1 medium-sized green pepper
2 oz. freshly squeezed lime juice
2 oz. freshly squeezed lemon juice
Hot peppers to taste
2 cups all purpose flour
2 tsp. baking powder
1 tsp. Lady Darling's Island Seasoning
Salt to taste
1 tsp. dried thyme leaves
1-3/4 cups water, approximately
Vegetable oil for deep-fat frying

> TIP:
> If seasoning is not to your taste after sampling the first fritter, add salt or pepper to the batter and continue frying.

Wash the conchs in cold water; cut into quarters and place into a **food processor** fitted with the knife blade. Cut the onion and green pepper into quarters and place into the processor with the conch.

Using the pulse setting, pulse only until the conch and vegetables are coarsely ground. Scrape into a **medium-sized bowl**.

In a **small dish**, mix together the lime and lemon juices. Crush the hot peppers into the juices; pour over the conch and vegetables.

Sift together the flour, baking powder, Island Seasoning, salt and thyme leaves. Combine with the conch mixture adding enough water to make a stiff batter.

Pour the oil into a **deep-fat fryer** *or deep pot* and heat. Drop the batter by teaspoonfuls into the hot oil and fry quickly until golden brown. Remove the fritters with a **slotted spoon** and drain on a **wire rack** over paper towels. Serve immediately "Au natural" or with *Tarter Sauce page 258.*

Sardine Stuffed Eggs

Sardine **Pâté** *page 58*
6 hard boiled eggs

In a **small bowl**, prepare the *Sardine Pâté*. Halve the boiled eggs, scoop out the yolks and add to the pâté mixing together thoroughly.

Fill the egg whites with the mixture rounding the tops. Arrange on a **serving platter**.

Sherry Beef Bites

Yield 24 appetizers

2 slices white bread
1/2 lb. extra lean ground beef
3 tbsp. finely chopped parsley
1 egg
Salt and pepper to taste
All purpose flour
2 tbsp. olive oil
1 tbsp. vegetable oil
1 medium-sized onion, finely chopped
1 lb. fresh tomatoes, skinned and chopped
1 tbsp. Champion Tomato Paste
1/2 cup Harvey's Dry Cocktail Sherry
Freshly chopped parsley

Tear the bread into pieces; place into a **large bowl** and soak in water for a few minutes, then squeeze out the excess liquid.

Combine the bread, beef, parsley, egg, salt and pepper, mixing gently until the consistency of smooth paste. Divide the mixture into 24 equal sized meatballs and roll each in flour.

Heat the oils in a **large non-stick skillet** and fry the meatballs so they are brown on all sides. Drain and remove to a **shallow dish**.

In the same skillet, sauté the onion until soft. Add the tomatoes, tomato paste and sherry allowing the sauce to bubble and thicken, stirring occasionally. Place the meatballs into the sauce and cook gently for 15 minutes.

Insert **cocktail picks**, sprinkle with parsley and serve as appetizers.

Fish Roe Stuffed Egg

Hard boiled eggs
Smoked fish roe
Mayonnaise
Freshly squeezed lemon juice
Hot peppers, crushed
Garlic clove, crushed

Halve the boiled eggs; remove the yolks and mash.

Remove the skin from the roe and discard. Place the roe into a **shallow dish**, mash thoroughly with a fork and combine with the yolk.

Add the mayonnaise, lemon juice, pepper and garlic mixing thoroughly. Pile back into the egg white halves, arrange on a **platter** and serve.

Fried Chicken Rissoles

Savoury Chicken Rissoles page 188
1-1/2 ounces of butter
Créole Sauce page 259

Prepare the Rissoles.

Heat the butter in a **large skillet** and sauté Rissoles, rotating for 5 to 6-minutes or until browned.

Drain on a **wire rack**; insert **cocktail picks** into each Rissole and arrange on a **serving platter** with a bowl of sauce for dipping.

Party Drummetts

16 four-inch wooden skewers
Ingredients for Mock Drumsticks page 189

Prepare drumsticks mixture; shape the mixture around the **4-inch wooden skewers** and fry. Arrange on a **serving platter** and serve with *Créole Sauce, page 259*.

Barbecue Party Drummetts

Prepare *Party Drummetts* above and brush on *1-1/2 cups Barbecue Poultry Sauce, page 261* before serving.

Rum Balls

Yield 2-1/2 dozen

1-1/2 cups vanilla or chocolate wafer crumbs
1/4 cup Ole Nassau Yer Ho Rum
1/4 cup honey
2 cups ground walnuts
Confectioners' sugar

In a **medium-sized bowl**, combine all ingredients except the sugar. Shape into 1-inch balls. Spread the sugar in a **shallow dish** and roll the balls in the sugar.

Serve or store in a **tightly covered container**.

Tamarind Guava Rum Balls

1/4 cup Tamarind Guava Paste page 366
1-1/2 cups chocolate wafer crumbs
1/4 cup Ole Nassau Yer Ho Rum
2 cups ground walnuts
Confectioners' sugar

Combine all ingredients except the Confectioners' sugar in a **medium-sized bowl**. Shape the mixture into 1-inch balls. Spread the sugar in a **shallow dish** and roll the balls in the sugar.

Serve or store in a **tightly covered container**.

Guinep Royale

2 lbs. guineps
1/2 to 1 cup sugar (according to tartness of fruit)
1/4 cup Ole Nassau Coconut Rum
1/4 cup Ole Nassau Pineapple Rum

TIP:
For year-round enjoyment, place marinated guineps into freezer bags and freeze.

Wash the guineps and using a **paring knife**, pierce the skin in the centre and remove dropping the fruit into a **large bowl with a cover**.

Stir in the sugar to taste, add the rums, cover and marinate for at least 1-hour, stirring occasionally and serve.

Guinep

The Guinep is native to South and Central America and the islands of the Caribbean. The erect, stately, attractive trees grow to heights of 25 to 40 meters.

The fruit clusters are branched, compact and heavy with nearly round, green fruits tipped with a small protrusion, suggesting at first glance small unripe limes. The skin is smooth, thin but leathery and brittle. The glistening pulp (aril) is salmon colored or yellowish translucent and juicy but very scant and somewhat fibrous, clinging tenaciously to the seed. When the fruit is ripe, the pulp is acid-sweet. To eat out of hand, the rind is merely torn open, the pulp-coated seed is squeezed into the mouth and the pulp is sucked from the seed.

Much work is required to scrape the pulp from the seed to make jam or marmalade, so usually the fruit is peeled and boiled, making a delicious cold drink. The white, crisp and starchy seeds are eaten after roasting and native inhabitants of Orinoco cook and consume them as a substitute for cassava. ✺

Guacamole

2 large ripe avocados
1 large ripe tomato, chopped
1 tbsp. finely chopped onion
1 clove garlic, crushed
2 tbsp. freshly squeezed lime juice
1 tbsp. chopped canned green chilies
1 tsp. salt
1/2 tsp. black pepper
Hot peppers to taste

Peel the avocados *page 29*; chop the pulp, place into a **large bowl** and mash. Add the remaining ingredients, mixing together thoroughly.

For a smoother dip, divide the mix into 3 batches; place into the bowl of a **blender** *or food processo*r and purée. To avoid dip turning dark, press the avocado seed into the dip, removing just before serving.

Use as a party dip with *Plantain Chips page 55*, potato chips or tostadas.

Clam Dip

1 medium-sized ripe avocado
1/2 cup minced clams and juice
2 tbsp. freshly squeezed lime juice
1 tsp. salt
Hot peppers to taste

Peel and mash the avocado in a **small bowl**. Add remaining ingredients, mixing well. Serve with crackers or chips.

Cream Cheese Dip

1 large ripe avocado
2 tbsp. freshly squeezed lime juice
8 oz. cream cheese, softened
1-1/2 tsp. salt
Hot peppers to taste

Peel and mash the avocado. Combine with remaining ingredients in a **small bowl**, mixing well. Serve with crackers or chips.

Avocado Bacon Dip

1 medium-sized ripe avocado
2 slices bacon
1 tbsp. freshly squeezed lime juice
1/2 tsp. salt
1 tsp. grated onion
Hot peppers to taste

Peel and mash the avocado and place into a **small bowl**. Fry the bacon until very crisp, crumble and add to the mashed avocado with remaining ingredients blending well.

Mango Dip

1 cup chopped ripe mango
2 tbsp. minced scallions
1-1/2 tbsp. freshly squeezed lime juice
1 tbsp. chopped fresh parsley
2 tbsp. chopped green or red pepper

Combine the ingredients in a the **bowl or a blender** and purée. Cover; chill for 2-hours and serve with *Breadfruit Chips page, 56* or chips of your choice.

Mango Salsa

1 cup diced ripe mango
2 tbsp. minced scallions
1-1/2 tbsp. freshly squeezed lime juice
1 tbsp. chopped fresh parsley
2 tbsp. chopped green or red pepper
Crushed hot peppers to taste

Combine the ingredients in a **small bowl** and mix thoroughly. Cover; chill for 2-hours and serve.

Salads & Dressings

Formal Dinner Menus

French Mushroom Soup
Bran Rolls
Avocado Salad
Broiled Grouper Filets
Bahamian Pigeon Peas & Rice
Medley of Mixed Vegetable
Fish Sauce
Guava Duff with Soka Rum
Sauce
White Wine
Petite Fours
Coffee & Island Blend Teas
Liqueurs & Special Blends

❀

Bahamian Conch Chowder
French Bread
Dill Seed & Cucumber Salad
Crown Roast of Lamb
Glazed Cornish Hens
Potatoe Au Gratin
Carrot Fritters
Mint Sauce
Ole Nassau Rum Cake
White & Red Wines
Coconut Squares & Benné Cakes
Coffee, Teas & Liqueurs

Okra Soup
Clover Leaf Rolls
Conch Salad in Tomato Cup
Roast Pork Calypso
Baked Chicken with Mango
Chutney
Potato Carrot Mash
Chinese Cabbage
Mushroom Gravy
Bananas With Sherry & Cream
White & Red Wines
Pineapple Drops & Rum Balls
Coffee, Teas & Liqueurs

❀

Pumpkin Soup
Benné Seed Sticks
Crawfish Salad on Bed of Lettuce
Baked Turkey with Corn Bread &
Oyster Stuffing
Fried Plantain
French Green Beans
Golden Gravy
Caribbean Sweet Potato Pie with
Coconut Icecream
White Wine
Peanut Cakes & Divine Fudge
Coffee, Teas & Liqueurs

Recipes

❋ **Tasty Salads**

Goombay Fruit

Avocado

Avocado, Orange Grapefruit

Dill Seed Cucumber in Sour Cream

Cabbage Slaw

Beet

Savoury Potato

Breadfruit

Macaroni

Mashed Potato

❋ **Seafood Salads**

Sir Clifford's Conch,

Quick Sliced Conch,

Crawfish, Crab Meat,

Shrimp, Spicy Tuna

❋ **Meat Salads**

Egg, Chicken,

Caribbean Chicken,

Holiday Turkey,

Corned Beef,

❋ **Salad Dressings**

Pina Colada Fruit

Avocado

Mint

Hot Benné Seed

Cucumber

Slaw (Sweet & Sour)

Goombay Fruit Salad

1 cantaloupe
3 bananas
Freshly squeezed juice of 1 lime
2 tangerines
1 papaya
2 mangoes
1-1/2 oz. sugar
1 tbsp. Ole Nassau Pineapple Rum
12 oz. strawberries
8 pitted cherries

Slash the cantaloupe down the section lines, but do not cut as far as the base. Carefully open like a flower and scoop out the seeds and some of the flesh. Drain off the juice and preserve in a **small bowl**. Chill the cantalope and juice for 1-hour.

Peel the bananas, slice and dip into the lime juice. Peel the tangerines, cut into segments and remove the seeds. Cut the papaya in half, remove the seeds and dice the flesh. Peel the mangoes; cut the flesh off the seeds and slice, preserving the juice.

Strain the melon juice; mix with the sugar, adding the rum and blending well. Set a few strawberries aside for decoration. Mix all of the fruits together with the juices and chill.

Just before serving, fill the cantaloupe with some of the fruit salad, place onto a **serving platter** and arrange the remaining fruit around the base decorating with the strawberries.

Variation

Serve salad in half pineapple after removing pulp.

Avocado Salad

Avocados
Anchovy paste
Lettuce
Tomatoes
French Dressing
Thin slices of onion

Peel the avocados and cut into 1-1/2 inch sections lengthwise. Arrange the lettuce leaves on **salad plates** placing the avocado sections on the lettuce.

Cut the tomatoes into wedges and thinly slice the onion. Arrange on the avocado and lettuce. Mix the dressing and anchovy paste (1/2-cup dressing to 1-tablespoon of paste) pour over the salad and serve.

Avocado, Orange and Grapefruit Salad

2 large ripe avocados
2 large oranges
1 large grapefruit
Lettuce leaves
Pina Colada Fruit Salad Dressing page 80

Peel the avocados and cut into 1-1/2-inch sections lengthwise.

Peel the oranges and grapefruit and remove the membrane and seeds, carefully preserving the sections.

Arrange the sections on **individual serving dishes** in a wheel design; pour on the dressing and serve.

Dill Seed Cucumber In Sour Cream

1 medium-sized cucumber, thinly sliced
1 tsp. salt
1/2 cup sour cream
1 tbsp. vinegar
1/2 tsp. ground white pepper
2 tbsp. chopped chives
1 tsp. dill seeds

Sprinkle the cucumber slices with the salt, place into a **salad bowl** and let stand for about 30-minutes. Drain thoroughly.

Combine the sour cream, vinegar, pepper, chives and dill seeds pouring over the cucumber. Chill and serve with garnish of radish or minced parsley.

Beet Salad

1 can (16 oz.) sliced or diced beets
1 tsp. vinegar
1 tsp. sugar
1/2 tsp. whole cloves
1/2 tsp. whole allspice
1 medium-sized onion sliced
1/2 tsp. salt

Drain the beets, reserving the liquid (at least 1-cup).

Combine the liquid, vinegar, sugar, spices and salt in a **2-quart sized saucepan**; bring to a boil. Add the beets. Remove from the heat, turn into a **serving bowl** with the liquid and chill.

When ready to serve, drain, remove the spices, separate the onion rings and mix into the beets.

Avocado

Grown in ancient times as a stable food by the Aztecs and Mayas of Mexico and Central America and introduced into northern South America long before the arrival of Europeans, the Avocado or Alligator Pear reportedly did not reach the West Indies until it was brought by the early Spanish explorers. It has become one of the most important foods of the Islands. Picked "right off the tree", it served as a vegetable, eaten with peas and rice and a meat dish which we call "relish". Or used to make desserts and pies.

Then too, its old colloquial names of Midshipman's Butter, Butter Pear or vegetable butter, suggest its use as a spread, and it does make a delicious sandwich filling when mashed and seasoned with vinegar, pepper, chopped onion and mayonnaise.

Halved avocado filled with delicacies such as crawfish, crab, conch and tuna salads is a gourmet delight. ❈

Cabbage Slaw

1/2 medium-sized cabbage, shredded
Slaw Dressing page 81

Shred the cabbage and place into a **large serving bowl**. Sprinkle with salt and pepper to taste. Toss gently with the *Slaw Dressing* and serve.

Savoury Potato Salad

2 lbs. potatoes, 3/4" dice
1/2 tsp. salt
Sauce
1/4 cup 1/4" dice onion
1/2 cup 1/4" dice green pepper
1/2 cup 1/4" dice celery
2/3 cup mayonnaise
1 tsp. mustard
1 tbsp. sweet relish
1 tsp. sugar
1/2 tsp. Lady Darling's Island Seasoning or to taste
1 small hot pepper (optional for spicy salad)
3 hard boiled eggs, 1 sliced, 2 chopped

Pour approximately 4-cups of water into a **3-quart sized saucepan**; place the eggs and salt into the water and set on to boil. Place the diced potatoes directly into the boiling water and boil until the potatoes are cooked just enough when tested with a sharp knife, but not soft.

Sauce

Place the chopped vegetables into a **large serving bowl**. Add the mayonnaise and remaining ingredients, mixing together well.

Turn the cooked potatoes and eggs into a **colander** and drain. Remove the eggs and place into a **small bowl** of ice cold water. Turn the hot potato into the serving bowl, mixing gently with the sauce. Taste-test and adjust the seasonings.

Peel the eggs and using an **egg chopper**, chop 2 and fold into the salad. Slice the remaining egg; arrange on top of the salad and sprinkle with paprika.

Macaroni Salad

2 cups uncooked macaroni
1 tbsp. salt
6 to 8 cups water
Sauce for *Savoury Potato Salad* *page 73*

Pour the water into a **3-quart sized saucepan** with the eggs and salt; bring to a boil. Add the macaroni and continue boiling for 6 to 8-minutes.

Turn the macaroni and eggs into a **colander** and drain. Remove the eggs and place into a **small bowl** of cold water.

In a large **serving bowl**, prepare the sauce for potato salad; turn the hot cooked macaroni into the bowl and gently mix together. Decorate and serve.

Mashed Potato Salad

3 large potatoes
1/4 cup chopped onion
1/4 cup chopped green pepper
1/4 cup chopped celery
1/2 cup mayonnaise
1 tsp. sweet relish
2 oz. milk
Salt

Peel the potatoes and, cut into cubes; place into a **2-quart sized saucepan** with enough water to cover. Add the salt, bring to a boil and cook until soft, about 20-minutes.

Sauce

In the bowl of a **blender**, combine the onion, green pepper and celery with mayonnaise and sweet pickle, add the milk and purée.

Turn the cooked potatoes into a **food mill** *or colande*r, drain and, using the food mill, mash immediately. Scrape into a **large serving bowl**.

While the potatoes are hot, gently stir in the sauce and salt to taste, mixing well. Serve hot.

Breadfruit Salad

1 firm-ripe breadfruit
1 tsp. salt
6 to 8 cups water
Sauce for *Savoury Potato Salad page 73*

Breadfruit Salad is made using the same ingredients and method as *Potato Salad* substituting 1 whole diced breadfruit.

Peel the breadfruit and cut into half *page 29*. Remove and discard the center membrane; cut into slices and then into 3/4-inch dice.

Pour enough water into a **3-quart sized saucepan** to cover the diced breadfruit; add the salt and eggs and bring to a boil. Add the breadfruit; cook until done when tested with a sharp knife. Turn into a **colander** and drain.

In a large **serving bowl**, prepare the sauce for potato salad; turn the hot breadfruit into the bowl and gently mix together. Decorate and serve.

Sir Clifford's Conch Salad

4 large conchs cut into 1/4" cubes
1/2 cup 1/4" dice celery
1/2 cup 1/4" dice green pepper
1/2 cup 1/4" dice onion
1 cup 1/4" dice ripe tomatoes
1/3 cup freshly squeezed lime juice
1/3 cup freshly squeezed lemon juice
Salt to taste
Hot peppers (bird or goat) to taste

Wash the conchs in cold water, cut into cubes, place into a **large serving bowl** and sprinkle with the salt.

Mix the lime and lemon juices together in a **small dish**. Crush the hot peppers into the juices; pour over the conch adding the diced vegetables and mix gently.

Taste-test and adjust the seasonings. Spoon into **salad cups** *or place on a bed of lettuce*. Serve with a small dish of lime juice and crushed peppers on the side.

Variation

Serve in half avocado or tomato star.

Quick Sliced Conch Salad

4 large conchs
1 large onion
1 medium-sized green pepper
2 ribs celery
1 cucumber
2 firm-ripe tomatoes
Freshly squeezed juice of 2 lemons
Freshly squeezed juice of 1lime
Salt to taste
Hot peppers (bird or goat) to taste

Wash the conchs thoroughly in cold water and cut into quarters. Cut the prepared vegetables into quarters.

Fit a **food processor** with disc for slicing. Begin by slicing the conch and then each vegetable. Remove to a **serving bowl** and sprinkle with salt.

In a **small dish**, combine the lemon and lime juices; crush the hot peppers into the juices and pour over the conch mix. Toss together gently; adjust the seasonings to taste and serve in **salad dishes** with a small dish of lime juice and hot peppers on the side.

Crawfish Salad

2 cups cooked crawfish, cut into 1/2" cubes page 32
1 cup 1/4" dice celery
1 tsp. minced onion
1 tsp. freshly squeezed lemon juice
2 tbsp. mayonnaise
Salt & ground white pepper to taste
Paprika

In a **medium-sized bowl**, mix together the crawfish, celery, onion, lemon juice, salt and pepper. Chill thoroughly.

Just before serving, drain and toss together with the mayonnaise. Sprinkle the top with paprika.

Crab Meat Salad

1 cup crab meat, cooked or canned
1/2 cup 1/4" dice celery
1/4 cup 1/4" dice green pepper
1/4 tsp. salt
1/4 tsp. ground white pepper
3 tbsp. freshly squeezed lemon juice
1/3 cup mayonnaise
Paprika

Flake the crabmeat, place into a **medium-sized bowl** and sprinkle with the lemon juice.

Add the diced celery, green pepper, salt and white pepper tossing gently with the mayonnaise. Chill and serve.

Shrimp Salad

1 cup cooked shrimp, 1/2" chunks
1 cup 1/2" dice celery
1 tsp. freshly squeezed lemon juice
1 tsp. minced onion
2 tbsp. mayonnaise
Salt and ground white pepper to taste
Paprika

In a **medium-sized bowl**, mix together the shrimp, celery and onion with the lemon juice, salt and pepper. Chill thoroughly.

Drain, and just before serving, toss together with the mayonnaise and sprinkle the top with paprika.

Chicken Salad

2 cups cold cooked chicken, cubed
1 tsp. freshly squeezed lemon juice
Salt and ground white pepper to taste
1/2 cup mayonnaise
1 cup diced celery
2 hard cooked eggs (optional)
1/2-cup diced ham or 1/2-cup seedless grapes (optional)

Boil the eggs; place into cold water; cool and chop using an **egg chopper**.

Cut the chicken into 1/2-inch cubes and place into a **medium-sized bowl**; sprinkle with the lemon juice, salt and pepper. Mix in the mayonnaise and celery. Carefully fold in the eggs.

Caribbean Chicken Salad

4 Servings

4 halves chicken breast
1 ripe plantain
1/4 cup olive oil
2 tbsp. freshly squeezed lime juice
1 tbsp. honey
2 tsp. Lady Darling's Island Seasoning
1 small onion, thinly sliced
1 medium-sized green pepper, thinly sliced
1 medium-sized red pepper, thinly sliced
1 head lettuce, torn for salad
1 ripe avocado cut into thin slices
1 ripe pineapple cut into 1-inch chunks

Wash the chicken, remove the skin and discard. Pat dry and cut into 1-inch chunks and place into a **large flat dish**. Peel the plantain and slice into 1/4-inch rounds.

Combine the olive oil, lime juice and honey in a **small bowl**, mixing together thoroughly. Divide the mixture in half.

Brush the chicken and the plantain with one half of the olive oil mixture and season with the Island Seasoning. Set aside.

Brush a **large non-stick skillet** with olive oil and heat. Over high heat, stir-fry the chicken and the plantains (in two batches) for about 5 to 6-minutes or until the meat is well done. Remove and let cool.

In a **large salad bowl**, toss together the onion, lettuce and remaining half of the olive oil mixture. Arrange on **four serving dishes** and top each with the chicken/plantain sauté, peppers, avocado and pineapple. Serve immediately.

Spicy Tuna Salad

1 can (6 oz.) tuna fish, drained
1 tbsp. freshly squeezed lime juice or lemon juice
1/4 cup 1/4" dice onion
1/4 cup 1/4" dice green pepper
1/3 cup mayonnaise
Hot peppers to taste
1 hard boiled egg, chopped (optional)

Place the drained tuna into a **small bowl** and sprinkle with the lime juice. Gently mix in the onion, green pepper, mayonnaise and crushed hot peppers to taste. Fold in the chopped egg if desired.

Holiday Turkey Salad

2 cups cold cooked turkey (holiday leftover)
1 cup 1/4" dice celery
1 tbsp. 1/4" dice onion
Salt and pepper to taste
1/2 cup mayonnaise

TIP:
A recipe for the turkey "left on the carcass" after a holiday meal.

Chop the turkey, especially the white meat into 1/2-inch chunks. Combine all ingredients in a **serving bowl** and toss lightly.

Variation

Add one of the following
Pineapple chunks
Seedless green grapes
1/2 cup pomegranate seeds
1/2 cup slivered almonds
1/2 cup dried apples with 1-tbsp. freshly squeezed lemon juice

Corned Beef Salad

1 can (12 oz.) corned beef
Hot peppers to taste
1 tbsp. freshly squeezed lime juice
1 tbsp. 1/4" dice onion,
1 tbsp. 1/4" dice green pepper
1 tbsp. 1/4" dice red pepper
2 tbsp. mayonnaise
Lettuce leaves and tomato wedges

Place the corned beef in a **medium-sized bowl** and break up with a fork in preparation to mix. In a **small dish**, crush the hot peppers into the lime juice and sprinkle over the beef.

Add the diced onion, peppers, and mayonnaise; mix together thoroughly.

Arrange the lettuce leaves and tomato wedges on **salad plates** topping with the corned beef mixture.

Egg Salad

3 hard cooked eggs
1/2 tsp. salt
1/2 tsp. ground white pepper
2 tbsp. mayonnaise
1 tsp. sweet relish

Boil the eggs (Tip *page 35*); chop using an **egg-chopper** and place into a **small serving bowl**. Add the salt and pepper mixing gently with the mayonnaise and the relish.

Piña Colada Fruit Salad Dressing

1 cup heavy cream
1/4 cup banana yogurt
1/4 cup pineapple juice
1/4 cup canned coconut milk
Freshly grated coconut

In a **medium-sized bowl**, whip the cream until thickened but not stiff. Fold in the yogurt, pineapple juice and coconut milk. Serve over fruit salads sprinkled with freshly grated coconut.

Avocado Salad Dressing

1 medium-sized ripe avocado
2 tbsp. heavy cream
1 tbsp. freshly squeezed lime juice
1/2 tsp. salt
1 tsp. prepared mustard
Hot peppers to taste

Peel the avocado; mash the pulp and place into a **medium-sized bowl**.

In **another bowl**, whisk together the remaining ingredients. Add to the bowl with the avocado and whisk thoroughly. Chill and serve.

Mint Salad Dressing

1/3 cup vegetable oil
1/3 cup chopped green onions
2 tbsp. lemon juice
1 tsp. dried mint leaves
2 cloves garlic, minced
1/2 tsp. salt
1/8 tsp. ground white pepper
1 bird pepper, crushed

Blend all ingredients in a **small bowl** and chill before pouring over vegetable salad.

Hot Benné Seed Dressing

1/4 cup vegetable oil
2 tsp. benné (sesame) seeds
2 tbsp. cider vinegar
2 tsp. sugar
1 tsp. soy sauce
1/4 tsp. garlic salt
1 bird pepper, crushed

Heat 2-teaspoons of the oil in a **small skillet**; add the benné seeds and cook over medium heat, stirring constantly, until the seeds are golden brown. Cool slightly.

Stir in remaining oil and remaining ingredients. Cook over medium heat, stirring constantly until the mixture boils. Pour over salad.

Cucumber Salad Dressing

1/2 cup finely chopped cucumber
1/4 cup finely chopped onion
1/4 cup cider vinegar
3 tbsp. vegetable oil
2 tbsp. sugar
1-1/2 tsp. caraway seeds
1/2 tsp. salt
1/2 tsp. paprika
1 bird pepper, crushed

Blend all ingredients in a **small bowl** and chill before pouring over vegetable salad.

Slaw Dressing
Sweet & Sour

1/2 cup mayonnaise
1 tbsp. finely chopped onion
1 tbsp. sweet relish
1 tbsp. vinegar
1 tsp. sugar
1 hard boiled egg, chopped (optional)

Mix the ingredients together in a **small bowl**. Taste-test for a sweet and sour balance adding more sugar or vinegar if needed. Gently mix in the chopped egg.

The Potato

One of the most important food plants developed in pre-Columbian America was the potato - f i r s t c u l t i v a t e d in the highlands of South America. Though the potato did not grow well in the tropics, the sweet potato thrived in both temperate and tropical zones. When Christopher Columbus returned to Queen Isabella, he did not say, "Your Majesty, I have brought you back an extraordinary treasure (because he was sent to look for gold) and it will change the world forever" and then hand her a potato. But he should have.

Breads & Rolls

Recipes

Bread Cups for Salads

Banana Doughnuts

Banana Biscuits

❋ *Muffins*

Guava, Molasses,

Banana Whole Wheat

❋ *Quick Breads*

Johnny Cake

Deluxe & Coconut

Rum Raisin Scones

Shortcakes

Cassava Coconut Pone

Corn Bread

Beer Cheese Corn Bread

Pineapple Loaf-a-Bread

Mango Bread

Banana Bran Bread

Tia Maria Jamaican Bread

❋ *Yeast Breads & Rolls*

Coconut Raisin Bread

Whole Wheat Bread

Dillie Dinner Rolls

Clover Leaf Rolls

Sesame Seed Bread Sticks

Coconut Bread Sticks

Pizza Crust

Guava Swirls

Petite Guava Duffs

Bread Cups For Salads

Yield 6 Cups
9 slices bread
Melted butter
Bake at 350ºF

Trim the crust from the bread slices and cut into halves diagonally. Melt the butter and brush halved slices on both sides.

Grease a **muffin tin** with butter and press the bread firmly into the cups. Bottoms will be flat and halved slices will cover sides and have 3 points upward. Place into the oven and toast.

Fill with seafood or meat salads.

Banana Doughnuts

Yield 20 Doughnuts
2-1/2 cups all purpose flour
2 tsp. baking powder
1/2 tsp. baking soda
1/2 tsp. ground nutmeg
2 tbsp. shortening
1/2 cup sugar
1 tsp. vanilla extract
2 eggs
1/2 cup mashed bananas
1/2 cup buttermilk
1/2 cup all purpose flour for rolling
Vegetable oil for deep-fat frying
Confectioners' sugar for dusting

Sift together the flour, baking powder, salt and nutmeg. In a **medium-sized mixing bowl** with **electric mixer**, cream the shortening and blend in the sugar. Add the vanilla and eggs beating until light and fluffy.

Mash the bananas in **another bowl** and combine with the buttermilk, stirring until well mixed. Add to the flour mixture in 3 or 4 portions, stirring just enough to mix after each addition. Place in a **covered dish** and chill for at least 1-hour.

Remove the dough to a floured **board** and knead lightly. With a floured **rolling pin**, roll out to 3/8-inch thickness. Cut out with a floured **doughnut cutter**.

Heat the oil in a **deep-fat fryer** *or a deep pot* with oil to cover and drop the doughnuts into the very hot fat. Fry quickly until golden brown; lift out using a **slotted spoon** and drain on a **wire rack**. Dust with Confectioners' sugar.

Banana Biscuits

Yield 12 Biscuits

2 large ripe bananas
1/3 cup butter, melted
1-1/2 cups all purpose flour
1/2 tsp. salt
2 tsp. baking powder
2 tbsp. sugar
1/2 cup raisins
1/4 cup Ole Nassau Banana Rum
Confectioners' sugar for dusting

Bake at 400°F

Peel the bananas; thinly slice one banana for tops of the biscuits and set aside. Mash the other banana and measure 1-cup of pulp into a **medium-sized bowl**. Stir the melted butter and rum into the banana pulp.

Sift together the flour, salt, baking powder, sugar and raisins. Add to the banana, mixing well. Add the rum mixing just enough to moisten. Turn onto a lightly floured **board** kneading until smooth.

With a floured **rolling pin**, roll the dough into a 1/2-inch thick rectangle and with a **2-inch cutter**, cut into rounds. Place onto a greased **baking sheet** and with fingers, make an indentation in the top of the biscuits pressing on one slice of banana.

Bake for about 20-minutes or until golden brown. Remove to a **wire rack** and dust with Confectioners' sugar.

Guava Muffins

3/4 cup fresh Guava Purée page 26 or canned guava, puréed
2 cups all purpose flour
1/2 tsp. salt
3 tsp. baking powder
1 cup milk
2 eggs, lightly beaten
3 tbsp. vegetable oil
Creamy Frosting page 314 (optional)

Bake at 400°F

In a **medium-sized bowl**, sift together the flour, sugar and baking powder. In a **small bowl**, combine the milk and eggs. Stir into the dry ingredients.

Stir in the oil and *Guava Purée* until the ingredients are just mixed.

Grease the **muffin tins** *or insert paper bake cups*. Fill each cup 2/3 full and bake for about 20-minutes. Remove to a **cooling rack**, allow to cool slightly and spread the *Creamy Frosting* over the top of each muffin.

Molasses Muffins

1-2/3 cups all purpose flour
3 tbsp. sugar
2 tsp. baking powder
1 tsp. ground ginger
1/2 tsp. salt
1/2 cup dark molasses
2 eggs, slightly beaten
1/4 cup vegetable oil
1/4 cup milk

Bake at 400°F

In a **medium-sized bowl**, mix together the flour, sugar, baking powder, ginger and salt. Make a well in the centre of the mixture.

In a **small bowl**, mix together remaining ingredients and pour into the well in the dry ingredients. Stir just until the ingredients are moistened.

Insert **paper bake cups** into **muffin tins** and fill each cup about 2/3 full. Bake for about 15-minutes or until centres spring back when touched lightly.

Banana Whole Wheat Muffins

Yield 12 Muffins

1 cup mashed ripe bananas
3/4 cup butter
3/4 cup sugar
1 egg
1/2 cup all purpose flour
1/2 tsp. baking powder
1 cup Whole Wheat flour
1 cup milk
1 tsp. baking soda

Bake at 400°F

In a **medium-sized mixing bowl** with **electric mixer**, cream the butter and sugar together until light and fluffy. Beat in the egg.

Sift together the regular flour and baking powder. Stir in the Whole Wheat flour and baking soda. Add the flour mixture alternately with the milk to the creamed mixture.

Grease the **muffin tins**, or *insert paper bake cups*. Fill 2/3-full and bake for 25-minutes or until the centre is set.

Johnny Cake

2 cups all purpose flour
3 tsp. baking powder
2 tsp. sugar
1 tsp. salt
1/3 cup vegetable shortening
3/4 cup water

Bake at 425°F

In a **medium-sized bowl**, sift together the flour, baking powder, sugar and salt. Cut in the shortening with a **pastry cutter**.

Make a well in the centre of the mixture; pour in the water mixing to a smooth dough. Turn onto a floured **board**, knead lightly and with a floured **rolling pin**, roll out into a 10-inch circle.

Place into a greased **iron skillet**, cover and over very low heat "bake on the stove top" for about 12 to15-minutes on each side. Serve hot with butter or guava jam.

To oven bake, place the dough into a greased **10-inch round baking pan** and bake for 25 to 30-minutes.

Journey Bread

(Also known as Johnny Bread or Johnny Cake)

In the early days of the American colonies, Johnny cakes, usually made of wheat flour and corn meal were originally called "journey cakes" because the circuit riders carried the bread with them on their travels to preach the gospel. Most likely, this custom came to the Bahamas with the 5,000 refugees that came here after being expelled from the new United States following the American Revolutionary War because of their unswerving loyalty to the King of England.

Johnny Cake Deluxe

2 cups all purpose flour
3 tbsp. baking powder
2 tbsp. sugar
1/3 cup butter
3/4 cup evaporated milk or whole milk
2 slightly beaten eggs

Bake at 425°F

Sift together the flour, baking powder, sugar and salt in a **medium-sized bowl**. Cut in the butter with a **pastry cutter**.

In a **small bowl**, whisk together the milk and eggs. Make a well in the center of the flour mixture and stir in the egg mix; gently mixing to a smooth dough.

Turn onto a floured **board**, knead lightly and with a floured **rolling pin**, roll out into a 10-inch circle. Place into a greased **10-inch round pan** and bake for 25 to 30-minutes. Serve hot with butter.

Coconut Johnny Cake

1 cup freshly grated coconut *page 24*
2 cups all purpose flour
3 tsp. baking powder
2 tsp. sugar
1 tsp. salt
1/3 cup vegetable shortening
3/4 cup canned coconut milk

In a **medium-sized bowl**, sift together the flour, baking powder, sugar and salt. Cut in the shortening with a **pastry cutter**. Mix in the grated coconut.

Make a well in the centre of the mixture; pour in the coconut milk mixing to a smooth dough. Turn onto a floured **board**, knead lightly and with a floured **rolling pin**, roll out into a 10-inch circle.

Place into a greased **10-inch iron skillet**, cover and over very low heat "bake on the stove top" for about 12 to 15-minutes on each side. (*Or place into a greased 10-inch round pan and bake at 425°F for 25 to 30-minutes*). Serve hot with butter or guava jam.

Rum Raisin Scones

1 cup all purpose flour
3 tsp. baking powder
1/2 tsp. salt
2 tbsp. sugar
2 oz. butter
1/4 cup raisins
1/4 cup Ole Nassau Chick Charney Rum
1/4 cup water

Bake at 400ºF

In a **medium-sized bowl**, sift together the flour, baking powder, salt and sugar. With a **pastry cutter**, cut in the butter until the mixture is the consistency of rice grains. Add the raisins; mix in the rum combined with the water handling the dough quickly and lightly.

Turn onto a floured **board** and with a floured **rolling pin**; roll out to 3/4-inch thickness. With a floured **2-inch round cutter**, cut into rounds. Place on an un-greased **baking sheet** and bake for 10 to 15-minutes. Serve warm or cold with whipped cream and *Guava Jam page 361*.

Shortcakes

2 cups all purpose flour
2 tsp. baking powder
1 tsp. salt
2 tbsp. sugar
1/3 cup vegetable shortening
3/4 cup buttermilk

Bake at 450°F

In a **small bowl**, sift together the flour, baking powder, sugar and salt. With a **pastry cutter**, cut in the shortening until mixture resembles rice grains. Make a well in the centre of the mixture and pour in the buttermilk.

Stir with a fork just until the mixture holds together. Gently form the dough into a ball and place onto a floured **board**. Knead lightly with finger tips, 10 to 15 times.

With a floured **rolling pin**, gently roll out the dough to 3/4-inch thickness. Cut out with a floured **3-inch cutter** *or with cut out and a knife*. Place the biscuits onto a greased **baking sheet** and bake for 10 to 15-minutes.

Corn Bread

1 cup Yellow Corn Meal
1 cup all purpose flour
2 tbsp. sugar
1-1/2 tsp. baking powder
1/2 tsp. salt
1 cup milk
1 egg, beaten
1/4 cup vegetable oil

Bake at 425°F

In a **medium-sized bowl**, combine the dry ingredients; add the milk and eggs and mix until blended. Stir in the oil mixing well.

Turn into a well-greased **8x10-inch pan** and bake for 25 to 30-minutes or until a knife inserted into the centre comes out clean.

Beer Cheese Cornbread

1-1/2 cups all purpose flour
1/2 cup Yellow Corn Meal
2 tbsp. sugar
1-1/2 tsp. baking powder
1 tsp. onion powder
3/4 tsp. baking soda
1/2 tsp. salt
2 cups Cheddar Cheese, grated
1 cup Kalik beer
2 eggs
1/3 cup vegetable oil
Bake at 350°F

Sift together the flour, corn meal, sugar, baking powder, onion powder and baking soda.

In a **medium-sized mixing bowl** with **electric mixer**, beat together the cheese, beer, eggs and oil. Add the dry ingredients and beat for about 2-minutes.

Turn into a greased **loaf pan** and bake for about 1-hour or until a knife inserted in the centre comes out clean. Serve warm or cold and refrigerate left-over cornbread.

Cassava & Coconut Pone

2 cups grated cassava *page 30*
2 cups freshly grated coconut *page 24*
1 tbsp. butter
2/3 cup sugar
1 tsp. baking powder
1/2 tsp salt
1 tsp. ground allspice
1 tsp. ground cinnamon
1 tsp. vanilla extract
3/4 cup milk
3/4 cup water
Bake at 350°F

Mix the grated cassava and coconut together in a **large bowl**. Cut in the butter with a **pastry cutter**, adding the sugar, baking powder, spices and vanilla. Add the milk and water, mixing well.

Turn the mixture into a well-greased **12x8-inch-baking dish**, and bake for 1-1/2 hours. Allow to cool slightly and cut into squares. Serve warm or cold.

Pineapple Loaf-a-Bread

1 cup finely chopped fresh pineapple with natural juices *page 25*
1-3/4 cups all purpose flour
2 tsp. baking powder
1/2 tsp. salt
1/4 tsp. baking soda
1/4 cup butter
3/4 cup brown sugar
2 eggs
3/4 cup chopped almonds
Creamy Frosting page 314 (optional)
Bake at 350°F

Prepare the fresh pineapple; slice and chop enough of the fruit to measure 1-cup, reserving the juice.

Sift together the flour, baking powder, salt and baking soda.

In a **small mixing bowl** with **electric mixer**, cream the butter and sugar together until light and fluffy. Beat in the eggs one at a time.

Stir in the pineapple and nuts. Turn into a well-greased **loaf pan** and bake for 1-hour. Remove, place onto a **cooling rack** and cool slightly. Spread the *Creamy Frosting* over the top.

Mango Bread

1/2 cup butter or margarine
1/4 cup sugar
1 egg
1/4 cup milk
2 cups all purpose flour
1 tsp. baking powder
1 tsp. baking soda
1/2 tsp. grated lemon rind
3/4 cup mashed ripe mango *page 27*
1/4 cup white raisins
1/2 cup raisins
1/2 cup chopped almonds
Bake at 350°F

In a **medium-sized mixing bowl** with **electric mixer**, cream together the butter and sugar. Add the egg and milk.

Sift together the dry ingredients and add to the egg mixture, mixing well. Stir in the lemon rind, mango, raisins and nuts.

Turn into a well-greased **loaf pan** and bake for 1-hour or until a knife inserted in the center comes out clean. Place onto a **cooling rack**, allow to cool and serve.

Banana Bran Bread

1-1/2 cups ripe bananas, mashed
1 cup bran
1-1/2 cups all purpose flour
2 tsp. baking powder
1/2 tsp. baking soda
1/4 cup butter, softened
1/2 cup sugar
1 egg
2 tbsp. milk
1/2 tsp. salt
1 tsp. vanilla extract
1/2 cup chopped walnuts
Bake at 350°F

In a **medium-sized mixing bowl** with **electric mixer**, cream the butter and sugar. Add the egg then the bran mixing well.

Combine the milk, mashed banana and vanilla in **another bowl** and add alternately with the sifted dry ingredients, beating thoroughly. Fold in the nuts. Turn into a greased **loaf pan** and bake for 1-hour.

Coconut Raisin Bread

Yield 3 Loaves

1/2 cup warm water (not hot)
2 pkg. active dry yeast
1-1/2 cups lukewarm canned coconut milk
1/4 cup sugar
1 tbsp. salt
3 eggs
1/4 cup soft butter
2 cups raisins
7-1/4 to 7-1/2 cups all purpose flour
Butter for brushing tops of loaves
Bake at 425°F

In a **large bowl**, dissolve the yeast in the warm water. Stir the lukewarm coconut milk, sugar, salt, eggs, shortening and half of the flour into the yeast. Mix until smooth *(or use bread maker according to manufacturer's instructions)*.

Add enough of the remaining flour to handle easily. Turn onto a floured **board** and knead. Cover with a dish-towel and allow rising in a warm place to double in size, 1-1/2 to 2-hours.

Punch down the dough, shape into 3 loaves and place into greased **loaf pans**. Brush the tops with butter, cover and allow rising again until double in size, 1-1/2 hours. Bake for 25 to 30-minutes.

Tia Maria Jamaican Banana Bread

2 cups all purpose flour
2 tsp. baking powder
1/2 tsp. salt
1/2 tsp. baking soda
1/2 cup butter or margarine
2 eggs
1/2 cup brown sugar
2 ripe bananas, mashed
1/2 cup Tia Maria

Dip

1/2 cup copped walnuts
1 pkg. (8 oz.) cream cheese, softened
3 tbsp. Tia Maria
Bake at 350°F

Sift together the flour, baking powder, salt and baking soda.

In a **medium-sized mixing bowl** with **electric mixer**, cream the b u t t e r and sugar until light and fluffy. Add the eggs and beat well, mixing in the Tia Maria.

With the mixer at low speed, add the dry ingredients alternately with the bananas, beating until smooth. Fold in the nuts.

Turn into a greased **loaf pan** and bake for 45 to 50-minutes or until a toothpick inserted comes out clean. Turn onto a **cooling rack** and allow to cool.

Dip

Meanwhile, in a **small mixing bowl** with the mixer, beat the cream cheese with the Tia Maria until light and fluffy. Serve with the *Banana Bread*.

Legend of Tia Maria

The legend of Tia Maria dates back to the Caribbean Colonial Wars of the 17th century. When the English navy stormed Jamaica, the Spanish settlers, along with the Spanish governor and his family, were forced to flee into the back-country. The governor's daughter, Adela, had time to save only her treasured black pearl earrings, wrapped for her in an old scrap of parchment by the family's housekeeper, an old woman lovingly called "Tia Maria". Days later, when Adela opened the package, she found a recipe scrawled inside. Maria had hastily recorded the family's secret formula for the Jamaican coffee liqueur.

For generations, the secret formula, named after the woman who saved it, was passed down as a gift from mother to daughter on the daughter's wedding day and is a tradition that continues to this day.

Whole Wheat Bread

1-1/4 cups warm water (not hot)
1 pkg. active dry yeast
2 tbsp. soft vegetable shortening
2 tsp. salt
1 tbsp. molasses
1 cup Whole Wheat flour
2 cups all purpose flour
Bake at 375°F

In a **large mixing bowl**, dissolve the yeast in the warm water. Add the shortening, salt, molasses and half the flour to the yeast. With an **electric mixer** set on medium speed, beat for 2-minutes.

Add remaining flour and blend in using a **large wooden spoon** *(or use bread maker according to manufacturer's instructions)*. Cover with a dishtowel and let rise in a warm place for 30-minutes.

Stir down the batter using the wooden spoon and spread evenly in a greased **loaf pan**. Cover and let rise for about 40-minutes. Bake for 45 to 50-minutes or until brown. Remove from the pan immediately and place onto a **cooling rack**.

Brush the top with melted butter. Cool before serving.

Global Exchange

The foods and plants which were growing on the Caribbean islands were unknown in Europe in 1492, such as corn, potatoes, tobacco and tomatoes. The potato can be credited with greatly increasing the European population and enabling large cities to be supported. Both potatoes and corn could be stored and transported, making it possible to feed people living in large cities and towns located great distances from farms. One can hardly imagine Ireland without the potato, or Italy without the tomato. In subsequent voyages, Columbus introduced barley, wheat, European grapes, pigs and rabbits to the Caribbean region. He also requested importation of almonds, honey, raisins, rice, horses, donkeys, sheep, and heifers.

Sapodilla

(Sapote or Naseberry)

The Sapodilla tree is native to Central America and the West Indies. For centuries, the Mayan Indians of Central America boiled the sticky, milkwhite latex of the (chickle) Sapodilla tree and chewed the gum. Now the modern world has adopted chicle as

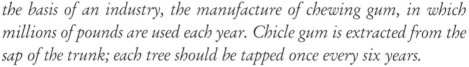

the basis of an industry, the manufacture of chewing gum, in which millions of pounds are used each year. Chicle gum is extracted from the sap of the trunk; each tree should be tapped once every six years.

The sapodilla or "Dilly" is grown from seed and is round in shape, about four inches in diameter with a reddish-brown skin varying in size and quality of its fruit. The flesh is yellowish to reddish brown and in many fruits is very fine, with smooth texture and sweet, rich flavour, while in others is a little grainy and over-sweet. The fruit is picked when mature but still hard and is held until it is just soft to the touch; it is then luscious eaten out of hand.

It is stated that the sapodilla is usable only as a fresh, raw fruit, unsuited for cooking. On the contrary, the fruit can be boiled and the juice made into a delicious syrup, added to breads, pancakes and cheesecakes. ✳

Dillie Dinner Rolls

Yield 4 Dozen

2 ripe sapodillas for 1 cup purée (or substitute 1 cup mashed yams)
1-1/2 cups warm water (not hot)
1 package active dry yeast (2 tsp.)
2/3 cup sugar
1-1/2 tsp. salt
2/3 cup vegetable shortening softened
2 eggs
7 to 7-1/2 cups all purpose flour

Bake at 425°F

In a **small bowl**, dissolve the yeast and 1-teaspoon of the sugar in the warm water. Using a **wire whisk**, whisk in eggs and the purée *page 27.*

In a **large bowl**, sift together the flour, remaining sugar and salt. Using a **pastry cutter**, cut in shortening until mixture resembles rice grains; make a well in the centre. Pour in the yeast mixture and with hands, mix the dough until easy to handle. Turn onto a floured **board** kneading until smooth *(or use bread maker according to instructions).*

Form the dough into a ball and return to the large bowl. Brush with oil, cover with a damp cloth and let rise in a warm place until double in size, 1-1/2 to 2-hours *or place in refrigerator overnight.*

About 2-hours before baking, punch down the dough, cut off pieces 1/3-the size of rolls desired and form into balls. Place the balls into a **large greased baking pan** about 1-inch apart. Cover and let rise in a warm place until double in size, 1-1/2 to 2-hours. Bake for 12 to 15-minute or until brown and serve warm.

Cloverleaf Rolls

Prepare **Dough** for *Dillie Dinner Rolls* and, after first rising, cut off pieces of dough about 1-inch in diameter and form into balls. Place 3 balls into each cup of greased **muffin tins**. Cover and let rise until double in size, 1-1/2 to 2- hours. Bake for 12 to 15-minutes. For a dark brown top, brush with Egg Glaze (an egg yolk beaten together with 1-teaspoon of fresh lemon juice) before baking.

Coconut Bread Sticks

Prepare **Dough** for *Dillie Dinner Rolls* and after first rising, cut off small pieces of dough and roll into sticks about 1/2x6-inches, and then roll in freshly grated coconut. Place onto greased **baking sheets**. Cover and let rise until double in size, 1-1/2 to 2-hours. Bake for 12 to 15-minutes.

Sesame Seed Bread Sticks

Prepare same as coconut sticks except roll in sesame seeds. Place onto greased **baking sheets**. Cover and let rise until double in size, 1-1/2 to 2 hours. Bake for 12 to 15-minutes.

Guava Swirls

Guava Filling page 333

Dough

1 tsp. (1/2 pkg.) active dry yeast
1/4 cup warm water (not hot)
3-1/2 to 3-3/4 cups all purpose flour
1 tsp. salt
1/4 cup sugar
1 egg
1/4 cup whole milk
3/4 cup lukewarm canned coconut milk
1/4 cup soft vegetable shortening
Vegetable oil for brushing the dough
Soka Hard Rum Sauce page 315
Bake at 350°F

Prepare the *Guava Filling* and set aside.

Dough

In a **large mixing bowl**, dissolve the yeast and 1-teaspoon of the sugar in the warm water. Using a **large wooden spoon**, mix in the milk, sugar, salt, shortening and half the flour. Continue mixing until smooth, adding just enough flour to handle easily.

Turn onto a floured **board**, kneading until smooth. Shape into a ball, return to the bowl and brush with oil. Cover with a damp cloth and let rise in a warm place until double in size, 1-1/2 to 2-hours.

Punch down the dough, place onto a floured board and with a floured **rolling pin**, roll out into an oblong of 1/4-inch thickness. Spread the filling evenly over the oblong to 1-inch of the sides.

Roll up tightly into a log, beginning at the wide end and brush the edges with water to seal, pinching together securely.

Cut the log into 1/2-inch thick slices and place on a greased **baking sheet**. Cover and let rise until double in size, 1 to 1-1/2-hours.

Bake for 25 to 30-minutes. Remove to a **cooling rack**, cool slightly and spread with *Soka Hard Rum Sauce*. Separate and serve warm or cold.

Petite Guava Duffs

Double batch of *Guava Filling page 333*

Dough

1/2 cup warm water (not-hot)
1 pkg. (2 tsp.) active dry yeast
1 cup milk, scalded
2/3 cup butter, softened
2 eggs
7 to 7-1/2 cups all purpose flour
1 cup sugar
1/2 tsp. salt
1 cup guava purée

TIP:
Dough may be
made the day before
and placed in refrigerator.
Remove 2 hours before
preparation of duffs.

Egg Wash

1 egg
2 tbsp. water

Soka Hard Rum Sauce page 315

Bake at 325°F

In a **small dish**, dissolve the yeast in the warm water. In a **1-quart saucepan**, scald the milk; melt in the butter and cool slightly. Beat together the eggs, yeast and milk mixtures.

In a **large bowl**, sift together the flour, sugar and salt. Make a well in the centre and stir in the egg mixture and guava purée blending to form a smooth dough.

Turn onto a floured **board** and knead for a few minutes. Form into a ball, brush with oil and place into the bowl. Cover and let rise in a warm place until double in size, 1-1/2 to 2-hours.

Prepare the *Guava Filling* and allow to cool.

Egg Wash

In a **small dish**, beat together the egg and water.

Punch down the dough; place onto the floured **board** and knead for a few minutes. Cut into four sections and, with a floured **rolling pin**, roll sections out to 1/4-inch thickness. Cut into 3x5-inch rectangles.

Place about 1-tablespoonful of filling on each rectangle and spread out. Brush edges with the egg wash and roll up pinching edges together securely. Place the duffs onto greased **baking sheets** with seams on top. Cover and let rise until double in size, 1-1/2 to 2-hours.

Bake for 20 to 25-minutes or until golden brown. Remove the duffs to **cooling racks** and while still warm, spread the *Soka Hard Rum Sauce* over tops and serve.

Notes

Soups &
Curries

Menus

✤

Caesar Salad
Pigeon Peas Soup & Dumplings
Vanilla Ice Cream with Mango
Syrup

✤

Lettuce Salad with Mint Dressing
Bahamian Conch Chowder
Clover Leaf Rolls
Mango Double Boiler Duff

✤

Greek Salad
Conch Au Vin
Barefoot Rice
Guava Upside Down Cake

✤

Tossed Salad with Dressing
Tej's Guyana Pepperpot
Corn Bread
Tamarind Chutney
Double Boiler Coconut Duff

✤

Lettuce & Tomato Salad with
Blue Cheese Dressing
Chicken Souse with Potato Cubes
Deluxe Johnny Cake
Mango Cheesecake

✤

Cabbage & Carrot Slaw
Smudder Pork Chops
Pork Seasoned Rice
Beet & Onion Slices
Guava Duff

✤

Tossed Salad with French Dressing
Stewed Fish with Potato Cubes
Cassava Pone
Half Sapodilla

✤

Recipes

❋ Soups
Avocado, Beer Cheese,
Creamy Cassava,
Onion Mushroom, Pumpkin, Okra,
Charline Cabbage
Cream of Potato
Green Pigeon Peas
Vegetable

❋ Chowders
Bahamian Conch,
Clam

❋ Hearty Soups
Holiday Turkey,
Pigeon Peas Soup & Dumpling,
Guyana Pepperpot,
Metagee from Guyana,
George's Chicken & Dumplin',
Conch Au Vin,
Turtle

❋ Stews
Hurricane Ham,
African Beef, African Chicken,
Mutton, Stewed Fish, Stewed Conch

❋ Curried Dishes
Chicken, Goat, Conch, Grouper

❋ Souses
Chicken, Turkey, Conch

❋ Smudder (Steamed) Dishes
Fish, Conch, Pork Chops,
Chicken, Mutton

Avocado Soup

1 large or 2 medium-sized avocados
1 tsp. freshly squeezed lemon juice
1/2 tsp. salt
1/2 tsp. crushed hot peppers
1 tbsp. finely chopped onion
1 tsp. lemon rind

Peel the avocados; mash the pulp and place into a **medium-sized bowl**. Add remaining ingredients, mixing thoroughly.

Place the mixture into the bowl of a **blender** *or a food processor* and purée. Turn into a **2-quart sized saucepan** and heat over very low heat, stirring, but do not cook. Serve immediately.

Pumpkin Soup

1 medium-sized pumpkin (about 4 cups cubed)
6 cups chicken broth
Salt to taste
3 slices bacon, chopped
1 medium-sized onion, chopped
2 ribs celery, chopped
1 sprig thyme
1 bay leaf
1 tsp. Lady Darling's Island Seasoning
Black pepper to taste
2 carrots, 1/2" dice
1 cup heavy cream

Cut open the pumpkin and remove and discard the seeds. Cut into sections; peel and cut into 1-inch chunks. Place into a **4-quart sized saucepan**, adding the chicken broth and salt.

Bring to a boil over high heat. Cover, and over medium-low heat, simmer for 45-minutes *(or pressure-cook for 15-minutes)*. Remove from the heat and allow to cool.

In 3 or 4 batches, place into the bowl of a **food processor** *or the bowl of a blender* and purée. Return to the pot and bring to a boil.

In a **large skillet**, fry the bacon and sauté the onion, celery and thyme. Turn into the pot; add the bay leaf, Island Seasoning and black pepper.

Reduce the heat, cover and simmer, stirring occasionally until the soup is thick, about 45-minutes. Add the vegetables and cream; simmer for an additional 10-minutes.

Boiling milk may be added to adjust consistency. Remove the bay leaf and the thyme sprig and serve immediately.

Beer Cheese Soup

1 cup of Kalik beer
1 cup grated Swiss cheese
2 cups beef broth
1/4 cup all purpose flour
1 tsp. ground white pepper
1/2 tsp. ground ginger
1 tsp. salt

Bring the beef broth to a boil in a **2-quart sized saucepan**. Remove from the heat.

Mix the flour with 1/2-cup of the beer and stir into the broth until smooth. Return to the heat and bring to a boil stirring until the mixture thickens.

Reduce the heat; stir in the cheese until it melts. Season with pepper, ginger and salt.

Stir in remaining beer. Remove from the heat, pour into soup dishes and serve immediately.

Onion Mushroom Soup

1 lb. fresh mushrooms, sliced
1 large onion, thinly sliced
2 tbsp. butter
2 tbsp. all purpose flour
4 cups beef broth
3/4 cup Harvey's Bristol Cream
1/2 cup shredded Gruyère cheese
6 slices French bread

Melt the butter in a **4-quart sized saucepan** and cook the mushrooms and onion until the onion is soft. Stir in the flour and cook, stirring for 1 or 2 minutes. Cover and simmer for 10-minutes. Stir in the Harvey's Bristol Cream.

Sprinkle the cheese on the bread slices and broil until melted.

Spoon the soup into **serving bowls** and place the toast on each serving of soup.

Creamy Cassava Soup

1 lb. cassava
1 lb. smoked ham or turkey
Water
1 large onion, chopped
1 large bay leaf
1 sprig of thyme
1 tsp. black pepper
Salt to taste
1 tsp. Browning Sauce
1-1/2 cups mixed vegetables (frozen)

Peel the cassava, cut into chunks and remove centre membrane *page 30*. Place into a **3-quart sized pot** with the smoked meat. Add enough water to cover, bring to a boil and cook for 30-minutes until the cassava is soft *(or pressure-cook for 15-minutes)*.

Cool, remove the meat to a **cutting board**; cut into small chunks and set aside.

In 3 or 4 batches, place the cassava with same water and onion into a **food processor** *or a blender,* and purée.

Return the cassava purée and chopped meat to the pot. Add the thyme, bay leaf, pepper, Browning Sauce and salt to taste. Cover, and cook over medium low heat, stirring occasionally for 15 to 20-minutes adding more water if necessary.

Add the vegetables and cook until soft, stirring to avoid settling of the soup at the bottom of the pot. Remove the bay leaf and thyme sprig and serve immediately.

Pre-Columbian Cultures

When the Europeans "discovered" the Americas in the 15th century, there were about thirty million people living in this hemisphere. These people were of very different cultures and lived in varied and separate societies. Some societies were as complex as those of the Aztecs, whose large cities were supported by innovative agricultural methods; or the magnificent mountain cities of the Incas, who practiced terrace cultivation. Corn's origin is believed to be on the Mexican plateau or in the highlands of Guatemala and dates back even further than the settlement by native people.

Cassava

Cassava, a starchy root covered with a brown bark, was the staple diet of the early Caribbean natives and is still an important item in the diet of many West Indians. The flesh which is white and hard, can be ground into flour and used to make bread.

The juice obtained from grated cassava root is flavoured with cinnamon, cloves and brown sugar to make cassareep, an essential component of a stew known as pepperpot. These tubers contain an amount of prussic acid, which must be removed by cooking, or pressing.

Other products made from cassava include laundry starch, tapioca and farina. ✻

Bahamian Conch Chowder

2 medium-sized conchs
3 slices bacon, chopped
1 medium-sized onion, 1/4" dice
1 medium-sized green pepper, 1/4" dice
1 stalk celery, 1/4" dice
1/2 tsp. dried thyme leaves
4-1/2 cups water
1 cup chopped tomato
2 tbsp. Champion Tomato Paste
1 bay leaf
1 tsp. Lady Darling's Island Seasoning
Salt & black pepper to taste
Hot peppers to taste
2 tbsp. margarine
2 tbsp. all purpose flour
1/2 cup milk
1 cup 1/4" dice carrots
1 cup 1/4" dice potato

Prepare conchs using Method Two *page 31.*

In a **large skillet**, fry the bacon until soft, add the diced onion, green pepper, celery and thyme leaves sautéing for 3 to 4-minutes.

Remove the sauté to a **3-quart sized saucepan** (preserving the fat in the skillet). Add the water to the pot.

Over high heat, sauté the conch in the skillet for 4 to 5-minutes. Reduce the heat add the chopped tomato and sauté for 4 to 5-minutes.

Turn the contents of the skillet into the pot and bring to a boil over medium high heat. Add the tomato paste, bay leaf, salt, Island Seasoning, black pepper and hot pepper. Reduce the heat, cover and cook for 15-minutes.

Melt the margarine in a **small saucepan** stirring in the flour until smooth. Remove from the heat, stir in the milk, and stirring continually, return to low heat, making a smooth sauce.

Slowly pour the sauce into the chowder as it cooks. Stir several times and adjust the seasonings. Add the carrots and potatoes; cover and simmer just until the vegetables are soft, 8 to 10-minutes. Remove the bay leaf and serve.

Clam Chowder

Prepare same as *Bahamian Conch Chowder* above except substitute 2-cups chopped clams for the conch.

Cream of Potato Soup

1 lb. potatoes, peeled and cubed
4 cups chicken stock or water with bouillon cubes
2 large onions, chopped
1 cup milk
1/2 cup cream
2 tbsp. butter
2 tbsp all purpose flour
1 bay leaf
Salt and ground white pepper to taste
Chopped parsley

Pour the chicken stock into a **large stockpot**; add the cubed potatoes and chopped onion.

Over medium-high heat cook until potatoes are tender. Allow to cool and pour into a **food mill** *or sieve* placed over a **large bowl** and pureé into the bowl with the stock.

In a **1-quart sized saucepan**, melt the butter and stir in the flour, cooking slowly for a few minutes.

Remove the saucepan from the heat and gradually stir in the milk. Return to medium heat and stirring vigorously, cook until the sauce thickens. Allow to cool a little.

Return the pureé to the stockpot; heat, then stir in the flour and milk mixture. Stirring, slowly add the cream.

Add the bay leaf and additional seasonings if desired. Cook for 10 to 15 minutes and serve garnished with chopped parsley.

Charline's Cabbage Soup

1/2 head medium-sized cabbage
2 onions
1 green pepper
2 scallions
2 ribs celery
2 carrots
1 can (8 oz.) tomato juice
1 can (16 oz.) tomatoes, chopped
1 tsp. dried thyme leaves
2 chicken bouillon cubes
1 bay leaf
1 tsp. Lady Darling's Island Seasoning
Water to cover
Salt and black pepper to taste

Wash, peel and chop the vegetables. Combine all ingredients in a **large stockpot**, adding water to cover and bring to a boil.

Reduce the heat, cover and simmer for about 45-minutes, stirring occasionally. Taste test, adding water and seasoning if necessary.

Holiday Turkey Soup

Carcass of holiday turkey with pan scrapings
Water to cover (about 5 to 6 cups)
2 chicken flavoured bouillon cubes
1 large onion, chopped
1 cup chopped okra (fresh or frozen)
1 sprig of thyme
1 large bay leaf
1 tsp. Lady Darling's Island Seasoning
Salt and black pepper to taste
2 ribs celery, chopped
2 carrots, chopped
1 large potato, peeled and cut into 1/4" dice

Remove whatever meat is left on the bones; cut into small chunks and set aside. Chop the bones of the carcass into sections and place into a **4-quart sized saucepan** along with the pan scrapings. Add the water, bouillon cubes, onion, okra, thyme sprig, bay leaf, salt, Island Seasoning and black pepper.

Bring to a boil. Cover and simmer over medium heat for 45-minutes, stirring occasionally. Remove the bones from the soup and discard.

Add the chunks of turkey meat, celery, carrots and potatoes and more water and seasonings if necessary. Cook for about 15-minutes. Remove the bay leaf and thyme sprig and serve.

Pigeon Peas Soup & Dumpling

3 cups soft cooked or canned pigeon peas, drained
3 conchs, fresh or dried
Stock from boiled or canned peas with additional water to measure 6 cups
1 oz. vegetable oil
3 slices bacon, chopped
2 medium-sized onion, chopped
1 clove garlic, finely chopped
1 tsp. dried thyme leaves
1 tsp. Browning Sauce
3 large potatoes, peeled and cut into 1" cubes
1 tsp. Lady Darling's Island Seasoning
Salt to taste
1 tsp. black pepper
Hot peppers to taste

Dumplings

2 cups all purpose flour
1 tsp. baking powder
1/2 tsp. salt
Water

Boil the peas *page 31*. Wash the conchs and prepare Method Two *page 31*. Drain and cut into 1-inch sized cubes and set aside.

In a **4-quart sized saucepan**, with a cover, combine the peas and stock and water.

Fry the bacon in a **large skillet** and remove to the pot, preserving drippings. Over high heat, quickly fry the conch in the skillet for 5 or 6-minutes. Remove directly to the pot.

Lower the heat under the skillet and sauté the onion and garlic with the thyme. Remove and add directly to the pot. Add the salt, Island Seasoning, black pepper and hot pepper to taste.

Bring the pot to a boil, reduce the heat, cover and cook for 35 to 40-minutes stirring occasionally.

Dumplings

In a **small bowl**, mix together the flour, baking powder and salt, adding just enough water (not all at once) to knead mixture to a smooth dough.

Place onto a floured **board** and with a floured **rolling pin**, roll out to thickness of about 1/2-inch and cut into 1x2-inch strips. Drop into the boiling soup individually.

Add the potatoes, cover and continue cooking for 12 to 15-minutes. Adjust the seasonings and serve immediately.

Pigeon Peas Soup & Dumpling Variation

Polenta Dumplings

1/2 cup Yellow Corn Meal
2 cups all purpose flour
1 tsp. baking powder
1/2 tsp. salt
1/2 cup water
1 tbsp. vegetable oil

In a **small bowl**, sift together the dry ingredients. Mix in the water and oil stirring to a stiff batter.

Drop by tablespoonfuls into boiling soup and continue cooking for 12 to 15-minutes.

Green Pigeon Peas Soup

1-1/2 cups green pigeon peas
3 to 4 cups water
1 - 12 oz. can tomato purée
2 scallions, chopped
Sprig of thyme
1 bay leaf
1/2 tsp. Lady Darling's Island Seasoning or to taste
Salt & black pepper to taste
1/2 cup long grain rice
1 cup firm-meat fish (mutton fish or grouper), cubed

In a **large stockpot**, combine the water, peas, tomato pureé, scallion, thyme and bay leaf and bring to a boil.

Add the seasonings to taste, rice and cubed fish. Simmer for about 30-minutes and serve.

Okra Soup

2 lbs. fresh okra (or frozen), chopped
3 slices bacon, chopped
1 large onion, chopped
1 sprig thyme
1 lb. smoked meat, 1/2" chunks
Water (approximately 5 to 6 cups)
1 large bay leaf
1 tsp. Browning Sauce
1 tsp. Lady Darling's Island Seasoning
Salt to taste
1 tsp. black pepper
Hot peppers to taste
2 cups corn cut fresh from the cob

Hot *Barefoot Rice* page 206

In a **large skillet**, fry the bacon and sauté the onion and thyme. Add the okra and continue to sauté for 5 or 6-minutes.

Combine the smoked meat and water in a **4-quart sized saucepan**.

Turn the sauté into the pot, add the bay leaf, Browning Sauce and seasonings and bring to a boil.

Reduce the heat, cover and simmer for about 45-minutes, stirring occasionally. Add the corn, adjust the seasonings and cook for another 10-minutes.

Remove the bay leaf and the thyme sprig. Serve immediately over hot *Barefoot Rice*.

Tej's Guyanese Metagee

2 lbs. pig's tails
2 lbs. salted beef
3 - 16 oz. cans coconut milk
1 large onion, cut into 1-1/2" chunks
2 scallions, chopped
2 cloves garlic, finely chopped
1/2 tsp. dried thyme leaves
1 whole goat pepper
1 green plantain
1 hard ripe plantain
1 lb. cassava
1 lb. red sweet potatoes
1 lb. yams (white sweet potatoes)

Dumplings

1-1/2 cups all purpose flour
1 tsp. baking powder
1/2 tsp. salt
1 tbsp. sugar
1/2 cup water, approximately

Wash the pig's tail and salt beef and cut into 1-inch chunks. Place into a **large stockpot with a cove**r, add enough water to cover the meat and boil until tender, about 1-1/2-hours *or pressure-cook for about 30-minutes*. Drain in a **colander**; place back into the pot and cover with water.

Add the coconut milk, onion chunks, chopped scallion, garlic, thyme leaves and whole goat pepper. Over medium high heat, bring to a boil.

Peel the vegetables and cut into large chunks. Place into the pot and cook until half-done.

Dumplings

In a **medium-sized bowl**, sift together dry ingredients and add water until dough becomes a dropping consistency. Drop by tablespoonfuls into the boiling soup. Cover and boil until dumplings are done, 15 to 20-minutes. Remove from the heat and discard the whole goat pepper.

To serve, arrange the vegetables and meat in layers on a **serving platter**.

Guyana Pepperpot

4 lb. cow heel, stew beef, pork or pig trotters
1/2 lb. salt beef or pig's tail
Freshly squeezed juice of I lime
Salt to taste
1 or 2 hot peppers
2 tbsp. brown sugar
1/2 cup cassareep
1 stick cinnamon
Few whole cloves
1 tbsp. vinegar

Barefoot Rice page 206

Cut the meat into pieces and wash well with the lime juice and salt. Place into a **4-quart sized stockpot** with water to cover and bring to a boil.

Put in the whole peppers with stems (remove before they burst *or they may be put into a Spice Bag page 367*). Add the cassareep, cover and allow to simmer until the meat is half-done.

Add the other ingredients and keep on boiling until the meat is tender and the liquid covers it. Serve with hot *Barefoot Rice*.

Guyana Pepperpot

This dish is an Amerindian specialty and has become one of the national dishes of Guyana. Its chief seasoning ingredient is cassareep: the thick syrupy residue from boiled cassava juice. The juice is extracted by grating the raw cassava, adding water and straining. Cassareep is seasoned with salt, pepper and sugar and is a preservative for meat. The pepperpot was heated day after day and portions removed for feeding the family. A new version of the pepperpot has emerged whereby 'greens', crab, shrimp, and pickled meats are cooked together in a soup. This pepperpot is also known as 'callaloo' in some of the islands. Callaloo has become a generic name for 'greens' as well as for 'greens-based' dishes. Pepperpot lasts for some time provided it is boiled up every day. Freshly cooked pieces of meat may be added and simmered in it. No onions, vegetables or starchy foods should be used in it.

George's Chicken & Dumplin'

1 stewing chicken, 3 or 4 lbs.
2 ribs celery, sliced
1 large onion, sliced
Salt to taste
Ground white pepper to taste
1/2 cup all purpose flour

Dumplings

1-1/2 cups all purpose flour
1-1/2 tsp. baking powder
1/2 tsp. salt
2 tbsp. vegetable oil
3/4 cup milk

Wash and clean the chicken, removing all the fatty parts. Cut into pieces as for frying and place into a **large stockpot**. Mix together 1/2-cup of flour and 1-cup of water; pour into the pot adding more water to cover.

Add the salt, pepper, onion and celery, and while stirring, bring to a boil. Reduce the heat, cover and, simmer for 15-minutes, stirring occasionally.

Dumplings

In a **small bowl**, sift together the flour, baking powder and salt. Stir in the milk and oil making soft dough and drop by teaspoonfuls into the simmering mixture. Adjust the seasonings.

Cover and cook for 20-minutes without lifting the cover then serve.

Conch Au Vin

4 large conchs
6 oz. button mushrooms, sliced
1 large onion, sliced
2 cloves garlic, finely chopped
4 slices bacon, chopped
2 tbsp. butter
2 tbsp. all purpose flour
Salt to taste
Pepper to taste
1 cup red wine
1 cup water
1 vegetable bouillon cube

Wash the conchs in cold water and cut into 2-inch sized chunks. In a **3-quart sized saucepan**, sauté the bacon and remove to a **flat dish**.

Sauté the mushroom, garlic and onion and remove to the dish reserving the bacon fat.

Coat the conch with the flour. Add the butter to the bacon fat and fry the conch until brown. Dissolve the bouillon cube in the water and pour over the conch pouring in the wine.

Return the vegetables and bacon to the saucepan adding the seasonings. Cover tightly and simmer for about 1-hour. Serve over hot *Barefoot Rice page 206* or cooked noodles.

Turtle Soup

3 lbs. turtle meat including bone, gristle and fat
3 cans (16 oz.) chicken bouillon or 3 cubes with 6 cups water
1 tbsp. whole allspice
1 tsp. whole cloves
1 tbsp. salt
Juice of 1 lemon, freshly squeezed
3 slices bacon, chopped
1 large onion, sliced
2 scallions, chopped
1 sprig fresh thyme or 1 tsp. leaves
1 large bay leaf
1 can (16 oz.) tomatoes, chopped
2 tbsp. all purpose flour
1/4 cup water
1 tsp. Lady Darling's Island Seasoning
Salt and black pepper to taste
Hot peppers to taste
1/2 cup Sherry

Wash the turtle parts thoroughly, chop into large chunks and place into a **large bowl**. Sprinkle with the salt and lemon juice and let stand for 10 to 15-minutes.

Pour off any remaining juices and place the meat into a **large stockpot** with the bouillon, whole spice, cloves and hot pepper. Bring to a boil over high heat, reduce the heat and cook for 20-minutes.

Cool and drain, preserving the stock. Discard the whole spice and the cloves. Peel off any soft shell and cut as much meat as possible from the bones; chop into smaller chunks. Discard the bones and return the meat with the stock to the pot.

Fry the bacon in a **large skillet** and remove to the pot preserving the fat in the skillet. Sauté the onion, scallion and garlic in the skillet for 5 to 6-minutes and, using a **slotted spoon**, transfer to the pot reserving the pan drippings. Sauté the tomato and transfer to the pot.

Mix the flour with the water and stir into the pot mixture and bring to a boil. Add the Island Seasoning, salt and pepper to taste. Reduce the heat, add the sherry and cook for 1-hour, adding water if necessary while cooking.

Serve with hot *Barefoot Rice page 206*.

Hurricane Ham Stew

2 dried conchs
1/4 cup butter
1 large onion, sliced
1/2 lb. sliced fresh mushrooms
1 can (10-1/2 oz.) bouillon or consommé
1-1/2 cups water (divided)
2 tbsp. all purpose flour
Salt to taste
1 cup sour cream

Wash the conchs thoroughly; place into a **bowl** with water to cover and soak overnight. Drain and cut into 2-1/2x3/4-inch strips.

Melt the butter in a **3-quart sized saucepan** and sauté the onion and mushrooms. Add the strips of conch, stir in the bouillon and 1-cup of the water.

In a **small dish**, mix the flour with the water and stir into the stew. Season with salt to taste and bring to a boil.

Reduce the heat, cover and simmer, stirring occasionally until the conch is tender, about 1-hour.

Stir in the sour cream, simmer for 10-minutes and serve over hot *Barefoot Rice page 206* or cooked noodles.

Hurricane Ham

A second name for the Conch is "Hurricane Ham" (Dried Conch). The reason for the nickname is: The Conch, after taken from the shell, is bruised and flattened out (tenderized), then hung into the sun. Day by day, the colour changes until the texture is that of a ham. After being cured, the meat is good for at least a year. This was usually done before the hurricane season, when weather prevented Out Islanders from travelling to the Capital to purchase food. At such times, the "Hurricane Ham" is at their disposal.

African Beef Stew

1-1/2 lbs. stew beef, cut into 1" cubes
2 tbsp. peanut oil
2 large onions, sliced
2 cloves garlic, chopped
2 large carrots, cut into 1/2" slices
2 tbsp. tomato purée
1 bay leaf
Dash of ground cloves
Hot pepper to taste
1 tsp. freshly squeezed lime juice
1-1/2 cups water
2 beef bouillon cubes
2 tbsp. creamy peanut butter
2 tbsp. all purpose flour
2 to 3 tbsp. water

Bake at 350°F

Heat the peanut oil in a **large skillet** and fry the beef, onion, garlic and carrot for about 5-minutes. Stir in the tomato purée and add the bay leaf, spices and seasoning together with lime juice, water and bouillon cubes.

Turn into a **covered 3-quart sized casserole dish**. Cover; place into the oven and cook for about 1-1/2-hours.

In a **1-quart saucepan**, mix together the peanut butter, flour and water until well blended. Cook over low heat for 5 to 6-minutes, stirring continuously. Remove the stew from the oven and stir in the peanut butter mixture blending well.

Return the casserole dish to the oven and bake for 15 additional minutes. Serve over hot mashed potatoes or *Barefoot Rice page 206*.

African Chicken Stew

Prepare same as *African Beef Stew* (above) except substitute *one 1-1/2 lb. chicken cut into 1-1/2" pieces* for the beef.

Mutton Stew

2 lbs. mutton (sheep or goat meat) cut into 1-1/2" cubes
2 tbsp. vegetable oil
1 large onion, sliced
1 lb. potatoes, peeled and cut into 1" cubes
2 tsp. dried parsley leaves
1 tsp. dried thyme leaves
1 bay leaf
1 tsp. Lady Darling's Island Seasoning
Salt to taste
Hot pepper to taste
3 cups water

Heat the oil in a **large Dutch oven** and over medium-high heat, brown the meat. Add the onion, parsley, thyme leaves, seasonings and water.

Reduce the heat, cover and simmer for about 1-1/2-hours or until the mutton is tender, stirring occasionally.

Add the potato cubes and continue to simmer until potatoes are done. Remove from the heat, discard the bay leaf and serve.

Stewed Fish

2 lbs. grouper or other firm-meat fish
Freshly squeezed juice of 1 lime
Salt
Hot peppers to taste

Stew

3 cups *Brown Flour Stew* page 266
1 large onion, sliced
1 tsp. dried thyme leaves
1 tsp. Lady Darling's Island Seasoning
Salt to taste
3 medium-sized potatoes peeled and cut into 1-1/2" cubes

Clean the fish thoroughly, cut into large chunks, place into a **flat dish** and sprinkle with salt to taste.

In a **small dish**, crush the hot peppers into the freshly squeezed lime juice and brush over the fish. Marinate for about 1-hour.

In a **4-quart sized saucepan**, prepare the *Brown Flour Stew*. Add the sliced onion and thyme leaves and bring to a boil over medium heat.

Remove the fish from the marinade and place into the pot. Add the potatoes and Island Seasoning to taste. Cover and cook for 15 to 20-minutes stirring several times.

Stewed Conch

Prepare *Stewed Fish* substituting *4 conchs cut into chunks*; prepared using Method Two *page 31* and adding freshly squeezed juice of 1 lime.

Curried Chicken

One 2 lb. chicken cut into 1-1/2" pieces
Salt to taste
1 tsp. curry powder
2 oz. vegetable oil

Sauce

3 slices bacon, chopped
1 large onion, sliced
1 cup fresh tomatoes, chopped
3 cups water (including any stock)
1 or 2 tbsp. curry powder
1 tbsp. all purpose flour
1 tsp. Lady Darling's Island Seasoning
Black pepper
Hot peppers to taste
2 medium-sized potatoes, peeled and cut into 1" cubes

Place the chicken chunks into a **large bowl**; sprinkle with salt and 1-teaspoon curry powder. Set aside to "take seasoning" for about 30-minutes.

Heat the oil in a **heavy 4-quart saucepan**; fry the chicken chunks and remove back to the bowl. Reduce the heat and sauté the onion. Add the tomatoes and continue to sauté. Stir in the water, fried chicken, curry powder and the seasonings to taste. Bring to a boil.

Reduce the heat, cover and simmer for about 20-minutes. Add the potato cubes and simmer until potatoes are done, about 10-minutes.

Curried Goat

Prepare same as *Curried Chicken* above except substitute *2 lbs. 2-inch pieces prepared goat meat.*

Curried Conch

Prepare same as *Curried Chicken* substituting *4 medium-sized conchs* prepared Method Two *page 31* and freshly squeezed juice of half lime.

Curried Grouper

Prepare same as *Curried Chicken* except substitute *2 lbs. grouper cut into large chunks and freshly squeezed juice of half lime.*

Chicken Souse

4 cups water
1 large onion, sliced
1 tsp. whole allspice
1 whole chicken, about 2 lbs.
3 medium-sized potatoes, peeled and cut into large chunks
4 tbsp. freshly squeezed lime juice
Hot peppers to taste
1 tsp. salt (or to taste)

Clean the chicken thoroughly; cut into 2-inch chunks and place into a **large flat dish**. Sprinkle a part of the salt and lime juice over the chicken and marinate for about 30-minutes.

Pour the water into a **4-quart sized saucepan**. Add the onion, whole all-spice, remaining lime juice and salt. Bring to a boil over high heat. Reduce the heat and boil for 10-minutes.

Remove the chicken from the marinade (discarde marinade). Place chicken into the saucepan, add the potatoes and hot peppers to taste. Cook until the potatoes are soft when tested with a sharp knife. Skim fat from the top of souse while cooking.

Adjust seasonings to taste and serve immediately with a small dish of lime juice and hot peppers on the side.

Turkey Souse

Prepare same as *Chicken Souse* above except substitute *1 turkey wing chopped into 1 or 2-inch chunks* for the chicken.

Conch Souse

Prepare same as *Chicken Souse* above except substitute *2 large conchs* prepared using Method Two *page 31* and cut into 2-inch chunks.

Smudder Fish

2 to 3 lbs. grouper or other firm-meat fish
Freshly squeezed juice of 1 lime
Salt & hot peppers
Gravy

2 oz. vegetable oil
1 large onion, sliced
2 tbsp. Champion Tomato Paste
3 cups water
1 tsp. dried thyme leaves
1 tsp. Lady Darling's Island Seasoning
Salt to taste
Hot peppers to taste

Clean the fish thoroughly; cut into large chunks place into a **large flat dish** and sprinkle with salt to taste.

In a **small dish**, crush the hot peppers into the freshly squeezed lime juice and brush over the fish. Marinate for about 1-hour.

Heat the oil in a **4-quart saucepan** and sauté the onion with the thyme leaves. Add the water, tomato paste, Island Seasoning and hot pepper to taste. Bring to a boil over medium heat.

Remove the fish from the marinade and add to the pot. Cover and simmer for about 20-minutes stirring several times.

Smudder Conch

Prepare same as *Smudder Fish* (above) substituting *4 medium-sized conchs* prepared using Method Two *page 31* and cut into large chunks.

Smudder Pork Chops

Prepare same as *Smudder Fish* (above) substituting *4 to 6 seasoned to taste and fried pork chops.* Omit the lime juice.

Smudder Chicken

Prepare same as *Smudder Fish* (above) substituting one *2 lb. chicken cut into pieces,* seasoned to taste and fried. Omit the lime juice.

Smudder Mutton

Prepare same as *Smudder Fish* (above) substituting *2 lbs. goat or sheep meet cut into 2-inch chunks,* seasoned to taste and browned. Cook for 1-1/2 to 2-hours.

Vegetable Soup

3 tbsp. butter
1 large onion, 1/2" dice
2 carrots, 1/2" dice
1 large tomato, peeled and chopped
3 to 4 cups water
1 large bouillon cube (chicken or beef)
1 tsp. Lady Darling's Island Seasoning
Salt & black pepper to taste
1 tbsp. butter
1 tbsp. all purpose flour
1 large potato, peeled and cut into 1/2" dice
1 cup chopped spinach, fresh or frozen

Melt the butter in a **large stockpot**; add the onion, carrots and celery. Cook slowly for about 10-minutes. Add the chopped tomato and continue to cook for a few minutes.

Add the water and bouillon cube and bring to a boil; reduce the heat.

Melt the butter in a 1-quart sized saucepan and stir in the flour. Stir into the soup.

Add the diced potatoes, adjust the seasoning and cook for 15 to 20-minutes. Add the chopped spinach; cook for about 5-minutes and serve.

"

Breakfast & Lunches

Menus

❋

Bahamian Boiled Fish
Barefoot Grits
Traditional Johnny Cake
Small Dish of Lime Juice with
Crushed Hot Peppers
Papaya Slices

❋

Corned Beef & Egg Mounds
Island Corn Grits with Butter
Sliced Tomatoes
Mango Slices

❋

Steamed Sardines
Barefoot Grits
Avocado Slices
Grapefruit sections rolled in
freshly grated coconut

❋

❋

Egg Stuffed Tomatoes
Fried Polenta Slices
Smoked Sausage Links
Half Sugar Apple

❋

Sapodilla Pancakes or Waffles
Mango Syrup
Crispy Fried Bacon
Pineapple Juice

❋

Family Breakfast Pie
Tomato Slices
Mango Chutney
Orange Juice

❋

Kalik Junkanoo Rarebit
Toasted English Muffins
Banana Pineapple Bacon

❋

Recipes

❋ **Breakfast Dishes**

Bahamian Boiled Fish

Mock Boiled Fish

Corned Beef & Grits

Corned Beef & Egg Mounds

Steamed Sardines

Deep Fried Eggs in Curry Sauce

Avocado & Eggs & Ham

Tomatoes Stuffed with Eggs

Laura's Banana Pancakes

Sapodilla Pancakes, Sapodilla Waffles

Carib Potato Pancakes

Banana Pineapple Bacon

Family Breakfast Pie

Kalik Junkanoo Rarebit

Green Banana Polenta, Coconut Polenta

❋❋ **Luncheon Dishes**

❋ **Fritters**

Cassava, Fish Roe Cassava, Corn, Fish

❋ **Sandwiches**

Banana Peanut Butter, Zippy Cheese,
Egg Salad, Avocado Eggs & Ham,
Corned Beef, Chicken Salad,
Holiday Turkey, Spicy Tuna

❋ **Avocado, Tomato Stars
& Bread Cups with Salads**

Crawfish, Shrimp, Spicy Tuna,
Egg, Chicken, Turkey,
Quick Stove Top Tuna Casserole
Baked Avocado Seafood
Breadfruit French Fried

❋ **Stuffed Baked Potatoes**

Corned Beef, Conch Chili,
Smoked Oyster

❋ **Quiches**

Bacon Coconut,
Curried Seafood

❋ **Tofu**

Fried, Chicken Sautéed,
With Crab Meat, Chili

❋ **Pizzas**

Conch, Individual

❋ **Burgers**

Jerk, Conch
Conch Chili
Conch Pockets
Jamaican Beef Patties

Boiled Fish & Grits

1 small grouper with "the head on"
2 limes
1 large onion, sliced
3 slices bacon, chopped
3 medium-sized potatoes, cut into 2" chunks
Salt to taste
4 cups water (approximately)
Hot peppers to taste
Barefoot Grits page 220

For the best "boil fish" the grouper has to be fresh. After the grouper is skinned and cleaned, all parts may be used for boiling including the head. You may prefer to use only the meaty parts.

Clean the fish thoroughly, cut into large chunks; place into a **large flat dish** and season with salt. Squeeze the juice of 1 lime into a **small dish**; crush the hot peppers into the juice and pour over the fish. Allow to "take seasoning" for about 30-minutes, turning several times.

Pour the water into a **4-quart sized saucepan**; add the onion, bacon, salt and juice of the remaining lime, also additional hot pepper to taste. Bring to a boil over high heat.

Remove the fish from the marinade and place into the pot together with the potato cubes. Reduce the heat, cover and cook until the potato cubes are done when tested with a knife.

Adjust the seasoning and serve immediately with hot *Barefoot Grits.*

Mock Boiled Fish

A recipe for left-over fried or broiled fish

2 cups water
1 large onion, sliced
Freshly squeezed juice of 1/2 lime
Hot peppers to taste
Salt to taste
Left-over fish
Potato cubes (optional)

In a **saucepan** *or skillet*, combine the water, onion, lime juice, hot pepper, salt and potato cubes and bring to a boil.

Reduce the heat; place the pieces of fish into the saucepan and gently simmer for about 10-minutes. Serve over hot *Barefoot Grits page 220* or *Johnny Cake page 88*.

Corned Beef Sauté & Grits
Fire Engine

Sauté
1 can (12 oz.) corned beef
1 tsp. freshly squeezed lime juice
1 tbsp. vegetable oil
2 tbsp. chopped onion
1/2 tsp. dried thyme leaves
1/2 cup water
2 tsp. Champion Tomato Paste
Hot peppers to taste
A few tablespoons of water
Barefoot Grits page 220

Place the corned beef into a **medium-sized bowl** and break up with a fork in preparation for cooking. Sprinkle with the lime juice.

Heat the oil in a **large skillet** and over medium heat; sauté the corned beef, adding the onion and thyme. Continue to sauté for 5 to 6-minutes. Stir in the tomato paste and crushed hot peppers to taste.

Add one to three tablespoonfuls of water for desired consistency and continue to cook, stirring. Cover, reduce the heat and cook for about 10-minutes. Serve over hot *Barefoot Grits* or on slices of toast.

Corned Beef & Egg Mounds

4 servings
Corned Beef Sauté (above)
4 eggs
Bake at 350°F

Prepare the *Corned Beef Sauté* using very little or no water.

Grease a **baking sheet**; divide the mixture into 4 sections and place onto the **baking sheet** to form 4 mounds. Make a depression in the centre of each mound.

Break the eggs, one in each depression and bake just until the eggs are set.

Sardines & Grits

1 can (4 oz.) sardines, drained
2 tbsp. vegetable oil
1 small onion, sliced
1 tbsp. Champion Tomato Paste
1/2 tsp. dried thyme leaves
1/2 tsp. Lady Darling's Island Seasoning
1 tbsp. freshly squeezed lime juice
Hot peppers to taste
Barefoot Grits page 220

Heat the oil in a **medium-sized skillet** and sauté the sliced onion and thyme leaves. Stir in the tomato paste; add the water, lime juice and seasonings, sautéing for a few minutes.

Gently place the sardines in the sauce, cover and cook for 5 or 6-minutes. Serve over *Barefoot Grits.*

Deep Fried Eggs In Curry Sauce

6 hard boiled eggs, peeled
1 cup all purpose flour
1/2 tsp. salt
1 egg, slightly beaten
1/4 cup milk
Vegetable oil for deep-fat frying
Curry Sauce page 257

Batter

Sift together the flour and salt. In a **small bowl**, combine the beaten egg and milk. Mix in the flour forming a stiff batter.

Dry the hard-boiled eggs thoroughly with **paper towels** and place into the batter coating completely.

Heat the oil in a **deep-fat fryer** *or deep pot.* Carefully remove the eggs from the batter using a **large slotted spoon** and gently place into the hot fat. Fry the eggs for 3 or 4-minutes or until golden brown, turning occasionally to brown evenly.

Remove with the slotted spoon, drain on paper towels and serve with *Curry Sauce.*

Avocado & Eggs & Ham

4 hard cooked eggs
1 cup mashed avocado
1/4 cup mayonnaise
1 tsp. prepared mustard
1 tsp. grated onion
1 tsp. freshly squeezed lime juice
1/2 tsp. salt
1/2 tsp. ground white pepper
4 slices of ham, heated
Avocado slices

Peel and mash the eggs; place into a **small bowl**. Blend in the mashed avocado and remaining ingredients except the ham slices.

Divide the mixture to form mounds in **four serving plates** surrounding with slices of ham and avocado. Serve with slices of toast.

Tomatoes Stuffed With Eggs

6 large firm ripe tomatoes
6 eggs
1 tbsp. parsley
4 oz. cooked ham
1 oz. butter
Salt & ground white pepper to taste
Bake at 350°F

Cut a slice from the top of each of the tomatoes; remove the pulp to a **bowl** and finely chop.

Separate the eggs; set the yolks aside and in a **medium-sized bowl**, blend the egg whites with the tomato pulp. Chop the parsley and ham; add to the mixture. Pack into the bottom of the tomato shells; place the egg yolks on the tops and season with salt and pepper.

Butter an **8x12-inch-baking dish** and stand the tomatoes in the dish. Bake until the egg yolks are firm and serve immediately.

Banana

Food of the ancients, no other fruit is today more widely known and valued, both as a food staple in the Tropics and as a dessert fruit, than the banana. Native to India and China, the Banana was cultivated and improved by aborigines before historic time. Indeed, few realize that it once had seeds, which filled it, leaving little room for pulp. The Portuguese found bananas in West Africa when they began their voyages of exploration in the fifteenth century and took this fruit to the Canary Islands then to the New World. Unripe green bananas are cooked and eaten as a starchy dish. ✽

See page 224 for plantains which resemble bananas in appearance and are used as a vegetable.

Laura's Banana Pancakes

1 cup Bisquick Baking Mix or Pancake mix
1/2 cup mashed ripe bananas
1/2 cup milk
1 egg

Combine ingredients in a **small bowl** and with **electric mixer** set on low speed, mix until blended.

Brush **griddle** *or large non-stick skillet* with butter; heat and drop spoonfuls of the mixture to form 4-inch pancakes. Brown on both sides and serve with syrup or *Guava Jam page 361.*

Sapodilla Pancakes

3 medium-sized ripe sapodillas
1 egg
2 tbsp. butter
1/4 cup sugar
1/4 cup coconut milk or whole milk
1 cup all purpose flour
1 tsp. baking powder
1/2 tsp. salt
1/2 tsp. ground cinnamon
3/4 tsp. ground nutmeg

Peel and mash the sapodillas. In a **small mixing bowl** with **electric mixer**, beat together the egg, butter, sugar and coconut milk. Fold in the mashed sapodilla.

Sift together the flour, baking powder, salt, cinnamon and nutmeg. Fold into sapodilla mixture.

Brush a **griddle** *or large skillet* with butter and drop spoonfuls of the mixture to form 4-inch pancakes. Brown on both sides and serve with *Sapodilla Syrup page 318.*

Sapodilla Waffles

Prepare *Sapodilla Pancake* batter (above) and pour into a large **pouring cup** *or pitcher*. Heat a **waffle iron** and brush with butter. Pour the batter into the centre of the hot iron and spread to cover the surface. Bake until the steaming stops; remove carefully with a fork.

Caribe Potato Pancakes

2-1/2 cups coarsely grated potatoes
1 tsp. salt
1/2 tsp. ground white pepper
2 slightly beaten eggs
1/2 tbsp. all purpose flour
1/2 tsp. curry powder
Vegetable oil 1/2" deep in skillet

Fit a **food processor** with the disc for shredding *or use a hand held grater*, coarsely grate the peeled potatoes and place into a **medium-sized bowl**.

Drain off all of the liquid from the potato and toss with the salt and pepper. Mix in the eggs, flour and curry powder.

Pour the oil into a **large skillet** and heat. Drop 2-tablespoonfuls of the mixture into the skillet to form each pancake and fry until golden brown on both sides. Serve immediately.

Banana, Pineapple & Bacon

Firm ripe bananas
Fresh or canned pineapple centre sticks
Bacon slices or very thin ham slices

Peel the bananas and cut into halves lengthwise. Place the pineapple stick between the banana halves.

Wrap the banana/pineapple with bacon strips. Place into a **baking pan** and place the pan under the low flame of **broiler**. Broil until the bacon is crisp, turning frequently. Serve immediately.

Kalik Junkanoo Rarebit

4 cups grated Sharp Cheddar cheese
1/2 tsp. prepared mustard
3/4 cup Kalik beer
3/4 cup salt
1/2 tsp. *Tamarind Paste page 366*
Dash of pepper sauce

Grate the cheese and melt in the top of a **double boiler** over hot, but not boiling water (do not allow the cheese to boil).

Stirring gradually, add the remaining ingredients. Serve at once over toast for breakfast or as a party dip.

Family Breakfast Pie

2 cups Corn Flakes cereal, crushed to fine crumbs
1 tbsp. butter, melted
1 medium-sized onion, thinly sliced
2 cups sliced fresh mushrooms
2 tbsp. butter
5 eggs, slightly beaten
1-1/2 cups shredded Swiss cheese
1/3 cup milk
1 tsp. salt
1/4 tsp. ground white pepper
3-1/2 cups potato cubes (about 1 to 1-1/4 lbs.)
1/4 tsp. ground thyme

Bake at 325°F

TIP:
To save time during the "morning rush hour", prepare potatoes the night before and place in refrigerator.

Place the cubed potatoes into a **3-quart sized saucepan**, with water to cover, add the salt and cook until soft when tested with a sharp knife. Turn into a colander and drain.

In a **bowl**, stir together the crushed cereal and 1-tablespoon of the butter, melted. Set aside.

Melt 2-tablespoons of the butter in a **large skillet** and sauté the onions and mushrooms until just tender. Turn into a **large bowl**. Add the eggs, milk, cheese, salt, pepper, thyme and potatoes and spread in a greased **9-inch pie pan**. Top with the cereal mixture.

Bake for about 40-minutes or until a knife comes out clean when inserted into the centre. Cut into wedges and serve warm.

Variation

Fry 8 slices of bacon until crisp; crumble and sprinkle over the pie before adding the cereal topping.

Oldest Influences

In the Caribbean, some of the oldest and most influential of our food habits stem from our aboriginal Amerindian (Carib and Arawak) heritage. Influences are evident in our preparation and use of cassava bread and corn - boiled, roasted or grated and used in various ways, including the now trendy "polenta". Cassava, a plant native to South America, produces a starchy root which was made into gruel or bread. The domestication of cassava was of enormous importance to tropical communities because the plant yields more food per acre than any other crop. When the European's sea biscuits became too spoiled on the long ocean voyages, a flour made of cassava was used to make into thin pancakes.

Green Banana Polenta

3 green bananas
1/2 tsp. ground cinnamon
2 cups water
1/2 tsp. ground nutmeg
1 cup canned coconut milk
1/2 cup Yellow Corn Meal
1/2 tsp. salt
1/2 cup sugar

Peel the green bananas, slice and place into the bowl of a **blender**. Add the water and coconut milk and purée until smooth.

Turn the mixture into a **2-quart sized saucepan**; add the salt, cinnamon, nutmeg and corn meal. Bring to a boil over medium heat, stirring constantly using a **large wooden spoon**. Reduce the heat, cover and cook for 20-minutes stirring occasionally.

Remove from the heat, stir in the sugar, and serve as breakfast porridge.

Coconut Polenta

1 cup Yellow Corn Meal
1/2 tsp. ground cinnamon
2 cups canned coconut milk
1/2 tsp. ground nutmeg
1 cup water
1/2 cup raisins
1/2 cup sugar

Combine all ingredients in a **2-quart sized saucepan**. With a **large wooden spoon**, begin stirring the mixture over medium high heat. Bring to a slow boil and about 6 to 8-minutes.

Keep the mixture moving and when it starts to boil, reduce to a very low heat. Cover and cook for 10 to 12-minutes, stirring frequently.

Place a **heat diffuser** under the pot to avoid the polenta sticking. Serve immediately.

Lunch Menus

❋

Half Avocado with Crawfish
Salad on
Bed of Lettuce & Tomato Slices
Tia Maria Jamaican Bread
Frozen Fruit Slushie

❋

Avocado Soup
Breadcup with Shrimp Salad
Coconut Breadsticks
Fox Hill Sapodilla Cheesecake

❋

Goombay Fruit Salad
Quick Stove Top Tuna Casserole
Crackers
Peach Turnover

❋

Conch Salad
Dillie Dinner Rolls
Corned Beef Baked Potato
Tortilla Sandwich Cookies

❋

❋

Buttered Asparagus Tips
Smoked Oyster Baked Potato
Corn on the Cob
Sawyer's Guava Jelly Roll

❋

Melon Salad
Bacon Coconut Quiche
Tomato Slices
Dillie Ice Cream Cup

❋

Avocado Salad
Tofu with Crab Meat
Banana Bran Bread
Petite Guava Duffs

❋

Beet Salad
Seafood Pizza
Paradise Pie a la Mode

❋

Conch Fritters

See *Conch Fritter* recipe *page 60*.

Cassava Fritters

1 lb. cassava, grated *page 30*
3 cloves garlic, chopped
1/2 medium-sized onion, 1/4" dice
1/2 green pepper, 1/4" dice
Hot peppers to taste
1 tsp. dried thyme leaves
1 tsp. freshly squeezed lime juice
1 egg
1 tbsp. cornstarch
1/2 tsp. baking powder
Salt to taste
Black pepper
Vegetable oil for deep-frying

Peel the cassava, cut into chunks and remove the centre membrane. Place into the bowl of a **food processor** fitted with the knife blade. Add the garlic, onion, green pepper and hot peppers and process for about 2-minutes.

Scrape the sides of the bowl with a **rubber scraper**; add the thyme, lime juice and the egg and process for another minute. Remove to a **medium-sized bowl**.

In a **small dish**, combine the cornstarch and baking powder and stir into the mixture. Season with the salt and pepper, mixing well.

Heat the oil in a **deep-fat fryer** *or deep pot*; drop the mixture by tablespoonfuls into the hot fat and fry the fritters until golden brown.

Remove with a **large slotted spoon**; drain on a **wire rack** and serve immediately with *Cocktail Sauce page 260*.

Fish Roe Cassava Fritters

Prepare same as *Cassava Fritters* above except mix *8 oz. mashed fish roe* into the batter.

Corn Fritters

1 cup freshly cut corn kernels or 1 cup frozen or canned corn
1 cup all purpose flour
1 tsp. baking powder
1/2 tsp. salt
2 slightly beaten eggs
2/3 cup milk
1 tbsp. vegetable oil
Vegetable oil for deep-frying

Sift together the flour, baking powder and salt. In a **small bowl**, with a **wire whisk**, whisk together the egg, milk and oil. Stir in the dry ingredients and mix to a smooth stiff batter. Stir in the corn.

Heat the oil in a **deep-fat fryer** or deep pot; drop the mixture by tablespoonfuls into the hot fat and fry until golden brown. Remove with a **large slotted spoon**; drain on a **wire rack** and serve with *Cocktail Sauce page 260*.

Fish Fritters

2 cups cooked fish
2 cups all purpose flour
2 tsp. baking powder
1 large onion, 1/4" dice
1 medium-sized green pepper, 1/4" dice
1 tbsp. freshly squeezed lime juice
Hot peppers to taste
1 tsp. salt
1 cup water (approximately)
Vegetable oil for deep-frying

Strip the fish into fine flakes and place into a **medium-sized bowl**. Add the diced onion, green pepper, salt and pepper to taste. In a **small dish**, crush the hot peppers into the lime juice and add to the bowl.

Sift together the flour and baking powder and fold into the fish mix with the water to make a firm batter.

Pour the oil into a **deep-fat fryer** or deep pot and preheat. Drop teaspoonfuls of the mixture into the hot oil, and fry until golden brown.

Remove the fritters with a **large slotted spoon**; drain on a **wire rack** over **paper towels** and serve with *Cocktail Sauce page 260*.

Banana Peanut Butter & Guava Jelly Sandwiches

4 Sandwiches

Spread
1 very ripe banana
3/4 cup peanut butter
1 tbsp. Sawyer's Guava Jelly
Slices of toast

Mash the banana in a **shallow dish**; mix together with the peanut butter and jelly just enough to blend. Spread on toasted slices of bread.

Zippy Cheese Sandwiches

Spread
2 cups grated Sharp Cheddar cheese
1/4 cup mayonnaise
1 tsp. prepared mustard
Hot pepper to taste
Slices of bread

Combine the spread ingredients in a **small bowl** mixing thoroughly. Spread generous amounts on slices of bread.

Avocado & Eggs & Ham Sandwiches

Spread
Avocado Eggs Spread page 131
4 slices of ham
Lettuce leaves
8 lightly toasted slices of bread

Prepare egg spread. Arrange the lettuce leaves on a slice of toast, add the ham slice and spread on generous amount of spread.

Meat Salad Sandwiches

Lightly toasted slices of Whole Wheat, Rye or other breads
Lettuce leaves
Tomato slices

For hearty sandwiches spread on generous amounts of one of the following meat salads :

Meat Salads page 75 to 79

Corned Beef Salad • Chicken Salad • Holiday Turkey Salad • Spicy Tuna Salad

If you need a quick fancy little lunch that looks like you spent hours preparing, use any of the recipes for Fish or Meat Salads served in either *Tomato Stars, Bread Cups For Salads,* or unpeeled avocado halves with tomato and cucumber slices.

You may find the references for these assorted dishes below.

❋ *Seafood Salads page 75 - 78*

Conch Salad • Crawfish Salad • Shrimp Salad • Crab Salad • Spicy Tuna Salad

❋ *Meat Salads page 78 - 79*

Chicken Salad • Turkey Salad • Egg Salad • Corned Beef Salad

Tomato Stars page 240
Bread Cups For Salads page 85
Un-peeled avocado halves *page 29*

Quick Stove Top Tuna Casserole

2 cups cooked macaroni
1 can (6 oz.) tuna fish, drained
1 can (10 oz.) cream of mushroom soup
10 oz. milk
1 can (6 oz.) mixed vegetable, drained
1 tbsp. freshly squeezed lime juice
1/2 tsp. onion salt
1 tsp. Lady Darling's Island Seasoning
Hot peppers to taste

Combine all ingredients in a **2-quart sized saucepan** mixing thoroughly. Stirring, bring to a boil over medium heat.

Reduce the heat, cover and cook for 10 to 12-minutes. Stir and serve.

Baked Avocado with Seafood

1 large avocado
2 tbsp. vinegar
1 tsp. garlic, finely minced

Creamed Seafood

1-1/2 cup *Cheese Sauce page 257*
1 can (6 oz.) tuna fish, drained or 1 cup crab meat, or 1 cup crawfish chunks
Grated Cheddar cheese
Seasoned bread crumbs
Bake at 375°F

Cut the un-peeled avocado into half and remove the seed. In a **small dish**, mash the finely minced garlic thoroughly in the vinegar.

Place 1-tablespoon of the garlic/vinegar into each half of avocado. Let stand for 1/2-hour brushing the vinegar over the inside and top several times.

Prepare the *Cheese Sauce* and gently mix in selected seafood. Pour off the vinegar from the avocado halves and fill with the creamed seafood.

Place onto a **baking sheet** lined with **wax paper**. Sprinkle tops with the grated cheese and bread crumbs. Bake for 15-minutes and serve immediately.

Breadfruit French Fries

1 firm ripe breadfruit
Salt
Vegetable oil for deep-frying

Peel and core the breadfruit *page 29* and cut into large slices. Place into a **3-quart sized saucepan** with water to cover; bring to a boil and cook for 10 to 15-minutes. Drain and allow to cool.

Cut the slices into strips for french-fries. Heat the oil in a **deep-fat fryer** *or deep pot*. Fry until golden brown, drain on a **wire rack**, sprinkle with salt and serve hot with Catsup if desired.

Corned Beef Baked Potato

4 large Idaho potatoes
Vegetable oil

Filling

Corned Beef Sauté page 129

Bake at 375°F or microwave for 8 to 10 minutes

Scrub, dry then prick the potatoes with a fork; rub with oil and bake until soft, about 50-minutes *or microwave*. Remove from the oven; cut a lengthwise slice from the top and scoop out most of the inside into a **large bowl** and mash.

Prepare the Corned Beef Sauté and mix together with the mashed potato. Pile back into the potato shells.

Bake for about 10-minutes *or microwave for about 3-minutes* and serve.

New World Crops

In addition to cassava, corn, potato and tomato, New World crops included beans, squash, cocoa and chile peppers, cooked in beautiful and useful clay pots that had been hardened by fire. The inhabitants cultivated cotton and learned to dye and weave cloth in bright patterns. They constructed buildings and created sculptures from stone. They made jewelry and ornaments from jade, and traded gold, silver, copper and bronze with other peoples.

Smoked Oyster Stuffed Potato

4 medium-sized baking potatoes
1 can (6 oz.) smoked oysters, drained
2 to 3 cups grated Cheddar cheese
3 tbsp. butter or margarine
1/2 cup light sour cream
2 green onions, finely chopped
or 1 tsp. dried chives
1/2 tsp. salt
1/2 tsp. black pepper
Hot peppers to taste
Paprika

Bake at 375°F or microwave for 8 to 10-minutes

TIP:

Prepare stuffed p o t a t o e s, bake for 40 minutes, place in freezer bags and freeze. When ready to serve, thaw and bake for 15 minutes or *microwave for 5 or 6 minutes.*

Scrub, dry then prick the potatoes with a fork; rub with oil and bake until soft, about 50-minutes *or microwave.* Cut each potato into halves lengthwise; scoop out the insides into a **large bowl** and mash.

Reduce the oven temperature to 350°F.

Add the cheese, onions, oyster, butter, sour cream, salt, black pepper and red pepper mixing well. Stuff each potato half with the mixture; sprinkle with paprika and place into a **shallow baking dish**. Bake for 15-minutes and serve immediately.

Curried Seafood Quiche

1 unbaked *9-inch Pie Shell page 271*
1 cup 1/2" chunks of crawfish
1 cup 1/2" chopped shrimps
1/2 tsp. curry powder
4 eggs, lightly beaten
2 cups heavy cream, scalded
1 cup grated Swiss cheese, packed
1/2 tsp. salt
1/2 tsp. ground thyme
1 medium-sized onion, chopped
1 medium-sized green pepper, chopped
1 large fresh tomato, chopped
Bake at 350°F

Prepare the pie shell and set aside. Combine the crawfish and shrimp chunks in a **bowl** and sprinkle with the curry powder.

In a **large bowl** combine the eggs, cream, cheese, salt and thyme. Mix in the chopped onion, sweet pepper tomato and seafood. Turn the mixture into the prepared *Pie Shell* and bake for 35 to 40-minutes until the centre is set. Serve hot or cold.

Bacon Coconut Quiche

1 - unbaked 9-inch Pie Crust page 271
4 to 6 slices bacon
4 eggs, lightly beaten
2 cups heavy cream, scalded
1 cup grated Swiss cheese, packed
1/2 tsp. salt
3/4 tsp. black pepper
3/4 tsp. ground nutmeg
1/2 cup freshly grated coconut or packaged shredded coconut
1 medium-sized onion, chopped
Hot peppers to taste

Bake at 350°F

Prepare the *Pie Crust* and prepare the fresh coconut *page 24*.

In a **large skille**t, half cook the bacon. Remove, chop and spread over the bottom and sides of the crust.

In a **medium-sized bowl**, combine the eggs, cream, cheese, salt, black pepper and nutmeg. Mix in the coconut, onion and hot peppers to taste.

Turn the mixture into the crust and bake for 35 to 40-minutes until centre is set. Serve hot or cold.

Fried Tofu

1 lb. firm tofu
1/4 cup soy sauce
1 clove garlic, minced
2 tsp. fresh ginger, crushed
Vegetable oil to grease the pan

Cut the tofu into 3x3x1/2-inch slices. Mix together the soy sauce, garlic and ginger in a **shallow dish** and coat the slices.

Brush a **large non-stick skillet** with oil. Over medium heat, pan fry the slices for about 5-minutes on each side. Remove the slices back to the shallow dish, brush again with soy sauce and serve immediately.

Ginger Sautéed Tofu

1 lb. firm tofu
1/4 cup vegetable oil
1/2 cup chopped pork, beef, chicken, shrimp or crabmeat
1 tsp. chopped ginger
1 tbsp. garlic, crushed
1 tbsp. bean paste (hot)
1-1/2 tsp. salt
1 tsp. sugar
1 tsp. sesame oil
1/2 cup soup stock
1 tbsp. cornstarch
1 tbsp. cold water
1 tbsp. chopped scallion

Cut the tofu into 1/2x1/2-inch chunks. Heat the oil in a **large non-stick skillet** and fry, stirring until tofu is golden. Remove to a **shallow dish** and set aside.

Reduce the oil in the skillet to 2-tablespoonfuls and heat. Stir-fry the chopped meat, adding the bean paste, garlic and ginger.

Finally, add the soup stock and tofu. Reduce the heat, cover and cook for a few minutes. Add the salt and sugar.

In a **small dish**, mix the cornstarch and water together. Stir in to thicken the stock. Remove to a **serving platter**, sprinkle with the scallions.

Tofu Chili

1 lb. frim tofu
1 large onion, 1/4" dice
2 cloves garlic, minced
2 tbsp. vegetable oil
1 can (10 oz.) chili beans
1 can (10 oz.) refried beans
3 cups tomatoes, fresh or canned
1 to 3 tbsp. chili powder (to taste)
1 tsp. fresh thyme leaves
1 tsp. Lady Darling's Island Seasoning
Salt & black pepper to taste
Hot peppers to taste
2 to 4 cups water

Crumble the tofu. Heat the oil in a **large non-stick skillet** and sauté the onion and garlic until tender. Add the tofu and sauté another few minutes.

Transfer to **4-quart sized saucepan** mixing together the remaining ingredients. Over medium-high heat, bring to a boil. Reduce the heat; adjust seasonings to taste, cover and simmer for 1-hour, stirring occasionally.

Conch Chili Baked Potatoes

Conch Chili page 150
Potatoes

Bake at 375°F or microwave for 8 to 10 minutes

Prepare the Conch Chili.

Scrub, dry, then prick the potatoes with a fork; rub with oil and bake until soft, about 50-minutes or microwave for 8 to 10-minutes.

Remove from the oven, and cut a lengthways slice from the top. Scoop out most of the potato, mash and combine with the chili.

Pile a generous amount of the chili mix back into the potato shells; return to the oven and bake for 10-minutes.

Conch Pizza

Pizza Sauce page 260
Pizza Crust page 273
2 conchs, thinly sliced page 32
1/2 tsp. oregano leaves
1/2 tsp. dried rosemary
Salt
Freshly squeezed juice of 1 lime
1 medium-sized onion, chopped
1 medium-sized green pepper, chopped
Black pepper
1/2 cup Parmesan cheese, grated
2 cups Mozzarella cheese, grated

Bake at 425°F

Prepare the Pizza Sauce; prepare the Pizza Crust and bake for 6 to 8-minutes.

Place the thinly sliced conch in a **shallow dish** and sprinkle with the salt and lime juice; let stand for a few minutes then drain.

Spread the sauce over the crust and place the conch slices, herbs and vegetables over the sauce. Season with the black pepper and sprinkle the cheeses on top. Return to the oven and bake for 15 to 20-minutes.

Conch ("Konk")

Claw-like horn

Conch emerging from its shell

Perhaps other than its natural beauty, nothing is more synonymous with The Bahamas than the "Conch", known as "the giant of the ocean without a bone". The Conch's home is a multicoloured shell, and its remarkable strength enables it to suck tightly into its shell, so that neither man nor fish can pull it out. Throughout history, the Bahamians have used conch for food, removing the conch from its shell by breaking into the pointed end of the shell and cutting the conch away with a knife. The shell is used to create jewelry, decorate gardens or as a landfill.

After the conch is taken from its shell it is diced and marinated in lime juice, hot peppers and seasonings to make the world famous conch salad or mixed in batter for a national dish, conch fritters. "Scorched Conch" is a favourite for Bahamians unable to wait for the time it takes to dice the fresh conch. Because conch is a mussel, when used in dishes requiring it to be cooked, it is a bruised (we beat the heck out of it), flattened and tenderized. Bahamian Conch Chowder is also a well know dish enjoyed around the world.

If conch is not available, substitute clams in some recipes. ✻

Individual Conch Pizzas

Yield 6 Individual Pizzas

2 medium-sized conchs, shredded page 32
3 English muffins
3 tbsp. butter, melted (divided)
1-1/2 cups Pizza Sauce page 260
1/2 medium-sized onion, chopped
1/2 medium-sized sweet pepper, chopped
1 tsp. salt
1/2 tsp. ground white pepper
1 tsp. freshly squeezed lime juice
1 tbsp. vegetable oil
6 slices Cheddar cheese

Melt 1-tablespoon of the butter in a **large skillet** and sauté the shredded conch, onion, sweet pepper, salt, pepper and lime juice for 4 to 5-minutes. Add the *Pizza Sauce*.

Split the muffins into halves and brush with remaining butter. Arrange on a **baking sheet** and toast under a broiler. Cover each muffin with the sauté and top with a slice of cheddar cheese.

Return to the broiler for a few minutes to melt the cheese and serve

Conch Burger

3 large conchs, finely ground page 32
1 medium-sized onion, chopped
1 medium-sized green pepper, chopped
Freshly squeezed juice of 1 lime
2 eggs, slightly beaten
1 cup Instant Mashed Potato Flakes
Salt
Hot peppers to taste
Vegetable oil for pan frying
Lettuce leaves, tomato slices (optional)

Place the finely ground conch into a **medium-sized bowl** and sprinkle with the lime juice, salt, crushed hot peppers, the slightly beaten eggs and potato flakes, mixing thoroughly.

Shape the mixture into burgers. Heat the oil in a **large skillet** and fry for 5 to 6-minutes on each side.

Gently remove the burgers, place on toasted buns and spread with *Cocktail Sauce page 260*.

Jerk Burgers

1 lb. ground beef or ground turkey
1 to 2 tsp. Powdered Jerk Seasoning
1 tbsp. vegetable oil

Form the ground beef into 1-inch thick burgers and place into a **flat pan**. Coat each burger with oil, then with the Jerk Seasoning. Marinate for about 30-minutes, turning a few times.

Place the burgers onto a **barbecue grill** over hot coals, under grill of oven *or in a non-stick skillet* and cook to individual taste. Remove, place on toasted bun, and serve with lettuce, tomato and other condiments. (No pepper needed).

Conch Chili

2 large conchs
1 large onion, chopped
1 green pepper, chopped
1 clove garlic, minced
1 can (16 oz.) chopped tomatoes, drained (preserve liquid)
1 tsp. oregano leaves
1 tsp. dried thyme leaves
1 to 2 tbsp. chili powder
2 tsp. salt
1 can (12 oz.) chili beans (preserve liquid)
1 can (12 oz.) Refried beans
Water
Hot peppers, optional
1 oz. vegetable oil

Wash and prepare the conchs Method Two *page 31*.

Heat the oil in a **large skillet** and sauté the conch, onion and green pepper for 5 to 8-minutes. Stir in the tomatoes, adding the seasonings.

Turn into a **3-quart sized saucepan**. Add the beans, and liquids. Bring to a boil over high heat. Adjust seasonings to taste. Reduce the heat, cover and cook for about 45-minutes.

Conch Pockets

Filling
2 large fresh conchs, shredded page 32
1 medium-sized onion, 1/4" dice
1 green pepper, 1/4" dice
1/2 tsp. dried thyme leaves
1 whole tomato, chopped
1 cup mixed frozen vegetables, thawed
1 tbsp. freshly squeezed lime juice
Salt to taste
Hot peppers to taste
Vegetable oil

Egg Wash
1 egg
2 to 3 tbsp. water

Crust
2 cups all purpose flour
3 tsp. baking powder
1/2 tsp. salt
1/3 cup vegetable shortening
1/2 cup milk
1 egg, well beaten

Bake at 400°F

Heat the oil in a **large skillet** and sauté the onion, green pepper and thyme. Add the shredded conch and sauté for 3 to 4-minutes. Stir in the tomato and continue to sauté adding the vegetables and lime juice. Season to taste and set aside to allow to cool.

Crust

In a **medium-sized bowl**, sift together the flour, baking powder and salt. With a **pastry cutter**, cut in the shortening until the mixture resembles coarse crumbs.

Make a well in the middle of the mixture; mix in the milk and beaten egg to form firm dough. Place onto a floured **board** and with a floured **rolling pin**; roll out to 1/4-inch thickness. Using a **cut out**, cut into 5-inch squares.

Egg Wash

In a **small dish**, beat together the egg and water.

Spoon 2-tablespoonfuls of the conch mixture into the centre of the squares. Brush the edges with the egg wash. Fold, overlapping the edges to form a seam pressing firmly together. Place on a greased **baking sheet**, seam side down.

Bake for 25 to 30-minutes until golden brown.

Jamaican Beef Patties

Crust

3-1/2 cups all purpose flour
1/2 tsp. baking powder
1 tsp. ground turmeric
1 tsp. salt
3/4 cup vegetable shortening, softened
1 cup (approximately) very cold water

Filling

1-1/2 lbs. lean ground beef
1 large onion, minced
3 scallions, minced
Hot peppers to taste
2 tbsp. vegetable oil
5 cups fresh bread crumbs
1/2 tsp. ground thyme
1 tsp. ground turmeric
Salt & Black pepper to taste

Bake at 400°F

Crust

In a **medium-sized bowl**, sift together the flour, baking powder, turmeric and salt. Using a **pastry cutter**, cut the shortening into the flour until the mixture resembles rice grains.

Gradually add just enough of the water to hold the dough together. Mix, and using hands, knead lightly into a ball. Brush lightly with oil and place back into the bowl, cover and chill.

Filling

In **another medium-sized bowl**, combine the onion, scallions and peppers with the beef, mixing well. In a **large skillet**, heat the oil over medium to high heat and sauté the meat mixture until brown (if necessary, drain off any excess fat or liquid).

Add the bread crumbs, thyme, turmeric, salt and pepper to taste, mixing well. Add the water, lower the heat and simmer for 20-minutes. The mixture should not be too moist or too dry. allow to cool completely.

Allow the dough to reach room temperature, place onto a floured **board** and with a floured **rolling pin**, roll out to about 1/4-inch thickness. Using a **Gourmet Cutter** *or a saucer* cut into 6-inch circles.

Place about 2 tablespoonfuls of the filling into the centre of each circle. Fold over and seal the edges using the cutter or tines of a fork. Place the patties onto an un-greased **baking sheet** and bake for 30 to 35-minutes. Serve hot, warm or cold.

Fish & Seafood

Menus

❊

Red Cabbage Salad
Samana Baked Red Snapper
with Conch Stuffing
Fried Breadfruit Slices
South Beach Mango Cheesecake

❊

Slices of Celery & Onion on
Beet Leaves with Nut Dressing
Fried Barbados Flying Fish
Rum Raisin Rice
Plantain Drops
Banana with Sherry & Cream

❊

Cabbage Slaw
Grouper Cutlets
Mango Chutney
Bahamian Pigeon Peas & Rice
Caribbean Guava Cobbler

❊

❊

Relishes & Pickles
Cracked Conch
French Fried Bread Fruit
Calypso Sauce
Cabbage Slaw
Avocado Pie

❊

Lettuce Leaf Salad with
French Dressing
Broiled Crawfish
Green Plantain Sauté
Buttered Mixed Vegetables
Coconut Ice cream

❊

Mixed Mince with Cabbage
Fish Seasoned Rice
Plantain Cakes
Pickled Almond Meats
Caribbean Pumpkin Pie

❊

Recipes

❁ Assorted Fish Dishes

Samana Baked Red Snapper in Conch Sauce

Fried Fish

Fried Barbados Flying Fish

Jamaican Salt Fish & Akee

Oven Fried Sword Fish

Oven Fried Scallops

Mahi Mahi (Dolphin)

Fried Fish Roe (Small)

Fried Fish Roe (Large)

❁ Grouper

Boiled, Abaco Baked,

Cutlets, Broiled Cutlets,

Fingers, Tamarind Guava Fingers,

Fillets with Banana Batter,

Fillets in Burnt Orange

❁ Salmon

Oven Fried Steaks,

Cakes, Stuffed Tomatoes

❁ Conch Dishes

Cracked, Spicy, Ginger, Guanabani,

Dumphries Creole, Rissoles,

Rissoles in Shrimp Sauce

❁ Crawfish

Broiled, In Beer Sauce,

Minced, Mixed Mince

❁ Shrimps

Carib Fried,

Shrimp Curry in a Hurry

Beer Battered,

Quick Curried,

Spiced Ginger

❁ Seafood

Seafood Casserole

❁ Turtle

Grilled Steaks

Pie

Samana Baked Red Snapper in Conch Sauce

1 large red snapper with "head on" (about 3 lbs.)
Salt
1 lime
Hot peppers to taste
4 tbsp. vegetable oil
Conch Sauce page 263
Bake at 325°F

Clean and wash the snapper, pat dry, place into a **large shallow pan** and season with salt. Squeeze the lime juice into a **small dish** and crush the hot peppers into the juice. Brush both inside and outside of the fish with the juice and marinate for about 1-hour.

Prepare the *Conch Sauce*. Remove the fish from the marinade and pat dry. Heat the oil in a **large skillet** and brown the snapper on both sides. Remove to a **shallow baking dish** brushed with oil.

Spoon a portion of the *Conch Sauce* on the inside and spread remaining over the fish. Cover the baking dish with foil wrap and bake for 30-minutes. Serve immediately, removing the foil at time of serving.

Fried Barbados Flying Fish

8 flying fish
2 limes
2 tsp. salt
1 medium-sized onion, chopped
2 tsp. ground thyme
1/2 clove garlic, chopped
2 eggs, lightly beaten
Hot peppers to taste
Vegetable oil 1" deep in skillet
Flour (approximately 4 oz.)

Clean and wash the fish thoroughly; pat dry. Place into a **large shallow pan** and season with 1-teaspoon of the salt. Squeeze the juice of 1 lime into a **small dish**; crush the hot peppers into the juice and brush over the fish. Marinate for 15-minutes, drain and pat dry.

Place the onion, thyme, garlic, remaining salt and crushed pepper into the bowl of a **blender**. Squeeze in the juice of remaining lime and purée. Rub the purée into the fish.

Beat the eggs in a **shallow dish**. Spread a dusting of the flour in the bottom of a separate **shallow dish**. Dip the fish into the egg, then into the flour. Pour the oil into a **large skillet** and heat. Fry the fish until crispy, about 5-minutes on both sides. Drain on a **wire rack** and serve immediately with slices of lime.

Fried Fish

For Bahamians, "fresh fish" would mean a trip to the fishing boats tied up at the dock – selecting a live fish from the "well" – having it cleaned and then taking it home to cook. The following recipe is the traditional method used to fry fish of various sizes. Large-sized fish would be scored and cut into halves. In the islands, fresh fish is always purchased and cooked "with the head on".

Use any of the following fish
Red snappers, Grey snappers
Jacks, Grunts or Porgies
Salt
Limes
Hot peppers
Vegetable oil 1" deep in skillet

Clean and wash the fish thoroughly and score on each side diagonally. Sprinkle with salt on the inside, outside and in the score and place into a **large flat pan**.

Squeeze a generous amount of lime juice into a **small dish** and crush the hot peppers into the juice. Pour over the fish and allow to "take seasoning" for as long as you like - all day or all night - but for at least 1 to 1-1/2 hours.

Pour oil into a **large skillet**, to a depth of about one inch and heat over high heat.

Remove the fish from the marinade and pat dry. Using a **long handle spatula**, place into the hot oil and fry very carefully - so as not to fry yourself - until the fish is golden brown about 5 to 6-minutes on each side. Drain on a wire rack placed over newspapers and serve hot.

Broiled Fish

Clean and season fish (above); arrange on grill of broiler and broil until crispy and brown on both sides.

Ackee

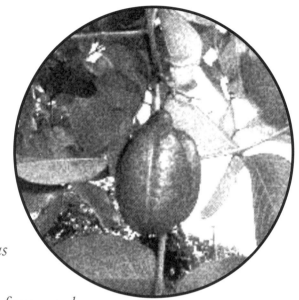

Captain Bligh, the same man who brought the breadfruit, brought the Ackee, a native of the Guinea Cost of West Africa, to the Caribbean in 1793 as food for the slaves.

Ackee trees are grown from seed and can reach heights of 40 feet. The attractive and colourful fruits, hanging from the trees like clusters of bells, turn yellowish, more or less suffused with red as they mature. In certain areas, the trees are used as ornamental or shade trees and, much like the breadfruit, it is not used as a food staple.

The ackee must be allowed to open fully or at least partly before it is detached from the tree. When it has "yawned", or is fully ripe, the fruits split open, revealing their three large, black seeds and creamy white arils or "meats" which has a somewhat nutty flavour. They are **cooked** while still fresh and firm, *usually parboiled* in salted water and cooked with salt fish. ❋

Salt Fish & Ackee

1 lb. salt fish
18 fresh or canned ackees
4 slices bacon cut into strips
1 large onion, sliced
1 medium-sized green pepper, sliced
3 tbsp. vegetable oil
Black pepper

Place the salt fish with cold water to cover into a **3-quart sized saucepan** and bring to a boil. Boil for 15-minutes. Remove the fish, reserving the stock in the saucepan.

Remove the pods, seeds and centers from the ackees *page 25*. Place into the saucepan with the fish stock and boil for 15-minutes. Drain, allow to cool and flake the fish, discarding the skin and the bones.

Fry the bacon strips in a **large skillet**, remove and set aside. Sauté the onion and green pepper in the bacon fat. Remove and set aside.

Sauté the fish and the ackee stirring in the onion and seasoning with black pepper. Just before serving, mix in the bacon strips.

Oven Fried Swordfish

Four 1" thick swordfish steaks
Salt
Freshly squeezed juice of 1 lemon
Ground white pepper
Seasoned bread crumbs
1 tbsp. vegetable oil
Lemon wedges

Bake at 450°F

Clean and pat each steak dry, place into a **shallow dish** and sprinkle with salt and pepper to taste. Brush with lemon juice and marinate for 30-minutes.

Spread the bread crumbs into a **shallow dish** and coat the steaks lightly with the crumbs. Arrange in a single layer on a **baking sheet** brushed with oil. Oven bake uncovered for 8 to 10-minutes, depending on thickness of steaks. Serve hot with lemon wedges.

Abaco Baked Grouper with Stuffing

1 small grouper (with the head on) or other large firm-meat fish
Salt
Freshly squeeze juice of 2 limes
Stuffing for Fish page 234
Hot peppers to taste
Bake at 325°F

Clean the fish and pat dry. Place into a **large shallow pan** and season with salt. Squeeze the lime juice into a **small dish**, and crush the hot peppers into the juice. Coat both the inside and outside of the fish with the juice and marinate for about 30-minutes.

Prepare the *Stuffing for Fish*. Remove the fish from the marinade and place into a **large baking dish** brushed with oil. Stuff, spreading any excess stuffing in the dish, and bake for 40 to 45-minutes.

Oven Fried Scallops

1 lb. scallops, fresh or frozen
4 tbsp. mayonnaise
2 cups fine seasoned crumbs
Paprika
Lemon wedges
Tartar Sauce page 258
Bake at 450°F

Defrost the scallops if frozen; drain and pat dry. Place into a **medium-sized bowl** with the mayonnaise and gently stir until evenly coated.

Spread the crumbs in a **shallow dish** and roll the scallops in the crumbs. Arrange in a single layer on a well-greased **baking sheet** and oven fry for 4 to 5-minutes for small scallops and 6 to 8-minutes for large scallops, just until the crust is golden.

Sprinkle with paprika and serve with lemon wedges and *Tartar Sauce*.

Mahi - Mahi
Dolphin

4 boneless dolphin fillets
Salt to taste
Freshly squeezed juice of 1 lime
Hot peppers to taste
1 tsp. fennel seeds
Vegetable oil 1/2" deep in skillet

Wash the fillets, pat dry and place into a **flat pan**. Sprinkle with salt; mash the peppers in the lime juice and brush over the fish. Sprinkle on the fennel seeds and let stand for a few minutes.

Heat the oil in a **large skillet**; quickly sauté the fillets until light brown on both sides, 6 to-8 minutes. Remove and serve immediately.

Fried Fish Roe
Small Fish

Roe of small fish
Salt to taste
Freshly squeezed lime juice to taste
Hot pepper to taste
Vegetable oil 1/2" deep in skillet

Remove the fish roe from the fish and clean. Sprinkle with salt and place into a **shallow pan**.

In a **small dish**, mix together the lime juice and crush in the peppers and garlic. Coat the roes and marinate for about 10-minutes.

Pour the oil into a **skillet** and heat over medium high heat. Fry the roe until crisp and brown. Serve hot "au natural".

Fried Fish Roe
Large Fish

Roe of large fish
Salt
Freshly squeezed lime juice to taste
Hot peppers to taste
Garlic cloves, crushed
Vegetable oil 1/2" deep in skillet

Clean the roe, place into a **saucepan** with water enough to cover and steam for 10-minutes. Drain, cool and slice into 1/2-inch slices. Place into a **shallow dish** and sprinkle lightly with salt on both sides.

Squeeze the lime juice into a **small dish**, and crush in the peppers and garlic. Brush on both sides of the roe slices and marinate for about 10-minutes.

Pour the oil into a **skillet** and heat over medium-high heat. Gently fry the slices until crisp and brown on both sides. Serve hot with *Cocktail Sauce page 260.*

Boiled Grouper

See *Boiled Fish & Grits page 128*

Broiled Grouper Cutlets

1-1/2" thick grouper cutlets
Salt
Ground white pepper
1 lime
Hot peppers to taste

Wash the cutlets; pat dry, arrange in a **flat pan** and sprinkle with salt and white pepper. Squeeze the lime juice into a **small dish** and crush the hot peppers into the juice. Pour over the cutlets and marinate for 1-hour.

Remove the cutlets from the marinade. Arrange in a **large shallow baking dish** *or broiling pan*. Place the pan under the broiler and broil for 6 to 8 minutes on each side, basting with juices from the dish. Serve immediately with your favourite seafood sauce or with *Mango Chutney page 363.*

Grouper Cutlets

Four 1" thick grouper cutlets
Freshly squeezed juice of 1 lime
Hot peppers to taste
Salt
2 eggs, beaten
Fine crumbs
Vegetable oil 1/2" deep in skillet

Wash the cutlets, pat dry, place into a **flat pan** and season with salt to taste. Squeeze the lime juice into a **small dish** and crush in the hot peppers. Pour over the cutlets and marinate for at least 1-hour.

Beat the eggs in a **shallow dish**. Spread the crumbs in **another shallow dish**. Dip the cutlets into the egg, then into the crumbs.

Pour the oil into a **large skillet** and heat. Fry the coated cutlets until brown, at least 4 to 5-minutes on each side. Serve with *Tamarind Mango Chutney page 364.*

Grouper Fingers

3 large grouper fillets
Salt
1 lime
Hot peppers to taste
1 cup all purpose flour
1 cup bread crumbs
Vegetable oil for deep-frying

Wash the grouper fillets and pat dry. Cut into 1/2-inch strips or fingers place into a **flat pan** and sprinkle with salt to taste.

Squeeze the lime juice into a **small dish**; crush the hot peppers into the juice and pour over the grouper fingers. Marinate for 1-hour.

Beat the eggs in a **shallow dish**. Spread the flour and the bread crumbs in **separate shallow dishes**.

Coat the fingers completely with the flour, dipping into the beaten egg, then in the bread crumbs. Place the coated fingers into refrigerator to set for 10 to 15-minutes.

Pour the oil into a **deep-fat fryer** or *deep pot* and heat until very hot. Place the fingers into the hot fat a few at a time and fry until golden brown. Remove, drain on a **wire rack** and serve hot with *Tarter Sauce page 258.*

Tamarind Guava Grouper Fingers

3 large grouper fillets
Salt
Tamarind Guava Paste page 366
1/2 cup all purpose flour
1/2 cup Yellow Corn Meal
Vegetable oil for deep-frying

Wash the fillets; pat dry, cut into 1-1/2-inch strips or fingers and place into a **flat pan**. Sprinkle lightly with salt, coat with the *Guava Tamarind Paste* and marinate for about 30-minutes.

Combine the flour and corn meal in a **shallow dish** and roll the fingers in the mixture. Pour the oil into a **deep-fat fryer** *or deep pot* and heat. Gently fry the fingers until golden brown, drain on a **wire rack** and serve.

Grouper Fillet in Banana Batter

Five 5-oz. grouper fillets
1 tbsp. ground white pepper
1 tbsp. salt
3 oz. freshly squeezed lemon juice

Batter

2 eggs
1/2 cup mashed banana
2 cups milk
1/2 cup all purpose flour
Vegetable oil 1/2" deep in skillet

Wash the fillets thoroughly and pat dry. Place into a **flat pan** and season with salt, pepper and lemon juice. Marinate for 30-minutes.

Batter

In a **medium-sized bowl**, combine the milk, eggs and mashed banana. Sift in the flour and with a **wire whisk**, whisk the mixture until smooth.

Dip the cutlets into the batter, coating both sides. Pour the vegetable oil into a **large skillet** and heat. Fry the cutlets over medium-high heat until the coating is golden brown, 5 to 6-minutes on each side, and serve immediately.

Note - Other firm meat fish fillet may be substituted for the grouper.

Hot Peppers

Bahamian Bird Peppers

The Red pepper reminds us that a significant part of African culinary practice consists of the condiments and seasonings used to prepare foods.

Jerk is a popular method in Jamaica of barbecuing well seasoned pork, chicken or fish. It can be traced to the Coromantee hunters of pre-slavery West Africa, who passed it on to the Maroons. They would roast seasoned pork over hot coals, in earthen pits that were covered with Pimento branches.

Peppers grow in abundance throughout the Caribbean and are an important ingredient in many of our recipes. Growing on small bushes, mature fruits are picked when they are green or red.

Familiar names of peppers are Cayenne, Chili and Pimento, but in the islands, you will find names like Bird Peppers and Scotch Bonnet or Goat Peppers. If you are an adventurer, when you visit the Caribbean, you will eat native dishes like the natives do – with lots of pepper. However, I would suggest a "mild" approach, especially with goat pepper. ✽

Grouper Filet In Burnt Orange

4 grouper filets
1 tsp. salt
1 tsp. ground white pepper
4 medium-sized oranges
1/2 cup olive oil

Wash the filets and pat dry. Place into a **flat pan** and sprinkle with salt and pepper on both sides. Set aside.

Wash the oranges and using a **potato peeler**, peel off strips of the rind until all of the rind of each orange is removed. Cut between the membranes, carefully removing the sections preserving the juice.

Heat the olive oil in a **large non-stick skillet**; add the strips of orange rind and sauté, stirring until dark brown. Remove and set aside.

Place the fish fillets in the hot oil and fry on both sides until crisp. Remove to a **serving dish**.

Add the orange sections and juice to the oil in the skillet. Cook over high heat for 1-minute. Add the salt and pepper to taste. Pour over the fish and top with the cooked orange peel.

Oven Fried Salmon Steaks

Four 1" thick salmon steaks
Freshly squeezed juice of 1 lemon
Salt
Ground white pepper
Seasoned bread crumbs

Bake at 450°F

Clean the steaks; pat dry, place into a **flat pan** and sprinkle with salt and pepper to taste. Brush with the lemon juice and marinate for 30-minutes.

Place the seasoned crumbs into a **shallow dish** and coat the steaks lightly with the crumbs. Arrange in a single layer on a well-greased **baking sheet** and oven bake uncovered for 8 to 10-minutes, depending on thickness of the steaks.

Serve hot with lemon wedges.

Salmon Cakes

1 can (14 oz.) pink salmon
Freshly squeezed juice of 1/2 lime
1 medium-sized onion, 1/4" dice
1 medium-sized green pepper, 1/4" dice
1 egg, slightly beaten
1/2 cup Instant Potato Flakes
Hot peppers to taste
Fine bread crumbs
Vegetable oil 1/4" deep in skillet

Drain the salmon and place into a **medium-sized bowl**. Remove the bones and skin and mash the salmon with a fork. Sprinkle with the lime juice and fold in the chopped onion and green pepper, egg and potato flakes. Add the hot peppers to taste, mixing gently.

Spread the bread crumbs on a sheet of **wax paper**. Using hands, form the mixture into 3-inch cakes and press into the crumbs coating completely.

Pour the oil into a **large skillet** and heat. Gently fry the cakes for about 5-minutes on each side. Drain on a **wire rack** and serve hot.

Salmon Stuffed Tomatoes

3 medium-sized tomatoes, chilled
1 can (14 oz.) pink salmon
1/2 cup 1/4" dice cucumber
2 tbsp. 1/4" dice onion
3/4 tsp. ground white pepper
1/2 tsp. salt
1/2 tsp. chopped pimento
1/2 cup mayonnaise

Cut off the tops of the tomatoes and scoop out the centers to make cups.

Drain the salmon and place into a **medium-sized bowl**. Remove the bones and skin and break up into small chunks. Gently mix in the cucumber, onion, seasonings, pimento and mayonnaise. Chill.

Fill the tomato cups with the chilled mixture. Serve on a bed of lettuce and garnish with cucumber slices.

Cracked Conch

4 medium-sized conchs
2 eggs, beaten
1/2 cup milk
1 tbsp. lime juice
1 tsp. Lady Darling's Island Seasoning
Hot peppers to taste
Flour
Vegetable oil for deep-frying
Salt to taste
Fresh lime juice & hot peppers

TIP:

Cracked conch is best serve immediately with a small dish of crushed hot peppers in lime juice, on the side.

Wash the conchs in cold water; cut into halves horizontally and tenderize Method One *page 31*.

In a **shallow dish** using a **wire whisk**, whisk together the eggs, milk and lime juice. Add the Island Seasoning and crush in hot peppers to taste, mixing together well. Spread enough flour to coat the conchs well on a sheet of **wax paper**. Heat the oil in a **deep-fat fryer** *or deep pot*.

Dip each piece of conch separately into the egg mix and then coat completely with the flour. Using a **long handle fork**, place immediately into the hot oil. Fry quickly until golden brown. Remove to a **wire rack** and sprinkle with salt to taste.

Guanabani Conch

4 large conchs
2 tbsp. freshly squeezed lime juice
3 cups fresh okra, diced
2 tbsp. White Wine
4 oz. butter
2 oz. fresh bread crumbs
1 large onion, chopped
Salt to taste
Ground white pepper to taste
Créole Sauce page 259
Bake at 350°F

Wash the conchs in cold water and prepare Method Two *page 31*. Place into a **flat dish**. Season the conch with the salt and pepper. Marinate in the lime juice and the white wine for 2-hours.

Melt the butter in a **large skillet** and sauté the onions and okra. Spread half the *Créole Sauce* on the bottom of a **3-quart sized casserole dish** and place the okra on top.

Drain the conch, placing it on top of the okra. Cover with more sauce and sprinkle with the bread crumbs. Bake for about 30-minutes.

Ginger Conch

2 fresh conchs, thinly sliced
2 cloves garlic, chopped
1 large onion, sliced
1 oz. fresh ginger, sliced
2 tbsp. sesame oil

Sauce

1 vegetable bouillon cube
1 cup water
1 tbsp. freshly squeezed lime juice
Salt to taste
Hot peppers to taste

Prepare the sliced conch *page 32*.

Sauce

In a **1-quart saucepan**, bring the water to a boil and dissolve the bouillon cube. Add the lime juice, salt and pepper and simmer for about 5-minutes.

Heat the oil in a **large skillet**; sauté the garlic and remove to a **flat dish**. Sauté the onion and remove to the dish.

Sauté the conch quickly; return the oil to the skillet, stirring in the sauce. Continue to sauté for about 2-minutes. Serve immediately over hot *Barefoot Rice page 206*.

Spicy Conch

2 large conchs, sliced *page 32*
3 scallions
1 sprig fresh thyme
Freshly squeezed juice of 1 lime
Hot peppers to taste
Salt
2 cups water

Cut the scallions into 1-inch pieces and place into a **2-quart sized saucepan** with the water adding the thyme, lime juice, peppers, salt and water. Bring to a boil and cook for about 10-minutes.

Place the thinly sliced conch into the boiling mixture. Remove from the heat; allow to sit for about 5-minutes and serve in **soup bowls**.

Dumphries Conch Créole

4 large conchs
2 oz. vegetable oil
4 slices bacon, diced
1 large onion, sliced
1 medium-sized green pepper, slivered
3 oz. Champion Tomato Paste
3 oz. tomato sauce
1 large fresh tomato, chopped
1 tsp. Lady Darling's Island Seasoning
Salt to taste
1 oz. freshly squeezed lime juice
1/2 tsp. dried thyme leaves
2 cups stock
Hot peppers to taste

Prepare the conchs Method Two *page 31*. Drain, preserving 2-cups of the stock and cut the conch into chunks.

Heat the oil in a **3-quart sized saucepan** and sauté the bacon. Stir in the onion and green pepper; continue to sauté for about 3-minutes. Add the fresh tomato and sauté for 3 additional minutes. Add the tomato paste and the sauce, thyme leaves, and the lime juice with the crushed pepper.

Add the stock and water, Island Seasoning, salt and the conch chunks. Cover and simmer over medium heat for 15 to 20-minutes.

Spicy Conch Rissoles

2 medium-sized conchs
1 tsp. salt
1 tbsp. freshly squeezed lemon juice
1 medium-sized onion chopped into 1" chunks
1/2 medium-sized green pepper cut into 1" chunks
1/2 tsp. dried thyme leaves
Hot peppers to taste
1 egg
4 cups water for boiling

Wash the conchs in cold water, cut into 1-inch chunks and sprinkle with salt and lemon juice. Place the conch, onion, green pepper, thyme, hot pepper and egg into the bowl of a **food processor** fitted with the knife blade and process for 2-minutes. Using a **rubber scraper**, remove the conch mixture to a **bowl**.

In a **2-quart saucepan**, bring the water to a rolling boil and drop the mixture by tablespoonfuls into the boiling water. After all of the mixture is spooned out into the saucepan, cook for 5-minutes.

Remove to a **flat dish** and serve with *Seafood Sauce page 260.*

Spicy Conch Rissoles In Shrimp Sauce

Spicy Conch Rissoles page 170
1 can (10 ozs.) Cream of Shrimp Soup
Cooked spaghetti

Prepare Rissoles. In a **2-quart sized saucepan**, prepare the Cream of Shrimp Soup according to directions, add Rissoles and cook over low heat for 5 to 6-minutes. Serve over cooked spaghetti.

Broiled Crawfish

Six 6 oz. crawfish tails
1 tsp. salt
1 tbsp. vegetable oil
Freshly squeezed juice of 1 lime
1 tsp. ground white pepper
1 tsp. Lady Darling's Island Seasoning

Drawn Butter

3 tbsp. butter
3 cloves fresh garlic
Broil at 400°F

Prepare the crawfish *page 32*; drain and let cool. Place the tails o n a **cutting board** with the soft side of shell on the board. With a **large sharp knife**, firmly cut through the top of the shell but do not com-pletely separate the tail while spreading flat.

Sprinkle the meat with the lime juice and then with the Island Seasoning, and white pepper.

Drawn Butter

Pass the fresh garlic through a **garlic press**. Melt the butter in a **small skillet** over low heat; add the garlic and heat for several minutes. Brush over the meat of the crawfish tails and sprinkle with paprika.

Arrange the tails on a **broiling pan**, place under the broiler and broil only until the tops are brown. Serve immediately with additional Drawn Butter if desired.

Crawfish

The snow white meat of the Crawfish, a delectable and tasty shellfish, is know to satisfy the most varied tastes. Cousin to the Maine Lobster, with two feelers instead of claws.

In the Bahamas, the season for harvesting the crawfish is from the beginning of April to the end of August.

Crawfish meat is more compact than that of the lobster and with true Bahamian artistry, crawfish can be prepared in many ways, broiled, roasted, baked, steamed, minced or made into tasty salads. ❇

Minced Crawfish

4 crawfish tails, in shells
Freshly squeezed juice of 1 lime
1 medium-sized onion, 1/4" dice
1 clove garlic, minced
1 medium-sized green pepper, 1/4" dice
1/2 tsp. dried thyme leaves
1 tsp. Lady Darling's Island Seasoning
Salt to taste
Hot peppers to taste
2 oz. vegetable oil

Prepare the crawfish *page 32* and remove the meat. Strip into thin shreds; place into a **bowl** and sprinkle with the lime juice.

Heat the oil in a **large skillet** and sauté the onion, green pepper, garlic and thyme for about 3-minutes. Add the crawfish shreds, Island Seasoning and hot peppers to taste. Continue to sauté for about 10-minutes, stirring often. Cover for the last few minutes of cooking.

Mixed Mince
Fish & Crawfish

1 lb. turbot or other firm-fleshed fish
2 tbsp. salt
Ingredients for *Minced Crawfish* (above)
2 cups shredded cabbage (optional)

Clean the turbot, place into a **3-quart sized saucepan**, with water to cover. Add the salt and lime juice and boil for about 10-minutes.

Drain and allow to cool. Strip the fish into thin shreds making sure to remove all of the bones. Combine with the stripped crawfish and prepare same as *Minced Crawfish*.

Add the cabbage during the last 5 or 6-minutes of cooking. Serve over hot *Barefoot Rice page 206*.

Crawfish In Beer Sauce

2 crawfish tails
2 tsp. butter
2 cloves garlic, minced
1/2 tsp. curry powder
1/2 tsp. salt

Sauce

1 tbsp. all purpose flour
1/2 cup Kalik beer
1/2 cup grated Sharp Cheddar cheese

Prepare the crawfish *page 32*; split into halves and remove the meat (preserve the shells). Cut into 1-inch chunks and sprinkle with the curry powder and salt.

Sauce

In a **1-quart saucepan**, mix together the flour, beer and cheese. Over low heat and stirring constantly, cook until the mixture thickens. Remove from the heat.

Heat the butter in a **large skillet** and sauté the seasoned crawfish chunks and garlic for 5 to 7-minutes. Spoon into the half shells and place onto **serving dishes**. Reheat the beer sauce and pour over the crawfish.

Caribe Fried Shrimp

1 lb. jumbo shrimp, shelled and deveined
1 egg
2 tbsp. cold water
1 tsp. freshly squeezed lime juice
Hot peppers to taste
2/3 cups Yellow Corn Meal
Salt to taste
1 tsp. curry powder
1/2 tsp. garlic powder
1/4 tsp. paprika
Vegetable oil for deep-frying

In a **small bowl**, beat the egg with the water, add the lime juice and crush in the hot peppers. In a **shallow dish**, combine the cornmeal, salt and seasonings.

Dip the shrimps into the egg mixture and roll in the corn meal until completely coated. Pour the oil into a **deep-fat fryer** *or deep pot* and heat. Fry the shrimps until golden brown. Drain on a **wire rack** and serve.

Shrimp Curry In a Hurry

2 cans (4-1/2 oz. each) medium-sized shrimp, drained
2 tbsp. butter or margarine
1 medium-sized onion, chopped
2 cloves garlic, minced
2 tbsp. all purpose flour
1-1/2 tbsp. curry powder
1/2 tsp. ground ginger
1 tsp. salt
2 cups chicken broth
1 cup milk
2 tbsp. freshly squeezed lemon juice
Shredded coconut

Barefoot Rice page 206

Over low heat, melt the butter in a **large skillet** and sauté the onion and garlic for 2 or 3-minutes. Stir in the flour, curry powder, ginger and salt.

Using a **wire whisk**, whisk in the chicken broth and milk and whisk vigorously until the mixture is smooth. Cook over low heat, stirring until the sauce thickens, 3 to 5-minutes. Add the shrimp and the lemon juice and continue cooking over low heat for 5-minutes, stirring occasionally. Serve over the hot *Barefoot Rice* topped with shredded coconut.

Beer Battered Shrimp

1-1/2 lbs. jumbo shrimps
1/2 tsp. salt
Freshly squeezed juice of 1 lime

Batter

1 cup all purpose flour
1 tsp. paprika
1/2 tsp. ground ginger
1 tsp. ground white pepper
1 tsp. salt
1 cup Kalik beer
1/2 cup all purpose flour for coating
Vegetable oil for deep-frying

Clean the shrimps and cut down the backs but not into halves. Open flat and sprinkle with salt and lemon.

Batter

In a **small bowl**, sift together 1-cup of flour, paprika, ginger, pepper and salt. Using a **wire whisk**, whisk in the beer until the mixture is the consistency of thin batter. Chill for about 10-minutes.

Spread remaining flour in a **flat dish** and coat the shrimps completely. Heat the oil in a **deep-fat fryer** *or deep pot*. With a **long fork**, dip each shrimp into the chilled beer batter and place carefully into the hot oil. Fry quickly until golden brown and crispy, about 2 or 3-minutes. Drain on a **wire rack** and serve immediately.

Quick Curried Shrimp

1-1/2 lbs. jumbo shrimp
1 tbsp. minced garlic
2 tbsp. olive oil
3/4 tsp. salt
3/4 tsp. curry powder
3/4 tsp. ground white pepper
1 cup Dry White Wine

Wash the shrimp, pat dry and place into a **shallow pan**. Sprinkle with the salt, curry powder and pepper and marinate for a few minutes.

In a **large skillet**, heat the oil with the garlic. Add the shrimp, and sauté over medium heat, stirring occasionally for 2 to 4-minutes. Add the wine and, over high heat, bring to a boil. With a slotted spoon, remove the shrimps to a **serving dish**.

Boil the wine mixture until it is reduced to 1/4-cup and slightly thickened. Adjust seasonings; pour the sauce over the shrimp and serve.

Spiced Ginger Scampi

20 pieces scampi or jumbo shrimps
1 tsp. chopped garlic
1 tsp. chopped onion
1 tsp. chopped ginger
8 oz. chopped fresh tomatoes
1/2 tsp. chopped mint leaves
1/2 tsp. chopped basil leaves
1 tsp. freshly squeezed lemon juice
1 tsp. chili sauce
1/2 oz. heavy cream
2 oz. butter
1 oz. Courvoisier
Salt and pepper to taste

Remove the scampi shells; devein and season with the salt, pepper and lemon juice. Let stand for 10-minutes.

Heat the butter in a **large skillet** and sauté the garlic, onions, ginger and tomatoes. Stir in the herbs continuing to sauté for a few minutes. Stir in the scampi, sprinkle with the courvoisier and flame until the scampi become reddish, then set aside.

Add the tomato purée to the **skillet** and reduce to desired consistency. Mix in the heavy cream, salt and pepper to taste.

Arrange the scampi on a **serving plate** and just before serving, sprinkle with additional chopped herbs if desired.

Grilled Turtle Steaks

4 turtle steaks, about 1-1/2" thick
Freshly squeezed juice of 1 lime
Salt
Ground white pepper or hot pepper to taste
1 oz. butter
2 tsp. parsley flakes

Clean the steaks well; pat dry and place into a **shallow pan**. Season with half the lime juice, salt and pepper to taste. Marinate for about 30-minutes.

Spread the softened butter on each side of the steaks. Grill under hot **grill** *or over hot coals* for 10-minutes on each side.

Place onto a **serving dish**, and pour the pan juices over the steaks. Sprinkle with the remaining lime juice and parsley. Serve hot.

Turtle Pie

Cassava Crust (double ingredients for top and bottom crust) *page 272*
2 carrots, 1/2" dice
1 lb. turtle meat
1 tbsp. all purpose flour
3 slices bacon
1 tbsp. water
1 medium-sized onion, 1/2" dice
1 tsp. parsley, finely chopped
1 scallion, 1/2" dice
1 tsp. dried thyme leaves
1 clove garlic, finely chopped
1/4 tsp. ground allspice
1 cup tomatoes, chopped
1 rib celery, 1/2" dice
1 tsp. Lady Darling's Island Seasoning
Salt to taste
Hot peppers to taste
1 tsp. black pepper

Bake at 350°F

Prepare the double cassava crust; roll out and line a greased **10-inch casserole dish** with the bottom crust. Roll out the top crust and set aside.

Wash the turtle meat, pat dry and chop into 1-inch chunks.

In a **large skillet**, fry the bacon and remove to a **large bowl**. Sauté the onion, scallion and garlic and remove to the bowl. Brown the meat; remove to the bowl. Sauté the tomatoes and remove to the bowl.

In a **small dish**, mix together the flour and water adding to the mixture in the bowl. Add the celery, carrots, parsley, thyme, allspice and seasonings to taste, mixing well.

Turn into the casserole dish lined with the crust and cover with the top crust. Fold the edge and flute. Cut slits in the top for steam to escape and bake for 45-minutes.

Turtle

There are many species of salt-water turtles in the waters of the Caribbean Sea, some mature upwards of 300 lbs. Some species are threatened, but the "green turtle" variety is still found in great numbers and several islands are experimenting with breeding in captivity. It is the meat of the green turtle and not the endangered species that is used in these recipes.

Seafood Casserole

1 cup crab meat, 1" chunks
1 cup crawfish, 1" chunks
1 cup shrimp, 1" chunks
1 tbsp. freshly squeezed lemon juice
Salt
Ground white pepper
3 cups Cheese Sauce page 257
3 whole tomatoes, chopped
1 medium-sized onion, chopped
1 medium-sized green pepper, chopped
1 cup fresh bread crumbs

Bake at 350°F

In a **large bowl**, mix the seafood together and season lightly with the lemon juice, salt and pepper.

In a **2-quart sized saucepan**, prepare the cheese sauce.

Grease a **3-quart sized casserole dish** and place a layer of the seafood mix in the dish, followed by a layer of tomatoes, then onion, green pepper and sauce.

Repeat the layers. Spread breadcrumbs over top and bake for 30-minutes.

Notes

Meat & Poultry

Menus

❋

Dill Pickles

Grilled Tamarind Guava
Chicken

Savoury Potato Salad

Sweet Peas

Carrot Fritters

❋

Dill Seed Cucumber in Sour
Cream

Jerk Chicken

Akara Bean Cakes

Wilted Greens

Stuffed Baked Sapodilla

❋

Celery with Avocado Stuffing

Chicken Rissoles in
Mushroom Sauce

Spaghetti

Coconut Brownies

❋

Corn Relish

Glazed Cornish Hens

Breadfruit Salad

Green Beans & Almonds

Honey Rum Baked Bananas

❋

Avocado Stuffed Celery

Barbecue Beef Strips

Brown Rice

Creamed Spinach

Mango & Pineapple Strudel

❋

Avocado, Orange Grapefruit
Salad

Corned Beef Cakes

Cabbage & Rice

Brussels Sprouts with
Cheese Sauce

Paradise Pie à la Mode

❋

Recipes

❂ **Chicken**
Oven Fried Bites,
In Coconut Batter,
Grilled Tamarind/Guava,
Jerk, Rotisserie Jerk,
Vegetable Stir Fry,
Pie with Cassava Crust,
Savoury Rissoles,
Rissoles in Mushroom Sauce,
Mock Drumsticks
Stove Top Baked Cornish Hens
Glazed Cornish Hens
Barbecue Pineapple Turkey Roll

❂ **Beef**
Barbecue Sesame Strips,
Steak & Kidney Pie,
Jerk Barbecue Ribs,
Jerk Roast, Sherry Bites
With Oriental Vegetables
Corned Beef Cakes
Baked Canned Corned Beef

❂ **Pork**
Jerk Chops,
Jerk Barbecue Ribs,
Stir Fry in Garlic Sauce,
Roast Calypso,
Jerk Roast,
Crown Roast of Lamb
Lemon & Garlic Lamb Chops

❂ **Land Crabs**
Andros Stuffed Baked,
Cakes,
Zesty Boiled,
Heritage Crab & Dough

Oven Fried Chicken Bites

1 lb. chicken breasts
1 to 1-1/2 cups bottled regular Italian Salad Dressing
1 to 1-1/2 cups Seasoned bread crumbs
Bake at 450°F

Wash the breasts thoroughly; pat dry and cut into 1-1/2-inch cubes. Place into a **shallow pan**; coat with the salad dressing and marinate for 15-minutes, stirring frequently.

Place the crumbs onto a sheet of **wax paper** and roll each chicken cube into the crumbs, coating completely.

Arrange in a single layer on a well-greased **baking sheet** and oven fry without turning for 8 to10-minutes.

Chicken in Coconut Batter

4 boneless chicken breasts
1 large fresh coconut, grated

Batter

2 eggs
1/4 cup all purpose flour (divided)
2 to 4 tbsp. canned coconut milk or whole milk
Salt
Ground white pepper
Vegetable oil for deep-frying

Break open the coconut and grate *page 24*.

Wash the chicken breasts thoroughly, pat dry, place into a **shallow pan** and sprinkle with salt and pepper to taste.

Batter

In a **small bowl**, beat the eggs; add 1-tablespoon of the flour, coconut milk, salt and pepper to taste.

Spread remaining flour in a **shallow dish** and spread the grated coconut in **another shallow dish**. Roll the breasts in the flour; dip into the batter, then into the grated coconut.

Heat the oil in the **deep-fat fryer** *or deep pot*, and using a **long fork**, place the coated chicken into the hot fat. Fry until golden brown and drain on a **wire rack**.

Grilled Tamarind Guava Chicken

4 boneless chicken breasts
Salt
Ground white pepper
Tamarind Guava Paste page 366

Wash the breasts thoroughly, pat dry, place into a **shallow pan** and sprinkle with salt and pepper to taste.

Coat the breasts completely with the paste and marinate for about 30-minutes.

Arrange on the **rack of barbecue grill** *or oven grill* and grill for 6 to 10-minutes on each side.

Azaleta's Mango Chicken

1 whole chicken about 2 lbs., cut into large chunks for stew
Salt and pepper to taste
Garlic powder to taste
1/2 cup Mango Chutney page 363 or 1/2 cup store bought chutney
1 cup chicken broth

Clean the chicken thoroughly, cut into chunks for stewing and season with salt, pepper and garlic. Mix chutney and broth together to make a gravy. Arrange chicken in a large **non stick skillet**; coat with the chutney mix, cover tightly and cook over very low heat for about 45-minutes. You add hot pepper for flavour if using the store bought chutney.

Pineapple Chicken

Prepare same as *Azaleta's Mango Chicken* (above) except substitute *Pineapple Chutney page 364* for *Mango Chutney*.

African Culinary Influences

By the early 1700's it was realized that, although some European foods were acceptable, slaves fared better when fed their customary food. Like religion, oral traditions, music, and dance, cuisine and culinary practices not only survived hard servitude but also enriched the cultures of the Americas. Fried chicken among other southern dishes reflects this African influence and even the seasoning of southern dishes is often far heavier than in northern recipes.

Chicken Vegetable Stir-fry

1/2 cup soy sauce
4 tbsp. sesame oil (divided)
2 tsp. sesame seeds
6 chicken breast halves
1 large onion, sliced
2 cups fresh broccoli flowerets
1/2 cup thinly sliced celery
1/2 lb. fresh snow peas
1/2 cup sliced fresh mushrooms
1 tbsp. cornstarch
1/2 cup water
Hot cooked brown rice

Remove the skin and bones from the chicken and slice into 2-inch strips.

In a **medium-sized bowl**, combine the soy sauce, 2-tablespoons sesame oil and the sesame seeds. Place the chicken into the bowl stirring to coat with the soy sauce and oils and marinate for at least 30-minutes.

Preheat a **wok** to medium high (325°F) *or a large skillet* over medium-high heat and stir-fry the marinated chicken for 2 to 3-minutes; remove back to the bowl.

Separate the onion slices into rings. Add 1-tablespoon of the sesame oil to the wok and stir-fry the rings and the broccoli for 2-minutes; remove to the bowl. Add remaining sesame oil and stir-fry the snow peas, celery and mushrooms for 2-minutes; remove to the bowl.

In a **small dish**, combine the cornstarch and water. Return the chicken and vegetables to the wok; add the cornstarch mix and, stirring constantly, cook until thickened. Serve over the Brown Rice.

Chicken Pie with Cassava Crust

Cassava Crust page 272
4 chicken breasts, boneless
1 medium-sized onion, chopped
1 clove garlic, minced
1 medium-sized green pepper, chopped
1 cup mixed vegetables
1 cup milk
1 can cream of chicken soup
1 oz. vegetable oil
1/2 tsp. dried thyme leaves
1 tsp. Lady Darling's Island Seasoning
Salt to taste
Black pepper

Bake at 350°F

Prepare the *Cassava Crust* and set aside.

Clean and wash the chicken breasts; cut into 1-inch cubes and sprinkle with half the salt, half of the Island Seasoning and black pepper.

In a **large bowl**, mix the canned soup with the milk until smooth.

Heat the oil in a **large skillet** and sauté the chicken cubes for 2 or 3-minutes. Stir in the onion, green pepper, garlic and thyme leaves. Stirring, continue to sauté for 3 to 5-minutes.

Combine the chicken sauté and the vegetables in the bowl with the soup, season to taste mixing thoroughly. Turn into a **deep casserole dish**.

On a floured **board**, with a floured **rolling pin**, roll out the crust and place over the top of the casserole dish. Flute the edges and make slits in the crust for steam to escape.

Bake for 35 to 45-minutes and serve immediately.

Savoury Chicken Rissoles

1 chicken breast (2 halves)
1 tsp. curry powder
1 carrot, chopped
1 rib celery, chopped
2 clove garlic, chopped
1/2 tsp. dried thyme leaves
1 tsp. salt
1/2 tsp. black pepper
1 egg
Hot peppers to taste
1 tsp. salt
4 cups water

Remove the chicken meat from the bones and cut into chunks. Fit a **food processor** with the knife blade; place the chicken and remaining ingredients into the bowl of the processor and process for 2-minutes, stopping to scrape the sides.

Pour the water into a **2-quart sized saucepan** and bring to a rolling boil. Drop the mixture by tablespoonfuls into the boiling water. After all of the mixture is spooned into the saucepan, cook for 5-minutes. Remove to a **serving dish** and serve with *Cocktail Sauce page 260* if desired.

Chicken Rissoles & Spaghetti

Prepare Rissoles; prepare *Créole Sauce (page 259)* place the Rissoles in the sauce and cook for about 10-minutes in sauce.

Serve over cooked spaghetti.

Barbecue Pineapple Turkey Roll

6 Servings

1 turkey roll
1 fresh pineapple for six slices page 25
Kahlúa Barbecue Sauce page 261

Cut six 1-inch thick slices from the turkey roll and brush with the barbecue sauce. Arrange in a **large baking dish**.

Brush the bottom of a **separate baking dish** with butter and arrange the pineapple slices in the dish. Set aside.

Grill the turkey slices for 10 to 15-minutes on each side and set aside.

Place the baking dish with the pineapple slices under the grill for 3-minutes and set aside. Place the grilled turkey slices onto the pineapple slices; coat with more sauce and serve hot.

Mock Drumsticks

Yield 8

8 six-inch wooden skewers
2 lbs. ground chicken or ground beef
1 medium onion, finely chopped
2 tsp. prepared mustard
1 tsp. Worcestershire sauce
2 eggs, beaten
1 tsp. salt
1 tsp. Lady Darling's Island Seasoning
Black pepper to taste
Hot peppers to taste
1 cup fine bread crumbs
1/3 cup vegetable oil

In a **medium-sized bowl**, mix together all ingredients except bread crumbs and oil. Divide the mixture into eight portions and shape around the **wooden skewers** to form drumsticks.

Spread the crumbs on a sheet of **wax paper** and carefully roll the drumsticks in the crumbs coating thoroughly.

Heat the oil in a **large skillet** and gently fry the drumsticks, turning carefully to brown on all sides. Reduce the heat, continue to cook for about 15-minutes, turning occasionally.

Stove Top Baked Cornish Hens

Two 1 lb. cornish hens
1-1/2 tsp. Lady Darling's Island Seasoning
Salt to taste
Ground white pepper to taste

Wash the hens thoroughly and cut into halves. Sprinkle both sides with the seasonings and place into a **large non-stick skillet** wing side down.

Cover the skillet, place on a **heat diffuser** and over very low heat, "pan bake" for 8 to 10-minutes. Turn the hens over; re-cover and continue to cook for about 15-minutes.

Variation

During the last 10-minutes of cooking time, coat the hens with *Tamarind Honey Glaze page 264* or *Barbecue Poultry Sauce page 261*.

Glazed Cornish Hens

Three 1 lb. cornish hens
Salt
Freshly ground pepper
1/4 cup butter, melted (divided)

Glaze

1/4 cup honey
1/2 cup Maker's Mark Bourbon
2 tbsp. of the melted butter

Bake at 350ºF

Remove the giblets from the hens and reserve for another use. Rinse the hens with cold water and pat dry. Sprinkle the cavity of each with salt and pepper.

Place the hens, breast side up, in a **shallow baking pan**; use 1/4-cup of the melted butter for the first basting.

Glaze

In a **small bowl**, combine the remaining melted butter, honey and bourbon.

Bake for about 1-1/2-hours brushing with the glaze every 15-minutes of baking time until the hens are tender.

Barbecue Sesame Beef Strips

One 3 lb. rump roast, sliced
1 tsp. black pepper
1 tsp. Accent seasoning
1 large onion, sliced
2 scallions, chopped
2 to 3 cloves garlic, finely chopped
2 tbsp. soy sauce
2 tbsp. sesame oil

Have the butcher slice the roast into 1/8-inch thick slices, *or while the roast is still slightly frozen; slice with a very sharp knife diagonally, across the grain*. Place the slices into a **large bowl with a cover** and sprinkle with the black pepper and Accent.

In a **small bowl**, mix together the remaining ingredients and pour over the beef slices. Cover and marinate overnight in refrigerator or for at least 6 hours at room temperature, turning the slices occasionally. Remove the slices from the marinade reserving the vegetables.

Place the slices on a **barbecue grill** *or oven grill* and grill until tender turning often. Grill the marinated vegetables and serve over the cooked beef.

English Steak & Kidney Pie

1-1/2 lb. steak for stewing
1/2 lb. beef kidney
Salt
Black peeper
2 tbsp. all purpose flour
1 cup beef stock or bouillon

Crust

1 cup all purpose flour
1-1/2 tsp. baking powder
1/2 tsp. salt
2 tbsp. vegetable shortening
1/3 cup milk

Egg Wash

1 egg
1 tbsp. water

Bake at 350°F

Cut the meat into 1-inch chunks; season with salt and pepper and coat with flour.

Heat the oil in a **large skillet** and brown the meat over high heat. Turn into a **3-quart sized saucepan**, add the stock, cover, and simmer over medium heat, for about 1-1/2 hours. Allow to cool.

Crust

In a **small bowl**, combine the flour, baking powder and salt. With a **pastry cutter**, cut in the shortening until mixture resembles rice grains. Mix in the milk to form a smooth dough.

Place onto a floured **board** and with a floured **rolling pin**, roll out into a 10-inch circle.

Turn the steak and kidney mix into a **9-inch pie dish** and cover with the crust.

Egg Wash

In a **small dish**, beat together the egg and water and brush the edge and over the top of the crust. Flute the edge and make slits in the top for stream to escape. Bake for 35 to 40-minutes and serve.

Jerk Chicken

1 whole chicken about 2 lbs., quartered
Salt to taste
1 to 4 tsp. Jerk Seasoning Paste, to taste
2 tbsp. vegetable oil

Clean the chicken thoroughly, cut into quarters, pat dry and place into a **shallow pan**. Coat with the oil rubbing the Jerk Seasoning into the meat well on both sides. Marinate for 1-hour, turning the chicken pieces a few times.

Place the quarters on the **barbecue grill** *or rotisserie* over hot coals *or under the grill of oven*. Grill until the chicken is thoroughly cooked basting with natural juices. Remove to a **serving dish** *or to a baking dish* and place into the oven to finish cooking.

Jerk Chicken Wings

Chicken Wings
Salt to taste
Powdered Jerk Seasoning, to taste

Clean chicken wings; pat dry, place into a **flat dish** and season with salt to taste. Dust with the powdered Jerk seasoning and let stand for about 15-minutes. Place the wings on a **barbecue grill** over hot coals *or under the grill of oven* and grill for 15 to 20-minutes.

Barbecue

When the Spanish arrived in the Americas, they found the Taino people of the West Indies cooking meat and fish over a pit of coal on a framework of green wooden sticks. The Spanish spelling of the Indian name for that framework was "barbacoa". Both the name for the framework and the method of cooking meats found their way to North America and were called "barbecue".

Jerk

Another Amerindian method of cooking was coating the freshly caught fish or bird with mud and baking it on charcoal placed in a pit dug in the sand. When done, the mud was scraped off taking with it feathers and scales. The present day method of cooking pork and chicken over an open fire, "jerking" in Jamaica, seems to be the modern day equivalent of this ancient cooking technique.

Jerk Barbecue Ribs

2 lbs. beef or pork ribs
Salt to taste
1 to 4 tbsp. Jerk Seasoning Paste, to taste
2 tbsp. vegetable oil

Clean the ribs, pat dry and place into a **large flat pan**. Coat with the oil. Rub the Jerk Seasoning into the meat well, on both sides and marinate for 1-hour, turning a few times.

Place the ribs onto a **barbecue grill** over hot coals *or under the grill of oven*. Grill until the meat is thoroughly cooked. Remove to a **serving dish** and brush with *Kahlúa Barbecue Sauce page 261* if desired.

Jerk Beef or Pork Roast

One 3 lb. pork or beef roast
Salt to taste
2 to 4 tbsp. Jerk Seasoning Paste, to taste
2 tbsp. vegetable oil
Bake at 350°F

Clean the roast, pat dry and place into a **large pan**. Coat with the oil. Rub the Jerk Seasoning paste and marinate for 1-1/2 to-2 hours.

Place the roast into a **large roasting pan**. Bake uncovered, basting occasionally until the meat is tender 2 to 2-1/2 hours. Serve immediately.

Jerk Pork Chops

4 centre cut pork chops
Salt to taste
1 to 4 tsp. Jerk Seasoning Paste, to taste
2 tbsp. vegetable oil

Clean the chops pat dry and place into a **large flat pan**. Coat with oil and rub the Jerk Seasoning into the meat well, on both sides. Marinate for 1-hour, turning the chops a few times.

Place the chops onto a **barbecue grill** over hot coals *or under the grill of oven*. Grill until the meat is thoroughly cooked.

Beef with Oriental Vegetables

1 lb. boneless sirloin steak
3 tbsp. soy sauce (divided)
2 tbsp. sugar
1/2 tsp. ground white pepper
1/2 tsp. dried onion flakes
2 tbsp. vegetable oil
1 tbsp. soy sauce
1/2 tsp. salt
1 carrot, thinly sliced
1 tbsp. sugar
1 rib celery, sliced
1 medium-sized onion, chopped
1 can (14 oz.) Chinese vegetables, drained
1 cup shredded cabbage
2 to 3 large fresh mushrooms, sliced
1 package (12 oz.) frozen Oriental vegetables
1/2 cup water
1 tsp. cornstarch

Hot Barefoot Rice page 206

Slice the partially frozen steak, diagonally across the grain into 3x1/4-inch strips and place into a **flat pan**.

In a **small bowl**, combine 2-tablespoons soy sauce, sugar, pepper and onion flakes; pour over the steak, stirring until coated.

Pour the oil around the top of a preheated **wok**, coating the sides and allow heating at medium high heat (325°F) for 1-minute. Stir-fry the steak strips for 2 to 3-minutes or until browned. Remove from the wok and set aside.

Combine the salt, 1-tablespoon of the soy sauce, and 1-tablespoon of the sugar, mixing well. Add the carrots, onion and celery to the wok, stir-fry for 2-minutes or until the vegetables are crisp-tender.

Add the steak, cabbage, Oriental vegetables, and mushrooms, stir-fry 1-minute. Stir in the soy sauce mixture.

In a **small dish**, combine the water and cornstarch mixing well. Add to the wok and cook for 1-minute, stirring constantly, until thickened. Serve over hot *Barefoot Rice*.

Corned Beef Cakes

1 can (12 oz.) corned beef
2 tbsp. chopped onion
2 tbsp. chopped green pepper
1 tsp. freshly squeezed lime juice
1/2 tsp. dried thyme leaves
Hot peppers to taste
1 egg, slightly beaten
1 cup Instant Mashed Potatoes Flakes, divided
Vegetable oil 1/4" deep in skillet

Place the corned beef into a **medium-sized bowl** break up with a fork in preparation to mix and sprinkle with the lime juice. Add the onion, green pepper, thyme leaves, hot peppers to taste and beaten egg. Mix together well, adding half the potato flakes.

Using your hands, pat the mixture into 3-inch cakes. Spread remaining potato flakes on a sheet of **wax paper**. Press each cake into the flakes on both sides.

Heat the oil in a **large skillet**; place the cakes into the hot oil and fry gently for about 4 to 5-minutes on each side. Drain on a **wire rack** and serve immediately.

Baked Canned Corned Beef

1 can (12 oz.) corned beef, chilled
1-1/2 tsp. whole cloves
1/4 cup brown sugar
1/2 cup crushed pineapple with juice

Bake at 325°F

Gently remove the beef from the can so that it remains whole; press in the cloves and place into a **small shallow pan**.

In a **small dish**, mix together the brown sugar and pineapple. Spread over the beef and bake for 15 to-20 minutes.

Stir Fried Pork in Garlic Sauce

1 lb. lean boneless pork
2 tsp. corn starch
1 tsp. salt
1 tbsp. plus 1 tsp. soy sauce
2 tsp. sesame oil
2 tbsp. vegetable oil
4 green onions, sliced
2 tsp. minced garlic
2 tsp. minced fresh ginger
4 large fresh mushrooms, sliced
1/2 cup sliced water chestnuts
Crushed hot peppers to taste
2 tbsp. water
2 tsp. cornstarch
2 tsp. soy sauce
2 tbsp. sherry
1 tsp. Hoisin sauce

Hot Barefoot Rice page 206

With a **large sharp knife**, slice the partially frozen pork diagonally across the grain into 2x1/4-inch strips and place into a **flat pan**. In a **small dish**, combine the cornstarch, salt and soy sauce. Pour over the pork, stirring until the meat is coated. Let stand 15-minutes.

Pour the sesame and vegetable oils around top of a preheated **wok** *or large skillet* coating the sides. Allow heating at medium-high (325°F) for 1-minute. Add the pork and, stir-fry for 3 to 4-minutes or until brown and remove the pork to the flat dish.

Stir-fry the onions, garlic, ginger, mushrooms, water chestnuts, and red peppers for 1-minute. Return the pork to the wok and stir-fry for an additional 2-minutes.

In a **small dish**, combine the water, 2-teaspoons of the cornstarch mixing well. Add remaining ingredients (except rice) to the wok. Cook for 1-minute, stirring constantly, until thickened. Serve over hot *Barefoot Rice*.

Roast Pork Calypso

1 bone-in pork loin roast, (3-1/2 to 4 lbs.)
1 tbsp. grated fresh ginger
3/4 tsp. salt
1/4 tsp. ground cloves
1/4 tsp. freshly ground pepper
2 cloves garlic, minced
1 bay leaf, crumbled
2 cups chicken broth
2/3 cup Tia Maria
1/2 cup pack brown sugar
1 tbsp. Tia Maria

Sauce

1-1/2 cups roasting liquid
1/2 teaspoon cornstarch
1 tbsp. lime juice

Bake at 375°F

Score the top fatty part of the roast with a **sharp knife** in a diamond pattern. In a **small bowl**, combine the ginger, salt, cloves, pepper, garlic and bay leaf rubbing the mixture over top of the roast.

Bring to room temperature and place the roast, fatty side up, in a **large roasting pan**; coat with the chicken broth and 2/3-cup of Tia Maria. Roast for 1-1/2 to-2 hours, basting often. (Allow 30-minutes per pound of meat).

In a **small dish**, mix together the brown sugar and 1-tablespoon Tia Maria and during the last 20-minutes of roasting, spread the mixture over top of the roast.

Continue roasting and basting until the meat thermometer reads 155°F to 160°F. (Tent the roast with aluminum foil if sugar begins to brown). Allow the roast to stand 10-minutes before carving.

Sauce

In the small dish, dissolve the cornstarch in the lime juice. Skim the fat from the roasting liquid. Measure the liquid adding water to make 1-1/2-cups. In a **small saucepan**, bring the liquid and cornstarch/lime juice to a boil over medium heat. Adjust seasonings to taste and serve over the sliced pork.

Crown Roast of Lamb

Serving 6 - 7

1 or 2 joints of loin approximately 12 to 14 chops
2 tbsp. butter, melted
Salt
Black pepper
Rice Dressing page 234
Bake at 300ºF

Have your butcher cut the loins and form into a round crown. Brush with the melted butter and season with salt and pepper to taste. Place into a **large flat baking pan**.

Wrap ends of each chop with foil for protection while baking.

Place into oven and bake for 30 to 35-minutes per lb.

Prepare the *Rice Dressing* and before last hour of cooking; fill the centre with the dressing and return to the oven to complete cooking.

Remove from the oven and place onto a **serving platter**; remove the foil protectors and decorate ends with **cutlet frills**.

Variation

An unfilled *Crown Roast of Lamb* may be cooked upside down omitting covers on each bone. When done, fill the centre with cooked dressing.

Lemon & Garlic Lamb Chops

4 lamb shoulder chops
1 tbsp. all purpose flour
1 tbsp. grated lemon peel
1/2 tsp. garlic powder
1 tsp. Lady Darling's Island Seasoning
1/2 tsp. black pepper
1/4 cup vegetable oil

Mix together the flour, lemon peel, garlic powder, Island Seasoning and black pepper in a **large plastic food storage bag**. Add the chops and shake to coat.

Heat the oil in a **large skillet**; add the chops and any remaining flour mixture. Fry over medium-high heat about 10-minutes, or until the chops are golden brown, turning over once. Drain on **paper towels**.

Crab Cakes

Land crabs & biters (4 to 6) enough to produce 1 lb. of picked crabmeat
or 1 lb. canned or frozen crab meat
1/4 cup finely chopped parsley
1/4 cup finely chopped scallions
1 tsp. Lady Darling's Island Seasoning
1/2 tsp. black pepper
1 tsp. dry mustard
Hot peppers to taste (optional)
1 egg
2 tbsp. Instant Mashed Potato Flakes
1/2 cup fine bread crumbs
1/4 cup butter
1/4 cup olive oil

Prepare the crabs *page 32* and place the bodies and biters into a **large saucepan** with water to cover. Bring to a boil and boil for about 5-minutes. Drain and allow to cool.

Break up the bodies and biters; pick out as much of the crabmeat as possible and place into a **medium-sized bowl**.

Add the parsley, scallions, and Island Seasoning, black pepper, mustard, hot peppers, egg and potato flakes mixing well.

Spread the bread crumbs on a sheet of **wax paper**. Shape the mixture into small cakes and roll in the crumbs.

Heat the butter in a **large skillet** and over medium heat; gently fry the cakes until golden brown on both sides.

Zesty Boiled Crabs

4 land crabs with biters
1 tsp. salt
1 tsp. whole allspice
1 bay leaf
Hot peppers to taste
3 cups Kalik beer

Remove the legs (discard) and remove the biters. Wash and scrub the whole crabs and biters thoroughly and place all into a **large stockpot**.

Pour the beer over the crabs; add the salt, allspice and bay leaf. Bring to a boil; reduce the heat and simmer for about 15 to 20-minutes or until the crabs are well done.

Remove to a **serving dish** and serve with *Cassava & Coconut Pone page 91*.

Andros Stuffed Baked Crabs

6 land crabs with biters
2 oz. butter
1/2 medium-sized onion, finely chopped
1/2 medium-sized green pepper, finely chopped
1-1/2 cups crisp bread crumbs
3/4 tsp. dried thyme leaves
Salt
Black pepper
Hot peppers, optional

Bake at 350°F

Scrub the crabs and biters, break open and clean, preserving the fat *page 32* (save the backs to be stuffed). Place the bodies and biters into a **large stockpot** with water to cover. Bring to a boil and boil for about 5-minutes. Drain and allow to cool.

Break up the bodies and biters; pick out as much of the crabmeat as possible and place into a **medium-sized bowl**.

Heat half the butter in a **large skillet** and sauté the onion and green pepper. Stir in the crab fat and sauté for several minutes. Turn into the bowl with the crabmeat mixing in the bread crumbs, thyme salt and pepper to taste.

Fill the crab backs with the mixture and place into a **shallow baking dish**, shell side down. Dot the tops of each with butter and bake until the stuffing is browned, 15 to 20-minutes. Serve hot.

Heritage Crab & Dough

4 land crabs with biters
1 tsp. salt
1 tsp. whole allspice
1 bay leaf
Hot peppers to taste
3-1/2 cups water

Dough

2 cups all purpose flour
3 tsp. baking powder
1 tsp. salt
1/4 cup vegetable shortening
1 cup water

Remove the legs (discard) and remove the biters. Wash and scrub the whole crabs and biters thoroughly and place all into a **large stockpot**. Add the water, salt, allspice and bay leaf.

Dough

In a **medium-sized bowl**, sift together the flour, baking powder and salt. Cut in the shortening and stir in the water to form soft dough.

Turn the dough into the pot and spread evenly over the top. Cover and bring to a boil. Reduce the heat and cook for 20 to 25-minutes. Serve immediately.

Award Winning Bahamian Beer
Distributed by Commonwealth Brewery
Nassau, Bahamas

Dinner
Side Dishes

Menus

❋

Tossed Salad with
Herb Dressing
Fried Fish
Conch Fried Rice
Broccoli with Cheese Sauce
Tropical Fruit Drops

❋

Cabbage Slaw with
Pineapple Chunks
Salmon Cakes
Hatchet Bay Rice
Sweet Peas & Baby Onions
Sapodilla Bundt Cake

❋

Water Cress Salad
Barbeque Pineapple Turkey Roll
Grilled Polenta Squares with
Mushrooms
Rum Raisin Ice Cream

❋

❋

Sliced Avocado with
Tomato Wedges
Calypso Pork Roast
Jamaican Peas & Rice
Ginger Fried Plantain
Guava Surprise

❋

Red & Green Cabbage Salad
Lemon & Garlic Lamb Chops
Wild Rice Cakes
Buttered Asparagus Spears
Miniature Bread Puddings

❋

Caesar Salad
Andros Stuffed Baked Crabs
Savoury Macaroni & Cheese
Buttered Baby Lima Beans
Merdina Carrot Cake

❋

Recipes

❋ Rice Dishes

Barefoot, Pigeon Peas, Black eyed Peas,

Jamaican & Peas, Crab & Rice,

Pepper Conch, Curried, Seafood,

Hatchet Bay (Original Dirty Rice),

Paella (Spanish Rice)

Rum Raisin, Seasoned,

Browned (for Fried Rice dishes)

Tamarind, Okra, Cabbage, Pumpkin, Casserole

Corned Beef Loaf, Rice Cakes

Brown Croquettes, & Fish Croquettes

❋ Baked Peas & Rice Dishes

Pigeon Peas, & Chicken,

& Shrimp, & Crab,

Black eyed Peas, Conch & Peas

❋ Fried Rice

Conch, Shrimp, Crawfish, Chicken,

Pork, Beef,

❋ Grits Dishes

Barefoot, Island Corn,

Pigeon Peas, Black eyed Peas

Cat Island Corn & Crab

Okra, Seasoned, Baked Curried,

Deep Fried Croquettes, Loaf

❋ Polenta Slices & Squares

Polenta, Grilled Squares,

Squares with Mushroom,

With Cheese Sauce, Spicy Corn Cups

❋ Plantain & Banana

Santa Maria Rings, Sauté

❋ Pasta Dishes

Savoury Macaroni & Cheese

Sauté Macaroni Bake, Seafood Bake

Seafood Stuffed Pasta Shells

❋ Casseroles

Breadfruit Cheese, Cassava, Conch & Beer, Crab Souffle, Potato Au Gratin

❋ Stuffings & Dressings

Island Corn Grits, Mashed Potato, Rice, Stuffing for Fish, Wild Rice,

Corn Bread & Oyster

Barefoot Rice

1 cup long grain rice
2-1/4 cups water
1 tsp. salt

In a **2-quart sized saucepan**, combine the water, salt and rice. Over medium heat, bring to a boil stirring several times. Cover and cook for 10-minutes.

Lower the heat, place a **heat diffuser** under the pot (to avoid the rice sticking) and cook for 10 to 15-minutes, stirring several times.

For fluffier rice, see Tip *page 40.*

Bahamian Pigeon Peas & Rice

1-1/2 cups boiled pigeon peas, drained *page 31 (reserve liquid)*
or 1-1/2 cups canned pigeon peas, drained
2 cups long grain rice
4-1/4 cups water including stock from peas
2 oz. vegetable oil
2 slices bacon, 1/2" dice
1 large onion, sliced
3 oz. Champion Tomato Paste
1 tsp. Browning Sauce
1 tsp. dried thyme leaves
1 tsp. Lady Darling's Island Seasoning
Salt to taste
Black pepper
Hot peppers to taste

In a **2-quart sized saucepan**, heat the oil, sauté the bacon for a few minutes, add the onion and thyme and continue to sauté adding the tomato paste.

Pour in the water; add the peas, Browning Sauce, salt, Island Seasoning and black pepper to taste. Add the hot pepper for more zest and stir in the rice.

Bring to a boil over medium heat, stirring occasionally. Cover and cook for about 10-minutes. Lower the heat and adjust seasonings to taste.

Over low heat, cook for an additional 10 to 15-minutes or until the rice is tender. Place a **heat diffuser** under the pot for the last 10-minutes of cooking time to avoid the rice sticking. However, the "pot-cake" or bottom of the rice is most delicious.

Pigeon Peas

Pigeon Peas, also known by other names like Gandules Verdes and Congo Peas, grow on a shrub-like plant, sometimes attaining a height of nine feet, and are capable of withstanding extreme droughts.

We are not sure of its origin. It could be Africa or India. However it is widely cultivated throughout the tropics, including the Caribbean.

The mature pods range in colour from light green to dark brown. The fresh picked peas are green and dried peas are dark brown, resembling small garden peas in shape and size. In the islands, pigeon peas are enjoyed in many traditional dishes, cooked with rice, grits or combined with dried conch in peas soup and dumpling. ❋

Black-eyed Peas & Rice

Prepare same as *Bahamian Pigeon Peas & Rice page 206* except substitute *black-eyed peas* for pigeon peas.

Conch & Peas & Rice

Prepare same as *Bahamian Pigeon Peas & Rice page 206* except add *2 cups shredded conch* while sautéing onion.

Baked Pigeon Peas & Rice

1-1/2 cups boiled pigeon peas, drained page 31 (reserve liquid)
or 1-1/2 cups canned pigeon peas, drained
2 cups long grain rice
4-1/2 cups water including liquid from peas
2 oz. vegetable oil
2 slices of bacon, diced
1 large onion, sliced
3 oz. Champion Tomato Paste
1 tsp. Browning Sauce
1 tsp. dried thyme leaves
1 tsp. Lady Darling's Island Seasoning
1/2 tsp. garlic powder
Salt to taste
Black pepper
Hot peppers to taste
Bake at 350°F

Select a covered **2-quart sized casserole dish with a cover**.

Heat the oil in a **large skillet**; sauté the bacon, onion and thyme leaves. Stir in the tomato paste, water, peas, rice and Browning Sauce. Add the Island Seasoning, garlic powder, salt and pepper to taste.

Mix together and turn into the casserole dish. Cover and bake for approximately 40-minutes or until the rice is tender.

Baked Black-eyed Peas & Rice

Prepare same as *Baked Pigeon Peas & Rice* (above) except substitute *black-eyed peas* for pigeon peas

Baked Peas & Rice & Chicken Or Seafood

Before baking pigeon peas or black-eyed peas & rice, place 4 to 6 seasoned chicken drumsticks on top of the rice or fold in 2-cups of chopped shrimp or crab meat.

Jamaican Peas & Rice

1 medium-sized coconut to make 1 cup coconut milk *page 25*
or 1 cup canned coconut milk
1-1/2 cups boiled pigeon peas, drained *page 31* (reserve liquid)
or 1-1/2 cups canned pigeon peas, drained
2 oz. vegetable oil
2 slices bacon, diced
1 large onion, sliced
1 clove garlic, minced
1/2 tsp. dried thyme leaves
2 cups long grain rice
3-1/2 cups water including stock from peas
1 tsp. freshly squeezed lime juice
Salt
Black pepper
Hot pepper to taste

Prepare the coconut milk.

Heat the oil in a **2-quart sized saucepan** and sauté the bacon. Add the onion and thyme and continue sautéing for 3 or 4-minutes. Add the coconut milk, peas, rice and remaining ingredients to the pot.

Bring to a boil over medium heat, stir and adjust the seasonings. Lower the heat; cover and cook for 20 to 25-minutes or until the rice is tender, stirring occasionally.

Place a **heat diffuser** under the pot for the last 10-minutes of cooking time to avoid the rice sticking.

Crab & Peas & Rice

3 land crabs with biters
2 cups long grain rice
4-1/4 cups water
2 oz. vegetable oil
2 slices bacon, diced
1 large onion, sliced
3 oz. Champion Tomato Paste
1 tsp. dried thyme leaves
1 tsp. Lady Darling's Island Seasoning
Salt to taste
Black pepper
Hot peppers to taste

Prepare crabs *page 32.*

Heat the vegetable oil in a **3-quart sized saucepan**; sauté the bacon for a few minutes. Add the onion and thyme; continue to sauté, adding the crab fat. Simmer for about 5-minutes stirring in the tomato paste.

Add the water, salt, Island Seasoning and black/hot peppers to taste. Stir in the rice adding the crab bodies and biters.

Cover; bring to a boil stirring occasionally. Lower the heat, taste-test and adjust the seasoning. Cook for 20 to 25-minutes until the rice is tender.

Place a **heat diffuser** under the pot for the last 10-minutes of cooking time to avoid the rice sticking.

East Indies / West Indies

History recorded Christopher Columbus' voyage as the discovery of the New World because he recorded the event in his diaries. As we know, Columbus did not know where he was when he made landfall, giving the islands a new identity "The West Indies", as he figured he was on the western side of the "East Indies" and the people were Indians.

Vegetable Fried Rice

1 cup long grain rice
Salt
1/4 cup sesame oil
1 or 2 tbsp. vegetable oil
3 cloves fresh garlic, finely chopped
1 large onion, sliced
1 small green pepper, sliced
2 stems celery, 1/2" slices
2 cups shredded cabbage
2 cups frozen mixed vegetables (thawed & drained)
Black pepper
Lady Darling Island Seasoning to taste
1 to 2 tbsp. soy sauce

Cook the rice same as *Barefoot Rice page 206* and allow to cool.

In a **wok** *or skillet,* heat half the sesame and vegetable oils over medium heat. Gently fry the garlic until it begins to turn brown; remove to a **large bowl**. Turn up the heat and stir-fry the onion slices for 1-minute; remove to the bowl. Stir-fry remaining vegetables one at a time, adding oils as necessary and removing to the bowl. Turn off the heat.

In the bowl, mix together the vegetables, rice and seasonings to taste. When ready to serve, return the mixture to the skillet for a few minutes stir-frying until thoroughly heated. Remove from the heat; stir in the soy sauce and serve immediately.

Curried Rice

1-1/2 cups long grain rice
2 oz. vegetable oil
2 tsp. curry powder
3-1/4 cups water
1 large onion, sliced
2 strips bacon, diced
Salt

Heat the oil in a **2-quart sized saucepan** and sauté the bacon. Add the onion and sauté for a few more minutes. Add the rice, water, curry powder and salt to taste.

Bring to a boil over medium heat. Stir, lower the heat, cover and cook for 20 to 25-minutes or until the rice is tender. Place a **heat diffuser** under the pot during the last 10-minutes of cooking to avoid the rice sticking.

Pepper Conch & Rice

2 large sized conchs, thinly sliced *page 32*
1/2 cup soy sauce
2 tbsp. cider vinegar
2-1/2 tbsp. cornstarch
1 tsp. sugar
2 small vegetable bouillon cubes
1/2 cup vegetable oil, divided
1/3 cup boiling water
2 cups sliced fresh mushrooms
2 cloves garlic, halved
2 medium-sized green peppers, slivered
1 large onion, sliced and separated into rings
1 can (8 oz.) water chestnuts, drained and sliced

Hot Barefoot Rice page 206

Prepare the conch.

In a **small dish**, combine the soy sauce, vinegar, cornstarch and sugar. Stir until the cornstarch dissolves.

In a **1-quart sized saucepan**, dissolve the bouillon cubes into the boiling water, and stir into the cornstarch mixture. Set aside.

Pour 2-tablespoonfuls of the oil around the top of a preheated **wok** *or large skillet* coating the sides; allow heating at medium high (325°F) for 1-minute. Stir-fry the garlic for 1-minute and discard. Stir-fry the conch for 2-minutes; remove and set aside.

Pour the remaining 2-tablespoons of the oil around the top of the wok, coating the sides; heat at medium-high for 1-minute. Add the mushrooms, green pepper, onion and water chestnuts and stir-fry for about 2-minutes.

Pour the cornstarch mixture over the vegetables in the wok and cook, stirring constantly, until lightly thickened.

Return the conch to the wok, stirring well. Serve over the hot *Barefoot Rice*.

Conch Fried Rice

1 large conch, for 2 cups sliced page 31
1 carrots, 1/4" slices
1 scallion, chopped
1 medium-sized onion, sliced
2 cloves garlic, minced
1/2 cup green peas
1/4 cup sesame oil
2 tbsp. soy sauce
1 tsp. Lady Darling's Island Seasoning
1 tsp. black pepper
2 cups Browned Rice page 215

Slice conch and season with the garlic, half of the sesame oil and half the soy sauce.

Heat the remaining sesame oil in a **wok** *or large non-stick skillet* and stir-fry the vegetables one at a time, removing to a **large bowl**.

Stir-fry the conch for about 3-minutes and stir in the *Browned Rice*. Stir in the vegetables; add the seasonings and cook for another 3-minutes. Remove from the heat; stir in the soy sauce and additional seasonings if desired.

Variations

Substitute 2-cups of the following uncooked meats for the conch
Chopped Shrimp
Chopped Crawfish
Slivered Chicken Breast
Strips of Pork
Strips of Beef

Hatchet Bay Rice
The Original Dirty Rice

2 cups long grain rice
4-1/2 cups water
1 large onion, chopped
2 oz. vegetable oil
2 slices bacon, diced
1/4 lb. chicken livers, chopped
1/4 lb. chicken gizzards, chopped
1 clove garlic, finely minced
1/2 tsp. dried thyme leaves
1 tsp. Lady Darling's Island Seasoning
Salt to taste
Black pepper
Hot peppers to taste

Bake at 350°F

In a **2-quart sized saucepan**, combine the water, rice, thyme and salt to taste. Cover, simmer for 15-minutes only and set aside.

Heat the oil in a **large skillet**, and sauté the bacon and onion. Add the chopped livers and gizzards; continue to sauté, stirring until brown. Add the garlic, Island Seasoning, pepper and, if necessary, additional salt. Turn into the saucepan with the rice, mixing well.

Turn into a greased **8x12-inch-baking dish** and bake for 20 to 25-minutes.

Rum Raisin Rice

1/2 cup golden raisins
2 tbsp. Ole Nassau Jack Malantan Rum
1 cup long grain rice
2-1/4 cups water
2 oz. diced pineapple
Salt

Soak the raisins and pineapple in the rum.

Pour the water into a **2-quart sized saucepan**; add the rice and salt to taste. Bring to a boil over medium heat and boil for 10-minutes.

Add the raisins and pineapple (drained); lower the heat and cook for 10 to 15-minutes or until the rice is tender. Place a **heat diffuser** under the pot for the last 10-minutes of cooking time to avoid the rice sticking.

Paella
Spanish Rice

2 tbsp. onion, chopped
2 cloves garlic, chopped
3 skinned tomatoes, cut into large chunks
1 cup uncooked rice
2 cups chicken stock
1 tsp. saffron (powder)
Salt to taste
Ground white pepper
1 lb. grouper chunks
1/2 lb. shrimps, chopped
1/2 lb. chicken, chunks

Bake at 350°F

Heat the oil in a **large skillet** and sauté the onion and garlic. Add the chunks of tomato and sauté for about 5-minutes.

Add the rice; continue to sauté adding the stock and saffron. Season to taste simmering for 5 to 10-minutes. Add the pepper, fish, shrimps and chicken mixing well.

Turn into a **3-quart sized covered casserole dish**, cover and bake for 35 to 40-minutes until the rice is tender. Serve immediately.

Browned Rice
For Fried Rice Dishes

1 cup long grain rice
2-1/4 cups water
1/2 tsp. salt
1 tsp. Browning Sauce

Combine ingredients in a **2-quart sized saucepan**; bring to a boil over medium heat stirring several times.

Cover and cook for 10-minutes. Lower the heat and cook for an additional 10 to 15-minutes. Place a **heat diffuser** under the pot for the last 10-minutes of cooking time to avoid the rice sticking.

Seasoned Rice

2 bouillon cubes (use flavor of choice)
1 cup long grain rice
2-1/4 cups water
1-1/2 tsp. Browning Sauce
1/2 tsp. garlic powder
Black pepper
Hot peppers to taste

Combine the water and bouillon cubes in a **2-quart sized saucepan**. Dissolve the cubes; stir in the rice and remaining ingredients. Over medium heat, bring to a boil.

Reduce the heat; stir, cover and cook for 20 to 25-minutes until the rice is tender. Place a **heat diffuser** under the pot for the last 10-minutes of cooking time to avoid the rice sticking.

Tamarind & Rice

1 cup half ripe tamarinds
2 cups long grain rice
2 tbsp. olive oil
2 tbsp. chopped onion
2 slices fresh ginger, crushed
1 tsp. ground white pepper
1/2 tsp. Lady Darling's Island Seasoning
Salt to taste
1 cup canned coconut milk
3-1/4 cups water

Prepare the tamarinds removing the seeds *page 26*; place into a **2-quart sized saucepan** with 2-cups of the water. Over medium heat, simmer for 5 or 6-minutes to allow to cool. Drain, preserving the liquid, cut into individual sections removing the seeds.

Heat the oil in a **large skillet** and sauté the rice until golden brown. Stir in the onion and ginger and sauté for a few more minutes.

Remove from the heat; stir in remaining ingredients and return to the pot with the tamarind and liquid, coconut milk and remaining water. Stir together well and adjust seasonings to taste.

Cover and over medium-low heat cook for 20 to 25-minutes or until the rice is tender. Place a **heat diffuser** under pot for the last 10-minutes of cooking time to avoid the rice sticking.

Okra & Rice

1-1/2 cup finely sliced fresh okras
1 cup long grain rice
2 oz. vegetable oil
2 slices bacon, chopped
1 medium-sized onion, sliced
1 tsp. dried thyme leaves
3 oz. Champion Tomato Paste
2-1/4 cups water
Black pepper
Hot peppers to taste
1 tsp. Lady Darling's Island Seasoning
Salt to taste

Heat the oil in a **2-quart sized saucepan** and sauté the bacon. Add the onion, okra and thyme and continue to sauté for 3 to 5-minutes. Stir in the tomato paste. Add the water, rice and seasonings to taste.

Over medium high-heat, bring to a boil, reduce the heat. Adjust seasonings to taste. Cover and cook for 15 to 20-minutes or until the rice is tender.

Place a **heat diffuser** under the pot for the last 10-minutes of cooking time to avoid the rice sticking.

Cabbage & Rice

Prepare same as *Okra & Rice* substituting *1-1/2 cups of shredded cabbage* for the okra.

Pumpkin & Rice

Prepare same as *Okra & Rice* substituting *1-1/2 cups of 3/4" dice pumpkin* for okra.

Tabaca/Tobacco

Columbus observed the Lucayans smoking the leaf of one of the plants that grew in abundance. He and his countrymen tried it and liked it, taking some home with them. But again he was confused, changing the name of this most enjoyable leaf. The Lucayans called the leaf "cohiba" and the fork-shaped nose-pipe "tabaca". Columbus called the leaf "tobacco"... and the rest is history.

Rice Casserole

2 cups long grain rice
2 oz. vegetable oil
2 slices bacon, diced
1 large onion, chopped
4-1/4 cups water
1/4 cup chopped green pepper
1 can (4 oz.) plum tomatoes
Hot peppers to taste
Salt
1/3 cup Sharp Cheddar cheese

Bake at 400°F

Heat the oil in a **large skillet** and sauté the rice stirring until it starts to colour. Stir in the bacon and onion; when the rice starts to brown, add the water and remaining ingredients except the cheese.

Cover and cook slowly over low heat until the rice is tender, about 15 minutes. Turn the mixture into a greased **8x12-inch-baking dish**, sprinkle with the cheese and bake for 15-minutes. Serve immediately.

Corned Beef & Rice Loaf

1 can (12 oz.) corned beef
1 oz. vegetable oil
2 tbsp. 1/4" dice onion
2 tbsp. 1/4" dice green pepper
1 tsp. dried thyme leaves
2 cups cooked long grain rice
1 can (10 oz.) tomato soup
1/2 tsp. Lady Darling's Island Seasoning
Salt to taste
Black pepper

Bake at 350°F

Break up the corned beef with a fork in preparation for cooking.

Heat the oil in a **large skillet**; sauté the corned beef, onion, green pepper and thyme for 4 to 5-minutes.

Add the tomato soup and seasonings to taste mixing gently. Turn the mixture into a greased **loaf pan** and bake for 30 to 35-minutes.

Wild Rice Cakes

1 cup Wild Rice mix
3 cups all purpose flour
1 cup Yellow Corn Meal
2 tsp. baking powder
1 tsp. salt
Butter and olive oil for frying

Cook the wild rice according to package instructions and allow to cool.

In a **large bowl**, combine the flour, corn meal, baking powder and salt mixing well. Fold the cooked rice into the mixture.

Grease a **large skillet** with butter (add olive oil as necessary) and heat. Drop spoonsful of the mixture onto the skillet to form flat cakes about 4-inches across. Fry on both sides until brown and serve hot.

Brown Rice Croquettes

2 cups cooked Brown Rice
2 eggs
1/8 tsp. ground allspice
1/8 tsp. poultry seasoning
1/4 tsp. salt
1 cup grated Parmesan cheese
3/4 cup Yellow Corn Meal
Vegetable oil for deep-frying

Mix together the rice, seasonings and cheese in a **medium-sized bowl**. Chill for 1-hour.

Shape the mixture into 1-inch sized croquettes (approximately 12 to 16). Spread the corn meal into a **shallow dish** and roll the croquettes in the corn meal.

Heat the oil in a **deep-fat fryer** *or deep pot*. Drop the balls into the hot oil and fry until golden brown. Drain on a **wire rack** over **paper towels** and serve.

From Africa to the Americas

When we prepare black-eyed peas or pigeon peas and rice, okra or desserts of banana pudding or yam pie sweetened with sorghum or molasses, we are savouring a taste of Africa. The vitality of these culinary traditions in the Americas is a testament to the richness of African cultures and a celebration of those Africans who shared that richness with their host societies.

Rice & Fish Croquettes

2 cups cooked fish
2 cups *Barefoot Rice page 206*
2 eggs, beaten
1 tsp. freshly squeezed lime juice
1 tsp. dried thyme leaves
Salt
Black pepper
Hot peppers to taste
Corn flakes rolled or bread crumbs

Flake the cooked fish and place into a **medium-sized bowl**. Add the cooked rice, eggs; lime juice, salt and peppers.

Form the mixture into 2-inch balls. Roll the corn flakes into crumbs and spread the flakes or bread crumbs on a sheet of **wax paper**. Roll the c r o q u e t t e s into the flakes coating completely.

Grease an **8x10-inch-baking dish**; arrange the croquettes in the dish and bake for 20-minutes.

Barefoot Grits

1 cup White Hominy Grits
2-1/2 cups water
Salt to taste

In a **2-quart sized saucepan**, combine the water, grits and salt.

Over medium-high heat, stirring continuously, bring to a boil and cook for about 5-minutes.

Reduce the heat, cover and cook for 10 to 15-minutes, stirring occasionally. Place a **heat diffuser** under the pot for the last 10-minutes of cooking time to avoid the grits sticking.

Island Corn Grits

1 cup island corn grits
3-1/2 cups water
1 tsp. salt

In a **2 quart-sized saucepan**, stir together the ingredients, cover and place over very low heat. Cook slowly for 15 to 20-minutes stirring occasionally.

Place a **heat diffuser** under the pot and continue to cook for another 15 to 20-minutes.

Bahamian Pigeon Peas & Grits

1 cup boiled pigeon peas, drained *page 31*
or 1 cup canned pigeon peas, drained
1 cup White Hominy Grits
2-1/4 cups water including liquid from peas
2 oz. vegetable oil
2 slices bacon, diced
1 medium-sized onion, diced
2 oz. Champion Tomato Paste
1/2 tsp. Browning Sauce
1/2 tsp. dried thyme leaves
1 tsp. Lady Darling's Island Seasoning
Salt to taste
Black pepper
Hot peppers to taste

Heat the oil in a **3-quart sized saucepan** and sauté the bacon for a few minutes. Add the onion and thyme and continue to sauté, adding the tomato paste.

Add water, peas, grits and remaining ingredients with salt and peppers to taste. Bring to a boil over medium heat stirring occasionally.

Cover and cook for 5-minutes. Stir, taste test and adjust the seasonings if necessary.

Reduce the heat and cook for 10 to 15-minutes. Place a **heat diffuser** under the pot for the last 5-minutes of cooking time to avoid the grits sticking.

Bahamian Black-eyed Peas & Grits

Prepare same *Bahamian Pigeon Peas & Grits* substituting *1-cup black-eyed peas* for pigeon peas.

Seasoned Grits

1 cup White Hominy Grits
2-1/2 cups water
1 large bouillon cube
1/2 tsp. Lady Darling's Island Seasoning
1/2 tsp. black pepper

Combine the ingredients in a **2 quart-sized saucepan** and place over very low heat. Cover and cook for about 10-minutes, stirring occasionally to blend ingredients completely.

Place a **heat diffuser** under the pot and continue to cook for about 10-minutes.

Cat Island Corn Grits & Crab

2 land crabs with biters
1 cup island corn grits
1 cup boiled pigeon peas, drained (reserve liquid)
or canned pigeon peas
3-1/2 cups water (including stock from peas)
2 oz. vegetable oil and the crab fat from crabs
2 slices bacon, chopped
3 oz. Champion Tomato Paste
1/2 tsp. dried thyme leaves
1 tsp. Lady Darling's Island Seasoning
Salt to taste
Black pepper
Hot peppers to taste

Prepare crabs *page 32* reserving the fat.

Heat the oil in a **2-quart sized saucepan** and sauté the bacon for a few minutes. Add the onion and thyme; continue to sauté adding the crab fat. Simmer for about 5-minutes stirring in the tomato paste.

Add the water, grits, Island Seasoning, salt, and black/hot peppers to taste. Add the crab bodies and claws.

Over medium heat, bring to a boil, stirring continually. Lower the heat, taste test and adjust the seasonings if necessary. Cover and cook over low heat for 30 to 35-minutes.

Place a **heat diffuser** under the pot for the last 10-minutes of cooking time to avoid the grits sticking.

Grits Croquettes

1 cup cooked, chilled White Hominy Grits
Black pepper
2 eggs
1-1/2 tsp. peanut oil
1/4 tsp. ground nutmeg
1 cup grated Sharp Cheddar cheese
1-1/2 cups soft bread crumbs
Vegetable oil for deep-frying

In a **medium-sized bowl**, mash the chilled grits with a fork and stir in the nutmeg and pepper to taste. Mix in the grated cheese and one egg. Shape the mixture into 2-inch croquettes and place onto a sheet of **wax paper**.

In a **small dish**, beat the remaining egg and peanut oil together. Dip the croquettes into the egg mixture, then roll into the bread crumbs.

Pour the oil into a **deep-fat fryer or deep pot** and fry the croquettes until golden brown. Drain on a **wire rack** and serve immediately

Crab Soufflé

2 land crabs with biters or 1-1/2 cups crab meat, flaked
2 tbsp. butter
2 tbsp. all purpose flour
1-1/2 cups milk
4 egg yolks, beaten
Ground white pepper
Salt to taste
1/2 cups finely grated Parmesan cheese
4 egg whites

Bake at 400ºF

Prepare the crabs and biters *page 32* and pick to produce 1-1/2 cups meat.

Make a sauce by melting the butter in a **2-quart sized saucepan**, stirring in the flour and cooking slowly for a few minutes.

Remove the saucepan from the heat and gradually stir in the milk. Return to medium heat and stir vigorously until the sauce thickens. Allow to cool slightly.

Stir in the beaten egg yolks, seasoning and pepper. Add the crab meat and the finely grated cheese.

Using a **wire whisk** *or electric mixer*, whip the egg whites until stiff. Carefully fold into the crab mixture.

Turn into a greased **soufflé dish** and bake for about 25 to 30-minutes or until risen and brown. Serve immediately.

Plantain

The plantain is a member of the banana family and must be cooked before eating. The individual fruits are bigger than a banana and are more clearly horn shaped. Plantains, high in carbohydrates, are less sweet than bananas and are served as a starchy vegetable or dried and ground into flour, playing the role that in other times was filled by potatoes or cereal grains. Being native to Africa, it follows that Caribbean people of African descent would include this delicious food in their diet. They are often boiled and served with meat; mixed into a hot casserole; cooked with plenty of spices, onion and peppers; cut into thin slices to produce delicious chips or just plain cut into slices, fried and eaten with a rice dish and fish. Anyone who has tasted fried plantains will want them again. ✻

Plantain Santa Maria

3 firm-ripe plantains
Vegetable oil for frying
1 egg

Filling

1 lb. ground beef or ground turkey
2 slices bacon, chopped
1 medium-sized onion, 1/4" dice
1 medium-sized green pepper, 1/4" dice
1 large tomato skinned and chopped
1 cup Refried beans
1/2 tsp. salt
1/2 tsp. black pepper
1 egg

Peel the plantains and cut each into 3-lengthwise slices. In a **large skillet**, pour the oil to 1/4-inch depth and heat. Turning carefully, fry the plantain slices until golden brown on both sides.

Remove, drain on **paper towels** and while still warm, curve the slices into rings securing with **toothpicks**. Set aside until cold.

Filling

Drain the oil from the skillet and reserve. Brown the ground meat, drain and place into a **large bowl**. Fry the bacon until soft; add the onion and green pepper sautéing for 3 to 4-minutes. Stir in the tomato and continue sautéing 3 or 4-minutes; remove to the bowl.

Add the Refried beans, salt and pepper to the bowl mixing thoroughly. Pack the meat mixture into the plantain rings.

In a **shallow dish**, beat the egg lightly; brush the tops and bottoms of the packed rings. Return the vegetable oil to the skillet and heat.

Gently fry the rings on tops and bottoms to a light brown. Remove to a **serving dish** and serve immediately.

Polenta Slices & Squares

3 cups Yellow Corn Meal or Polenta Flour
9 cups water
2-1/2 tsp. salt
2 tbsp. butter

In a **heavy 4-quart sized saucepan**, combine the corn meal, water and salt. Using a **large wooden spoon** and stirring constantly, bring to a boil over medium-high heat. This will take 6-8 minutes. Keep the mixture moving to avoid lumps.

When the mixture starts to bubble, reduce the heat immediately. Place a **heat diffuser** under the pot, cover and continue to cook for 10-minutes, stirring frequently.

• **For slices**: Remove from the heat. Stir in the butter. Turn onto a **greased board** *or baking sheet* forming a mound. Cool completely. Slice into 1-inch thick slices of varying lengths across the mound.

• **For slices with cheese or meat sauce**: Arrange the slices in a greased **baking dish**; top with cooked vegetables, cheese or meat sauce and **Bake at 350°F** for 15 to 20-minutes.

• **For squares**: Turn cooked *Polenta* into a large flat pan; cool and cut into 4x1-inch thick squares. Fry in hot olive oil until golden brown. Remove to a **serving platter** and serve as a side dish with meat, vegetables or cheese topping.

• **For barbecue squares**: Place squares onto a **barbecue grill**, turning gently until grilled on both sides. Serve with shish-ke-barbs.

Polenta Squares with Mushrooms

Polenta Squares (above)
2 tbsp. olive oil
4 cups sliced mushrooms
2 cloves garlic, minced
2 tbsp. chopped parsley
1 tsp. salt
1/2 cup Marsala Wine (or sweet wine)

Prepare the squares; fry or grill and set aside (keep warm).

Wash and slice the mushrooms. Heat the oil in a **large skillet** and sauté the mushrooms until golden brown. Add the salt, garlic and parsley and sauté for a few more minutes.

Stir in the wine; continue to sauté stirring in the cream and mixing well. Place the squares onto a **serving dish**; spread the mushroom mixture over the squares and serve.

Polenta with Cheese Sauce

Cooked *Polenta page 226*
1 cup of Gorgonzola cheese or Blue cheese
1 cup of Parmesan cheese
2 tbsp. butter
1-1/2 cups cream
Bake at 350°F

Cook *Polenta;* pour onto a greased **board** forming a mound and cool. Cut into 1-inch thick slices of varying lengths.

Grate the cheeses in a **food processor** *or with a hand held grater.* Melt the butter in a small saucepan and stir in the cream and cheeses until melted.

Grease a **large casserole dish** and arrange a layer of *Polenta Slices* in the bottom. Pour the cheese mixture over the slices, alternating sauce and slices, ending with cheese sauce. Bake for 15 to 20-minutes.

Polenta Spicy Corn Cups

4 cups cooked *Polenta page 226*
1 can (16 oz.) sweet corn, drained or 2 cups fresh cut or frozen corn
2 slices bacon, chopped
2 tbsp. 1/4" dice onion
2 tbsp. 1/4" dice green pepper
1 tbsp. ground white pepper
Olive oil
Bake at 350°F

Prepare *Polenta* and turn into a **large bowl**.

In a **large skillet**, sauté the chopped bacon; stir in the onion, and green pepper, sauté for a few more minutes. Turn into the bowl with the polenta, adding the corn and white pepper.

Brush the **muffin tins** with olive oil and spoon the mixture into the cups, making a depression in the center of each. Cool completely (may be prepared ahead and refrigerated overnight).

Turn the muffin tins upside down to remove the polenta cups and place into a greased **baking sheet**. Spoon meat, fish or cheese fillings into centre of cups and bake for 15 to 20-minutes.

Savoury Macaroni & Cheese

2 cups uncooked macaroni
6 to 8 cups water
1 tsp. salt
2 cups grated Sharp Cheddar cheese
1 medium onion, 1/4" dice
1 medium green pepper, 1/4" dice
2 celery stalks, 1/4" dice
2 eggs, slightly beaten
1-1/2 cups evaporated milk or whole milk
1/2 tsp. dried thyme leaves
2 tbsp. butter
1 tsp. Lady Darling's Island Seasoning
Ground white pepper
Hot peppers to taste
Seasoned bread crumbs

Bake at 325°F

In a **2-quart sized saucepan**, bring the water to a boil, add the salt and macaroni (a pat of butter will avoid boiling over). Cook for 6 to 8-minutes. Turn into a colander; drain and turn into a **large bowl**. Mix together with the remaining ingredients except the bread crumbs.

Grease a **deep medium-sized casserole dish**. Turn the mixture into the dish sprinkle the top with crumbs and bake for 40 to 45-minutes until the centre is set.

Sauté Macaroni Bake

2 cups uncooked macaroni
6 to 8 cups water
Salt
1/2 cup chopped onion
1/2 cup chopped green pepper
1 clove garlic, minced
1/2 cup vegetable oil
1 can (16 oz.) tomato juice
2 tbsp. Salsa Sauce
1 tsp. salt
1/2 tsp. black pepper

Bake at 350°F

Heat the tomato juice in a **small saucepan**.

Heat the oil in a **large skillet** and over low heat; sauté the macaroni, onion, green pepper and garlic, stirring occasionally until the macaroni turns slightly yellow.

Bring the juice to a boil. Stir into the macaroni mixture adding the remaining ingredients.

Turn into a greased **2-quart sized casserole dish with a cover**. Cover and bake for 40-minutes.

Variation

Before turning into casserole dish fold in *2 cups of chopped crawfish, shrimp, crabmeat or fish.*

Seafood Stuffed Pasta Shells

1 cup diced raw seafood, fish, crawfish or shrimp
2 tbsp. butter
1 cup fresh bread crumbs
1/2 cup heavy cream
1 tbsp. chopped fresh parsley
1 egg, slightly beaten
Salt & pepper to taste
6 to 8 large pasta shells
1 cup grated Parmesan cheese

Bake at 350ºF

Wash the seafood, pat dry and cut into 1/4-inch dice. Heat the butter in a **medium-sized non-stick skillet** and cook seafood quickly for 1-minute.

In a **medium-sized bowl**, toss the bread crumbs in the cream and mix in the cooked seafood, parsley, egg and seasonings. Refrigerate for about 15-minutes.

Cook the pasta shells according to package direction and drain. Stuff the shells with the chilled mixture, place into a greased **baking dish** and bake for 20-minutes. Remove to a serving platter.

In a **small saucepan**, melt the grated cheese, pour over the baked shells and serve immediately.

Breadfruit & Cheese Casserole

4 cups 3/4" dice firm-ripe breadfruit
2 cups grated Sharp Cheddar cheese
1 medium-sized onion, 1/4" dice
1 medium-sized green pepper, 1/4" dice
2 ribs celery, 1/4" dice
2 eggs, slightly beaten
1-1/2 cups evaporated milk or 1-1/2 cups whole milk
2 tbsp. butter
1/2 tsp. dried thyme leaves
1/2 tsp. Lady Darling's Island Seasoning
Salt to taste
Ground white pepper to taste
Hot peppers to taste

Bake at 350ºF

Prepare breadfruit *page 29*.

In a **medium-sized bowl**, mix together all ingredients and taste test. Turn into a **deep casserole dish** and bake for 40 to 45-minutes.

Cassava Casserole

2 lbs. cassava
1 tbsp. salt
1 tbsp. whole allspice
Hot peppers to taste
1 medium-sized onion, quartered
4 to 6 cups water
3 slices bacon, chopped

Bake at 350°F

Peel the cassava and cut into 1-inch thick slices *page 30*. Place into a **3-quart sized saucepan** with water to cover. Add the allspice, onion, bacon, salt and hot peppers. Bring to a boil; reduce the heat, cover and cook until the cassava is soft. allow to cool.

Drain off the liquid, preserving 1-cup, and discard the allspice. Fit a **food processor** with the knife blade. Divide the cassava into three batches.

Pour 1/3-cup of the liquid into the bowl of the processor with each batch of the cassava. Using the pulse method, process for about 2-minutes until the mixture is smooth.

Remove to a **large bowl**; mix thoroughly and adjust the seasoning. Turn the mixture into a greased **2-quart sized casserole dish** and bake for 30 to 35-minutes.

Conch & Beer Casserole

Cassava Crust page 272
2 large conchs
1/2 cup all purpose flour (divided)
1 tsp. ground white pepper
1 tsp. salt
1 tsp. dried thyme leaves
1/4 cup vegetable oil
1 large onion, 1/2" dice
2 carrots, 1/2" dice
2 potatoes, 1" cubes
2 tbsp. Champion Tomato Paste
1-1/2 cups Kalik beer
1 clove garlic, minced
1 bay leaf
1 tbsp. freshly squeezed lime juice
Hot peppers to taste

Bake at 400°F

Prepare the Crust, roll out and set aside.

Wash the conchs thoroughly in cold water and cut into 1-inch chunks.

In a **medium-sized bowl**, mix together 1/4-cup of the flour, white pepper salt and thyme leaves. Coat the conch chunks completely with the mixture.

Heat the oil in a **large skillet** and brown the chunks on all sides. Transfer to a **large stockpot**. In the skillet, sauté the onion, carrots, celery and potatoes until lightly brown; place into a bowl and set aside.

Sprinkle remaining 1/4-cup of flour over the drippings in the skillet, stirring constantly until lightly browned. Stir in remaining ingredients and bring to a boil. Reduce the heat, cover and simmer for 45-minutes.

Remove from the heat, stir in the vegetable oil and turn into a **deep casserole dish**. Cover with the crust, fold under the edges, flute and make slits in the top for steam to escape. Bake for about 40-minutes until the crust is brown.

Potato Au Gratin

2 large potatoes, 1/2 dice
Salt to taste
White Sauce page 257
2 tbsp 1/4" dice onion
2 tbsp. 1/4" dice green pepper
Fine bread crumbs
Butter

Bake at 400°F

Place diced potatoes into a **2-quart sized saucepan** with water to cover; add salt and cook just until potatoes are done when tested with a sharp knife. Drain and cool.

Prepare the *White Sauce.*

In a **large bowl**, gently mix together the cooled potatoes, sauce, onion and green peppers. Turn into a greased **casserole dish** and cover with bread crumbs.

Dot with butter and bake until the crumbs are brown, about 35-minutes.

Variation

To prepare *Potato Au Gratin* with cheese, substitute *Cheese Sauce page 257* for the *White Sauce.*

Island Corn Grits Stuffing

3 cups hot cooked *Island Corn Grits page 220*
3 slices bacon, chopped
1 medium-sized onion, 1/4" dice
1 medium-sized green pepper, 1/4" dice
2 stalks celery, 1/4" dice
1 tsp. dried thyme leaves
1/2 tsp. Lady Darling's Island Seasoning
1/2 tsp. black pepper

Cook the grits.

In a **large skillet**, fry the chopped bacon; add the diced vegetables and thyme leaves; sauté for 5 or 6-minutes. Remove from the heat and stir in the hot grits. Add the Island Seasoning and black pepper to taste, mixing thoroughly. Use to stuff poultry or fish.

Mashed Potato Dressing

3 large potatoes cut into large chunks
1 medium-sized onion, 1/4" dice
1 medium-sized green pepper, 1/4" dice
2 slices bacon, 1/4" dice
1 clove garlic, minced
1/2 tsp. basil
2 tbsp. butter
1 tsp. salt
1/2 tsp. black pepper

Cook the potatoes until well done. Turn into a **food mill** or a *colander* placed over a **medium-sized bowl** and drain. Using the food mill, mash the potatoes and add the butter while potatoes are still hot.

In a **medium-sized skillet**, sauté the bacon, then add the onion, green pepper and garlic with basil and sauté lightly. Turn into the mashed potatoes. Add salt and pepper to taste. Stuff into chicken, duck or other poultry.

Rice Dressing

1 cup long grain rice
2-1/4 cups chicken broth
Salt
1 bay leaf
2 tbsp. butter
1/2 cup finely chopped onion
1/2 cup finely chopped celery
1/4 cup finely chopped green pepper
1 clove garlic, minced
3 tbsp. chopped parsley
1/2 cup chopped chicken liver

In a **2-quart sized saucepan**, combine the rice, broth, salt and bay leaf; bring to a boil. Stir, cover and simmer over medium heat for 20-minutes and cool slightly.

Heat the butter in a **large skillet**; sauté the onion, celery, green pepper and garlic for about 5-minutes. Add the liver and continue to sauté, stirring until it loses its red color. Stir the liver mixture and parsley into the rice.

Dressing can be used to stuff a small turkey, a 3 to 4 lb. chicken or 3 Cornish hens.

Stuffing for Fish

2 oz. butter
1 small onion, 1/4" dice
1 small green pepper, 1/4" dice
2 cups soft cubes of bread
1 tbsp. finely chopped chives
1 tsp. parsley flakes
1/2 cup fish stock
2 tbsp. minced ham
Salt
Black pepper

Melt the butter in a **large skillet** and sauté the onion and green pepper. Remove to a **large bowl** and toss together with remaining ingredients

Stuff into the cavity of large seasoned fresh fish and bake according to the selected recipe.

Wild Rice Stuffing

6 slices bacon
1-1/2 cups cooked Wild Rice
1 cup sliced celery
1/2 cup walnuts
1/2 cup chopped onion
1-1/4 cup beef broth
1 cup dry, seasoned bread cubes
1 egg slightly beaten
3/4 cup raw cranberries, chopped
4 tbsp. Maker's Mark Bourbon

Bake at 350°F

In a **large skillet**, fry the bacon until crisp, drain and crumble. Pour off all but 2-tablespoonfuls of the drippings.

Sauté the celery and onion in the drippings until tender; turn into a **large bowl**. Add the bread cubes, cooked rice, cranberries, walnuts, broth and egg. After mixing thoroughly, add the bourbon. If the stuffing is dry, add more bourbon or water.

Bake in a **10-inch round casserole dish** for 30-minutes.

Corn Bread & Oyster Stuffing

Corn Bread page 90, omit the sugar in recipe
3 slices bacon, chopped
1 medium-sized onion, 1/4" dice
1 medium-sized green pepper, 1/4" dice
2 stalks celery, 1/4" dice
1 tbsp. poultry seasoning
1/2 tsp. Lady Darling's Island Seasoning
1/2 tsp. black pepper
1 pint oysters, drained and chopped
1-1/2 cups chicken stock

Crumble the cooled *Corn Bread* into 1/2-inch chunks and place into a **large bowl**.

In a **large skillet**, fry the chopped bacon; add the diced vegetables, sauté for 5 or 6-minutes. Turn into the bowl with the corn bread and gently mix in the seasonings and chopped oysters. Stir in the chicken stock and use to stuff a turkey or 2 roasting chickens.

P. W. Albury & Sons Limited

The present company in Nassau is the continuation of a business, J. S. Johnson & Co., that was started over 100 years ago by W.C.B. Johnson. It was bought by Paul W. Albury in 1959 and re-named P. W. Albury & Co. During the Second World War, the factory produced for "The War effort". This allowed Mr. Albury to train in canning and processing. As a result, this experience influenced his decision to take a risk in the tomato business, as he felt this was a better choice of livelihood over a teacher's salary. The company is presently at #28 Fifth Terrace, Centerville.

Mr. Albury coined the name CHAMPION BRAND during his take-over in 1959, and the company has produced tomato paste, pigeon peas, and tomato sauce which are used in many recipes, including our favourite native dish "Peas and Rice". In contributing to The Bahamas economy, the company purchases ripe tomatoes from local and Family Island farmers. The finished product is sold throughout The Bahamas. Presently, the firm is operated by James W. Albury (son of Paul W. Albury) and granddaughters Caroline & Charlotte.

Vegetables

Menus

Tomato & Sweet Pepper Salad
with Benny Seed Dressing
Turtle Soup
Seasoned Rice
Mango Crepes & Ice Cream

Spinach Salad
Stewed Conch with Carrots &
Potatoes
Island Corn Grits
Tamarind Mango Chutney
Ole Nassau Rum Cake

Sweet Peas & Baby Onions
Hurricane Ham Stew
Noodles
Guava Rind Pickles
Pineapple Roly Poly

Green Beans with French Dressing
Curried Goat
Barefoot Rice
Fried Plantain
Tamarind Mango Chutney
Pina Colada Cake

Chopped Spinach & Herb
Dressing
African Beef Stew
Mashed Potato
Carrot Fritters

Recipes

Spicy Harvard Beets

❋ **Tomato**

Star, Curry Fried Green,
 Crumb Bake,
Stuffed,
Chinese Cabbage
Skillet Slaw with Bacon Top
Stuffed Cabbage Rolls
Stuffed Green Peppers

❋ *Plantain*

Fried, Ginger Fried
 Cakes, Drops
Baked, Green Sauté
Green Banana Sauté
Ginger Mashed Potatoes
Potato Carrot Mash
Potato Croquettes

❋ **Breadfruit**

French Fried,
Sliced with Bacon,
Stuffed
Akara (African Bean Cakes)
Pineapple Sweet Potato Drops
Sweet Potato in Orange Shells
Sweet Potato with Orange Peel
Fu Fu

Spicy Harvard Beets

1 can (14 oz.) sliced or cubed beets, drained (preserve juice)
1/2 cup liquid (beet juice and water)
1 tbsp. cornstarch
1-1/2 tbsp. sugar
1/2 tsp. salt
2 tbsp. vinegar
1 tsp. whole allspice

In a **2-quart sized saucepan**, combine all ingredients except the beets, mixing thoroughly.

Stirring constantly, bring to a boil and boil for 1-minute. Add the beets and cook over low heat, for 4 to 5-minutes. Remove the whole spice seeds and serve hot.

Tomato Star

Place the tomato stem end down, on a **cutting board** making 5 or 6 downward slashes without cutting through the bottom. Gently spread the sections to form a star.

Fill between the slices with selected salad mixture.

Curry-Fried Green Tomatoes

4 large green tomatoes
1/2 tsp. curry powder
1/2 cup Yellow Corn Meal
1 tsp. black pepper
1 tsp. salt
Vegetable oil for pan frying

Slice the tomatoes into 1/2-inch thick slices. On a sheet of **wax paper**, combine the corn meal, curry powder, salt and black pepper. Press the slices into the mixture, coating both sides.

Pour the oil into a **large skillet** to 1/2-inch depth and heat. Place the coated slices into the pan and gently fry, until golden on both sides. Serve immediately.

Tomato Crumb Bake

4 ripe tomatoes, sliced
1 cup Seasoned breadcrumbs
1 tbsp. butter
1/2 tsp. curry powder
1/2 salt
1/2 tsp. black pepper

Bake at 350°F

Grease a **casserole dish** with butter. Sprinkle half of the crumbs over the bottom of the dish and arrange the slices on top of the crumbs. Sprinkle with salt and pepper to taste. Spread remaining crumbs on top of the tomato and bake for 30-minutes or until crumbs are brown.

Stuffed Tomato

4 firm-ripe tomatoes
1 cup bread crumbs
1 tsp. salt
1 tsp. black pepper

Bake at 400°F

Wash the tomatoes; cut a slice from the stem end, removing as much of the pulp as possible without piercing the skin. Drain off the juice.

In a **small bowl**, mix the pulp with the salt and pepper folding in the bread-crumbs. Spoon the mixture into the tomato shells, place into a buttered **baking dish** and bake for 20-minutes.

Seeds of Change

Historians have noted that four of the most important seeds of change from the Americas were tomatoes, yams, corn and the lowly potato. "If you imagine the Italians without tomatoes, the Africans without maize and the Irish, Germans and Russians without potatoes to eat, the importance of American food crops becomes self-evident.

Chinese Cabbage

3 cups shredded cabbage
2 tbsp. butter
1 stalk celery, 1/4" dice
1 small green pepper, 1/4" dice
1 small onion, 1/4" dice
1 tsp. salt
1/2 tsp. black pepper
1 tbsp. water

Heat the butter in a **large skillet** and sauté the celery, green pepper and onion for 2 to 3-minutes. Stir in the cabbage and sauté for about 3-minutes.

Add the salt, black pepper and water, cover tightly and steam for 5-minutes, stirring several times. Serve immediately.

Stuffed Cabbage Rolls

4 to 6 large cabbage leaves
1 cup cooked rice
Mixture for Savoury Chicken Rissoles page 188
1/2 cup water
3/4 cup tomato purée
1/2 cup sour cream

Prepare the Rissoles mixture, steps one and two. Place into a **medium-sized bowl** and fold in the cooked rice.

Separate and wash the cabbage leaves. In a **3-quart sized saucepan**, bring the salted water to a boil; cook the leaves for 3-minutes and drain.

Grease an **8x10-inch covered casserole dish**; *or use heavy foil to cover*, place one or two tablespoonsful of the meat mixture on each cabbage leaf. Roll up carefully, and fasten with **toothpicks**. Place the rolls into the casserole dish, close together.

Mix together the purée and water; pour over the rolls. Cover and bake for 30-minutes. Remove to a **serving dish**. Mix the sour cream with t h e l i q u i d remaining in casserole dish and serve over the cabbage rolls.

Skillet Slaw with Bacon Top

4 cups shredded cabbage
4 slices bacon
1 tsp. salt
1/2 cup vinegar
1 tbsp. brown sugar
1/2 cup chopped parsley
1 tbsp. finely chopped onion

In a **large skillet**, fry the bacon until crisp, remove, and crumble.

Add the vinegar, salt, sugar, and onion to the fat in the skillet heating thoroughly.

Remove the skillet from the heat, add the cabbage and parsley and toss together. Turn into a **serving dish**, top with the bacon and serve immediately.

Stuffed Green Peppers

6 medium-sized green peppers (firm)
2 cups cooked rice
2 cups diced cooked chicken (or canned)
1 cup celery, 1/4" dice
1/4 cup onion, 1/4" dice
2 tbsp. pimento
1 tsp. curry powder
1/2 tsp. salt
1/4 tsp. ground white pepper
2 ripe tomatoes, peeled and mashed
1/2 tsp. dried thyme leaves
1 tbsp. olive oil

Bake at 350°F

Remove the tops and seeds of the green peppers. Pour 2-cups of water into a **3-quart sized saucepan**, add the salt and bring to a boil. Place the peppers into the pot and partially cook for about 5-minutes. Remove and drain.

Heat the oil in a **large skillet** and sauté the onion and celery for a few minutes. Add the tomatoes and continue sautéing for a few minutes. Stir in the pimento, rice, chicken, curry powder, thyme leaves, salt and pepper to taste; remove from the heat.

Stuff the peppers with the mixture and place into a greased **10x8-inch baking dish**. Pour a small amount of water around the peppers and bake for 30-minutes.

Fried Plantains

Serves 6

3 ripe plantains (soft to the touch)
Vegetable oil 1/4" deep in skillet

Cut off tips of the plantains, peel and cut into halves around then cut each half into 3 lengthwise slices.

Heat the oil in a **large skillet** over medium high heat. Gently fry the plantain slices turning until golden brown, about 3-minutes on each side. Drain on **paper towels** and serve immediately.

Ginger Fried Plantain

1 ripe plantain
1 oz. fresh ginger
2 tbsp. butter

Cut off tips of the plantains, peel and cut into halves around then cut each half into 3 lengthwise slices. Peel the ginger and thinly slice.

Heat the butter in a **large skillet** and sauté the ginger slices for a few minutes. Add the plantain slices and fry until golden brown 3 or 4-minutes on each side.

Plantain Cakes

3 firm-ripe plantains
1/2 tsp. baking powder
1/2 tsp. ground cinnamon
Vegetable oil 1/2" deep in skillet

Cut off and discard the tips of the plantains. Place the un-peeled plantains into a **3-quart sized saucepan** of boiling water to cover; boil until soft, about 15 to 20-minutes.

Drain, cool, peel and mash the plantains. Place into a **medium-sized bowl** mixing in the baking powder and cinnamon. Shape the mixture into small flat cakes.

Heat the oil in a **large skillet** and gently place the cakes into the hot oil. Fry until golden brown on both sides. Serve immediately.

Plantain Drops

Over-ripe plantains are very sweet but usually too soft to fry normally. Using this recipe, you will never throw away another plantain, no matter how dark and spotted although thought "too ripe" to fry.

Over-ripe plantains
Cinnamon
Equal parts butter & olive oil for frying

Slit the skin of the plantain; scoop the pulp into a **bowl** and mash. Add a small amount of cinnamon, mixing well.

Heat the butter and olive oil in a **skillet** over medium heat and drop the mixture by tablespoonfuls into the hot fat. Fry for 3 or 4-minutes on each side and gently remove directly to serving plates.

Green Plantain Sauté

2 green plantains
1 oz. butter
1 tbsp. curry powder
1 tsp. salt
1 tsp. ground white pepper
1 cup canned coconut milk
2 tbsp. freshly grated coconut
1/2 cup water

Peel the plantains carefully by scoring the skin with the tip of a sharp paring knife. Cut each plantain into 3 lengthwise slices.

Heat the butter in a **large skillet**, sprinkle in the curry powder and fry for 2 to 3-minutes. Add the plantain slices, brown lightly and sprinkle with salt and pepper.

In a **small dish**, mix together the coconut milk, grated coconut and water. Pour over the plantain in the skillet.

Simmer over low heat for 30-minutes, basting with the pan gravy. Remove to a **serving dish** topping with the pan gravy and serve hot.

Green Banana Sauté

Prepare same as *Green Plantain Sauté* (above) except substitute *3 large green bananas* for plantain.

Baked Plantain

Ripe plantains

Bake at 350°F or Microwave for 4 to 5 minutes

Wrap un-peeled plantain in **foil**; place on a **baking sheet** and bake for about 20-minutes. *Or wrap the un-peeled plantain in wax paper; bake in microwave for 5 to 7-minutes depending on size.*

Ginger Mashed Potatoes

1 lb. potatoes, peeled and cubed
1 carrot, peeled and cut into chunks
1 tsp. chopped fresh ginger
1 tsp. salt
2 tbsp. butter
1/2 cup orange juice

Place the potatoes and carrots into a **2-quart sized saucepan** with water to cover adding the chopped ginger and salt. Cook until soft.

Turn into a **food mill** *or colander*, drain and mash using the food mill.

Scrape into a **glass-serving bowl** mixing in the butter and orange juice. Serve immediately.

Potato Carrot Mash

2 medium-sized potatoes
2 medium-sized carrots
1/2 tsp. salt
2 tbsp. butter
1/2 tsp. ground ginger

Cut peeled potatoes and carrots into 1-inch chunks. Place into a **2-quart sized saucepan** with water to cover. Add the salt and cook until soft. Turn into a **food mill**, drain and mash.

Turn into a **bowl**, stir in the butter and ginger mixing thoroughly. Serve as a side dish or use as stuffing for poultry or fish.

Potato Croquettes

2-1/2 lbs. potatoes
1/2 cup butter, room temperature
1-2/3 cups Parmesan cheese
1 clove garlic, minced
3 tsp. freshly chopped parsley
3 eggs (2 separated for whites)
Salt
Black pepper
Flour
Olive oil 1/2" deep in skillet
Bread crumbs

Peel the potatoes, cut into large cubes and place into a **3-quart sized saucepan** with water to cover. Add the salt, bring to a boil and cook until soft, about 20-minutes.

Turn into a **food mill** placed over a **large bowl** *or into a colander*, drain; and with the food mill, mash. Add the butter, cheese, parsley, garlic, 1 egg, salt and pepper mixing well. If the mixture is too loose, add a little flour and shape into croquettes.

Separate the whites of 2 eggs into a **shallow bowl**. Place a layer of flour on a sheet of **wax paper** and a layer of crumbs on another sheet of wax paper.

Heat the olive oil in a **medium-sized skillet**. Gently roll each croquette in the flour; dip into the egg white, then into the breadcrumbs.

Fry in the hot oil until brown, about 1-minute per side. Drain on a **wire rack** over **paper towel** and serve.

French Fried Breadfruit

1 firm ripe breadfruit
Salt
Vegetable oil for deep-frying

Peel, core and cut the breadfruit into slices and boil *page 29*. Allow to cool; pat dry and cut slices into french-fries strips.

Heat the oil in a **deep-fat fryer** *or deep pot*. Fry until golden brown, drain on a **wire rack**, sprinkle with salt and serve hot with Catsup if desired.

Breadfruit

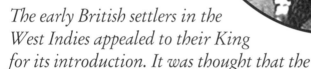

Breadfruit, rich in carbohydrates and vitamins A, B and C, originates from the South Pacific and has been described as "bread growing on trees".

The early British settlers in the West Indies appealed to their King for its introduction. It was thought that the large Fruit would provide food for the slaves brought from Africa to the Caribbean to work on the sugar plantations. Their appeal was heard and there followed the ill-fated voyage of H.M.S. Bounty, which, under Captain Bligh, sailed from England in 1787 bound for Tahiti. The Captain's deep concern for his breadfruit cuttings at the expense of his crew led to the famous "Mutiny on the Bounty". Not so well known is that there was a second voyage in 1791 which succeeded, bringing to the West Indies not only the breadfruit but also the Ackee and a number of other tropical plants.

When the breadfruit is unripe and roasted it is most bread-like. When fully ripe, it is soft and the pulp is yellow and resembles the sweet potato in flavor. It can be boiled, baked, steamed, fried, made into salads or made into soup or "poi". ✽

Sliced Breadfruit With Bacon

1 firm-ripe breadfruit
Salt
Ground white pepper
3 slices bacon, chopped
1 medium-sized onion, sliced
2 tbsp. vinegar
1 oz. vegetable oil

Wash the un-peeled breadfruit and place into a **3-quart sized saucepan** with water to cover *page 29*. Cook for 40-minutes.

Turn into a **colander**; drain and allow to cool slightly. Peel, core and slice into 1-inch thick slices. Place onto a **serving platter** and sprinkle with salt and pepper to taste and keep warm.

Heat the oil in a **large skillet** and sauté the chopped bacon and onion. Spread over the breadfruit slices and serve immediately.

Stuffed Baked Breadfruit

1 firm-ripe breadfruit
Salt
1/2 oz. vegetable oil
1/2 lb. ground beef
1/2 lb. ham, finely chopped
1 tomato, peeled and chopped
1 medium-sized onion, chopped
Black pepper

Bake at 350°F

Peel the breadfruit *page 29*; cut in half and scoop out the centre membrane. Place into a **3-quart sized saucepan** with water to cover. Bring to a boil and cook for about 15-minutes.

While the breadfruit is cooking, heat the oil in a **large skillet**. Brown the beef, drain, add the ham and sauté. Add the tomato, onion, salt and pepper, continuing to sauté.

Remove the breadfruit from the boiling water and place into a greased **shallow baking dish**. Stuff centres with the meat mixture and bake for 45-minutes. Slice and serve.

Pineapple Sweet Potato Drops

1 fresh pineapple, cut into 1/2" slices *page 25*
or 1 can (16 oz.) pineapple slices
3 cups mashed red sweet potatoes or yams
2-1/2 tbsp. butter
1 tsp. salt
1/8 tsp. ground white pepper
Pinch of ground nutmeg and cinnamon, (together 1/8 tsp.)
2-1/2 tbsp. brown sugar
1-1/2 cups crushed corn flakes

Bake at 350°F

In a **medium-sized bowl**, combine the mashed sweet potato, butter, seasonings and brown sugar.

With a **rolling pin**, roll the corn flakes to crumbs on a sheet of **wax paper**.

Place 2-tablespoonfuls for each drop on the corn flake crumbs and roll into balls.

Place a ball on each pineapple slice and place onto a greased **baking sheet**. Bake for 20-minutes.

Sweet Potatoes In Orange Shells

4 servings
5 medium-sized red sweet potatoes or yams
5 large oranges
4 tbsp. cream
1 oz. butter
1 oz. brown sugar
1/4 tsp. salt

Scrub the potatoes; place into a **3-quart sized saucepan** with water to cover and bring to a boil. Cook until soft when tested with a sharp knife. Turn into a **food mill** or *colander*, drain and cool.

Peel the potatoes and mash using the food mill. Turn into a **large mixing bowl**.

Slice the tops off 4 oranges and scoop out the flesh without breaking the skins. Cut the peel sliced from the tops into strips for decoration.

Squeeze the juice from the pulp. Grate the rind of the fifth orange on the fine side of a **hand held grater**.

In a **small dish**, combine 4-tablespoons the orange juice and the grated rind mixing well. Add to the potato mixture.

Add the cream, butter, sugar and salt to the mixing bowl and, with **electric**

mixer, beat until well blended. Beat in the juice and rind mix.

Spoon the mixture into the orange shells, place into a greased **flat baking dish** and bake for 20-minutes. Place on a **serving dish** and decorate with the orange strips.

Sweet Potatoes With Orange Peel

6 medium-sized red sweet potatoes or yams
2 tbsp. grated orange peel
2 tbsp. brown sugar
2 tbsp. butter
3 tbsp. cream
Bake at 325°F

Scrub the potatoes, place into a **3-quart sized saucepan** with water to cover and bring to a boil. Cook until soft when tested with a sharp knife. Drain and allow to cool.

Scoop out the pulp leaving a 1/4-inch layer in the potato skin. Place the pulp into a **food mill** placed over a **medium-sized bowl** and mash. Add the orange peel, sugar, butter and cream, mixing well.

Spoon the mixture back into the skins and place into a greased **casserole dish**. Bake for 15 to 20-minutes serving immediately.

Fu Fu
Sweet Potato Cakes

2 medium-sized yams (white sweet potato)
1 small onion, chopped
1 tsp. minced garlic
1 egg
1/2 cup evaporated milk
Salt
3 tbsp. butter
2 tbsp. olive oil

Peel the yams and cut into 1-inch sized chunks. Place into a **2-quart sized saucepan** with 1/2-cup of water; cook for about 20-minutes and drain.

Turn into the bowl of a **food processor** fitted with the knife blade, add the onion and garlic, process for 1-minute. Remove to a **medium-sized mixing bowl**; beat in the egg, milk and salt until the mixture is smooth. Form into small cakes.

Heat the butter and olive oil in a **large skillet**; gently place the cakes into the skillet and fry until brown on both sides. Serve immediately.

251

Akara
Black-Eyed Pea Fritters

3 cups dried black-eyed peas
1 onion, chopped
1/2 tsp. salt
1/2 green pepper, chopped
1/2 red pepper, chopped
Bird peppers or cayenne pepper to taste
1/2 tsp. fresh gingerroot, chopped
Peanut oil for deep-fat frying

Clean the black-eyed peas under running water. Place into a **bowl with a cover**, add enough water to cover and soak overnight. After soaking, rub peas together between your hands to remove the skins. Rinse to wash away the skins and any other debris; drain in a colander.

Place into the bowl of a **food processor** *or grinder* and process into a thick paste. Add the chopped onion and peppers to bowl of the processor and mix together.

Remove the mixture to a **medium-sized bowl**; add enough water to form a smooth, thick batter that will cling to a spoon. Add the salt and hot peppers to taste and allow batter to to stand for a few hours or overnight in the refrigerator (doing so improves the flavour).

Heat the oil in a **deep-fat fryer** *or deep pot*. Make the fritters by scooping up a spoon full of batter and using another spoon to quickly push it into the hot oil. Deep fry the fritters until they are golden brown; turn frequently while frying.

Serve warm with hot sauce or *Créole Sauce page 259.*

Akara
(African Bean Cake)

Black-eyed Peas were cultivated in the Mediterranean region in ancient times, and have been grown all over Africa for centuries. In Western Africa they are used as the basis for a batter from which fritters are made.

The fritters, known as Akara, are commonly prepared at home for breakfast, for snacks, or as an appetizer or side dish. They are also "fast-food" sold by vendors on the streets and in the market places. These fritters take an entire day to prepare, as the peas have to soak overnight, then ground into a thick paste and mixed with onion and peppers to form a smooth batter. The batter has to stand for a few hours or overnight to improve the flavour before deep-frying in peanut oil

In time, the descendants of Africans in The Bahamas substituted flour for the black-eyed peas, added chopped conch and lime juice, creating the "Bahamian Conch Fritter". ✸

Notes

Meat
Sauces &
Gravies

Recipes

❈ Sauces

White, Cheese,
Curry, Deluxe Curry,
Mint, Nut,
Tarter,
Tamarind Guava,
Cocktail, Creole,
Guanahani, Pizza,
Barbeque Poultry,
Tamarind Barbeque,
Kahlúa Barbecue,

❈ Seafood Sauces

Avocado, Fish,
Ginger Fish,
Fish Roe,
Seafood,
Ginger,
Tamarind Butter,
Conch

❈ Marinades & Glazes

Beer Marinade
Harvey's Marinade
Tamarind Honey Glaze

❈ Gravies

Roux,
Brown,
Golden,
Brown Flour Stew

Avocado Seafood Sauce

1 ripe avocado
1 clove garlic, finely minced
1 tbsp. wine vinegar
Freshly squeezed juice of 1 lime
4 tbsp. olive oil
1 tsp. salt
Black pepper
1/4 tsp. crushed red pepper

Peel the avocado and mash the pulp with a fork.

Place immediately into the bowl of a **blender** with remaining ingredients, mixing thoroughly. Serve with fish or other seafood.

White Sauce

1/4 cup butter
1/4 cup all purpose flour
1/4 tsp. salt
1/4 tsp. ground white pepper
1 cup milk

Melt the butter over low heat in a **small heavy saucepan**. With a **wooden spoon**, stir in the flour, salt and pepper, stirring until the mixture is smooth.

Remove from the heat and stir in the milk. Return to the heat and bring to a boil, stirring constantly. Boil for 1-minute. (Add more milk for medium or thin sauce).

Cheese Sauce

1 cup *White Sauce* (above)
1/4 tsp. dry mustard
1/2 cup Sharp Cheddar cheese

Prepare *White Sauce*, stirring in the dry mustard and cheese until the cheese is melted.

Curry Sauce

1 cup *White Sauce* (above)
1/2 tsp. curry powder (or to taste)

Prepare *White Sauce* except sauté the curry powder in the butter before adding the flour.

Deluxe Curry Sauce

1 cup mayonnaise
1/2 cup sour cream
1 tbsp. red wine vinegar
1 tbsp. olive oil
2 tsp. curry powder (or to taste)
1/4 tsp. salt
1 clove garlic, crushed
1 tsp. grated onion

Combine all ingredients in a **small bowl** mixing together thoroughly. Chill.

Mint Sauce

2 tbsp. chopped fresh mint leaves
1/2 cup vinegar
2 tbsp. sugar
3/4 tsp. salt
Small amount of crushed hot pepper

Place the chopped mint into a small **covered dish**.

Heat the vinegar, sugar, salt and pepper together in a **1-quart saucepan** and pour over the mint. Chill.

Nut Sauce

2 tbsp. pecan nut meats
2 tbsp. blanched peanuts
1/4 cup freshly squeezed lemon juice
1/4 cup olive oil
3/4 tsp. salt
3/4 tsp. paprika

Pound the nuts to a paste and place into a **small bowl**. Blend in the remaining ingredients mixing well. Cover until ready to serve.

Tarter Sauce

1/2 cup mayonnaise
1 tsp. onion purée
2 tbsp. sweet relish
1 tsp. minced parsley
2 tsp. finely chopped pimento

Combine ingredients in a **small bowl**, mix well and serve with seafood.

Créole Sauce

1 small onion,1/4" dice
1/2 green pepper, 1/4" dice
2 gloves garlic, finely chopped
1/2 tsp. curry powder
1 tsp. dried oregano
2 oz. Champion Tomato Paste
2 tbsp. finely chopped fresh parsley
1/2 tap salt
1 tsp. black pepper
1/2 tsp. curry powder
Hot peppers to taste
2 tbsp. olive oil
1 cup tomato juice

Heat the oil in a **large skillet** and sauté the vegetables. Add the curry powder, oregano, tomato paste, parsley and spices and hot peppers to taste. Stir together well, remove from the heat and cool.

Combine the sautéed mixture with the tomato juice in the bowl of a **blender** and purée. Return to the skillet and simmer for 10-minutes.

Guanabani Tomato Sauce

1 stalk of celery, 1/4" dice
1/2 medium-sized onion, 1/4" dice
1 carrot, 1/4" dice
2 1lbs. fresh tomatoes, peeled and chopped
1 oz. Dry White Wine
4 oz. margarine
1 tsp. chopped parsley
1 tsp. basil
2 oz. vegetable oil
1/2 tsp. dried thyme leaves
2 bay leaves
1 clove garlic, chopped
A pinch of rosemary

Heat the oil in a **large skillet** and sauté the chopped vegetables. Add the chopped tomatoes and continue to sauté.

Mix in the herbs, wine, salt and pepper to taste simmering for 20 to 30-minutes. Cool, turn the mixture into the bowl of a **blender** and purée.

Cocktail Sauce

1 cup mayonnaise
3 tbsp. tomato ketchup
1 tbsp. vinegar
1 tsp. *Tamarind Paste page 366*
1 tsp. freshly squeezed lemon juice
1 tbsp. onion juice or purée

Combine all ingredients into the bowl of a **blender**, purée and chill.

Pizza Sauce

3 cups tomato sauce (canned or bottled)
3/4 tsp. oregano leaves
3/4 tsp. rosemary
1/2 tsp. garlic powder
1/8 tsp. ground thyme
1/2 tsp. salt
1/2 tsp. black pepper

Combine the ingredients in a **2-quart sized saucepan** and simmer for 6 to 10-minutes. Allow cooling and spread on crust according to pizza recipe.

Seafood Sauce

2 cups chopped tomatoes
1 medium-sized onion, chopped
1/2 green pepper, chopped
2 tbsp. vegetable oil
1-1/2 cups fish or conch stock
1 tsp. freshly squeezed lime juice
1 tsp. vinegar
Black pepper

Heat the oil in a **large skillet**; sauté the onion and green pepper for 4 to 5 minutes. Add the tomatoes and continue to sauté, stirring constantly, for about 5 minutes.

Turn into a **2-quart sized saucepan**. Add the stock, lime juice, vinegar and black pepper. Bring to a boil, reduce the heat and simmer for 15-minutes. Cool, turn into the bowl of a **blender** and purée.

Barbecue Poultry Sauce

1-1/4 cups orange juice
3 tbsp. freshly squeezed lime juice
2 oz. melted butter
3 tbsp. chopped parsley
1 tbsp. dry mustard
1 clove garlic, minced
3 tbsp. soy sauce
3 tbsp. honey
Salt

In a **bowl**, mix all ingredients together except the salt (which should be added just before serving). Pour the mixture into the bowl of a **blender** and purée.

Kahlúa Zesty Barbecue Sauce

1 tbsp. butter
1/3 cup minced onion
3/4 cup chili sauce
1/4 cup Kahlúa
2 tbsp. brown sugar, packed
1 tbsp. Tamarind Paste page 366
1/4 tsp. salt
Hot peppers to taste

Melt the butter in a **1-quart saucepan**, and sauté the onion until translucent. Blend in remaining ingredients and simmer for 5-minutes, stirring several times.

Ginger Fish Sauce

1 cup White Wine
1 large onion, sliced
1 oz. ginger, sliced
2 slices of bacon, chopped

In a **1-quart saucepan**, simmer the onion in the wine for about 10-minutes.

Meanwhile, in a **non-stick skillet**, fry the bacon; add the ginger and sauté for a few minutes.

Pour the wine and onion into the bowl of a **blender** and purée. In **small bowl** mix together the purée and ginger sauté. Pour over fish and bake.

Fish Roe Sauce

4 oz. fresh fish roe
2 tbsp. butter
2 tbsp. all purpose flour
1 cup water
1 small bouillon cube
Salt to taste
Ground white pepper to taste

Clean the roe, place into a **saucepan**, cover and steam for 10-minutes. Drain, cool, remove the skin and mash thoroughly with a fork.

In a **1-quart saucepan**, melt the butter over low heat and stir in the flour until well blended. Continue to stir, cooking until the mixture is smooth.

Remove from the heat, gradually stirring in the water. Add the bouillon cube. Bring to a boil, stirring constantly, and boil for 1-minute.

Blend in the seasonings and mashed fish roe, simmering for a few minutes. Serve over hot seafood.

Ginger Seafood Sauce

1 cup White Wine
1 large onion sliced
1 oz. ginger, sliced
2 slices of bacon, chopped

In a **1-quart saucepan**, simmer the onion in the wine for about 10-minutes. Let cool.

Meanwhile, in a **large skillet**, fry the bacon and sauté the ginger for a few minutes.

Pour the simmered wine and onion into the bowl of a **blender** and purée. Add the purée to the saucepan with the bacon/ginger sauté mixing thoroughly. Pour over fish or other seafood in preparation for baking.

Seafood Tamarind Butter

2 oz. butter
2 oz. *Tamarind Paste* page 366
1/4 cup celery, 1/4" dice

Combine the ingredients in a **small dish**, mixing well. Chill and serve over cooked fish or seafood.

Conch Sauce

1 large conch, shredded
1 tbsp. butter
1 medium-sized onion, chopped
1/4 tsp. ground thyme
Freshly squeezed juice of 1 lemon
3 tbsp. cream
1/2 tsp. Champion Tomato Paste
1 tsp. Lady Darling's Island Seasoning
Salt to taste
Hot peppers to taste

Prepare conch.

Melt the butter in a **large non-stick skillet** and over high heat; sauté the conch and chopped onion for about 3-minutes. Reduce the heat, stir in the tomato paste, cream and lemon juice and simmer for a few more minutes.

Remove from the heat and add the Island Seasoning, salt and hot peppers to taste.

The Arawaks

Like other groups in the Americas, the Arawaks were also farmers, learning how to farm about 9,000 years ago. It was an important development when they acquired the skills for the different uses of seeds, fruits, and roots, and how to cultivate them. When Columbus' ships landed in what is now the West Indies, he traded with "the people" and took corn home with him to Spain. From Spain, corn was introduced to other Western European farmers, and eventually was distributed throughout the world. The Native American's name for corn was MA-HIZ, which early settlers began to call Maize. The Americans also shared their methods for preparing corn with the settlers, including corn bread, corn pudding, corn soup and fried corn cakes.

Beer Marinade

1 medium-sized onion, 1/4" dice
2 carrots, 1/4" dice
1 rib celery, 1/4" dice
1/4 cup vegetable oil
4 cups Kalik beer
1 tsp. dried thyme leaves
1 tsp. whole allspice
1 bay leaf
1 tsp. salt
1 tsp. black pepper
Hot peppers to taste

Heat the oil in a **large skillet** and sauté the diced vegetables for about 5-minutes. Stir in the beer, spices and seasonings; bring to a boil, stirring.

Reduce the heat, cover and simmer for 20-minutes. Cool completely, serve over meat or seafood.

Harvey's Marinade

1/4 cup light soy sauce
1/2 cup Harvey's Bristol Cream
1/2 tsp. grated fresh ginger
Green onions, chopped

In a **small bowl**, mix ingredients together thoroughly and marinate chicken, fish or red meat for 15-minutes to 1-hour before cooking.

Tamarind Honey Glaze

1/2 cup pineapple juice
1 tbsp. Tamarind Paste page 366
1/2 tbsp. Ole Nassau Chick Charney Rum

In a **1-quart saucepan**, combine the pineapple juice and Tamarind Paste. Over medium heat, simmer for 5-minutes. Add the rum and continue to simmer for another 5-minutes.

Brush over poultry, meat or seafood and bake.

Roux

Method One

1/2 cup all purpose flour
2 cups cold water
1 to 2 tsp. Browning Sauce

Spread the flour evenly in a **small heavy skillet** and over medium high heat, stirring, brown the flour but do not burn. Let cool.

In a **2-quart sized saucepan** combine the browned flour and cold water, stir until flour is dissolved. Over medium-high heat, stirring, bring to a boil. Add the Browning Sauce according to taste.

Method Two

1/2 cup all purpose flour
2 cups of cold water
1 to 2 tsp. Browning Sauce

Spread the flour in a **shallow dish** and place in a hot oven until the flour is browned. Cool. (See Tip *page 38*). Follow step two in **Method One**.

Method Three

1/2 cup all purpose flour
1/2 cup vegetable oil
2 cups very hot water
1 to 2 tsp. Browning Sauce

Combine the oil and flour in a **medium-sized skillet** and over medium-high heat, stir continuously until the flour is browned.

Meanwhile heat the water until very hot but not boiling. Remove the skillet from the heat; quickly stirring in the water until the mixture is smooth. Add the Browning sauce.

Brown Gravy

2 to 4 tbsp. Roux (above)
1 cup cold water
1/4 tsp. onion powder
1/4 tsp. garlic powder
1/4 tsp. ground thyme
Lady Darling's Island Seasoning to taste
Black pepper to taste

In a **1-quart saucepan** combine all ingredients and bring to a slow boil, stirring. Simmer for about 10-minutes.

Brown Flour Stew

Roux **Method Three** *page 265*

1 large onion, sliced
1 tsp. dried thyme leaves
1/2 tsp. Lady Darling's Island Seasoning
1 tsp. black pepper

Prepare the *Roux*; add the onion, thyme leaves, seasonings, vegetable and pieces of meat or seafood, cooking until meat is done.

Golden Gravy

1 cup chicken broth or 2 small boullion cubes
1/2 tsp. Worcestershire sauce
1/8 tsp. salt
3 tbsp. vegetable oil
3 tbsp. all purpose flour
1/4 tsp. ground white pepper
1 cup milk

In a **1-quart saucepan**, prepare the broth; stir in the Worcestershire sauce and salt and set aside to cool slightly.

Heat the oil in a **small skillet** over low heat. Stirring constantly, blend in the flour and pepper, heating until the mixture bubbles.

Remove from the heat and slowly add the seasoned chicken broth, stirring constantly. Thoroughly blend in the milk and return to the heat.

Cook rapidly, stirring constantly for 1 or 2-minutes. Serve with meat or poultry.

Pastries
Pies &
Tarts

Recipes

❋ **Crusts & Pie Shells**

Coconut, Crumb,

No Need to Knead,

Pie Shell 9-inch, Double

Corn Meal Pastry

Cassava Crust – 9-inch

Seasoned Crust for Meat Pies

9-inch Meat Pie Crust

❋ **Turnovers (Fried Pies)**

Peach, Apricot, Apple,

Mince Meat

Rum Raisin Nut

❋ **Fresh Tropical Fruit Turnovers (Fried Pies)**

Guava, Pineapple,

Coconut, Dilly

❋ **Tarts (9x12-inch)**

Coconut, Pineapple

Dilly, Green Mango

Fruit Puffs

Bananas In Blankets

Crispy Sapodilla Rollups

❋ **Pies**

Paradise (Green Mango)

Avocado Lime

Cocoa Rum

Caribbean Sweet Potato

Bahamian Pumpkin

Tequilime

Fruity Yogurt

Key Lime Rum

Mango

Rum Pineapple Custard

Sapodilla

Soursop

Sugar Apple

Nutmeg

The nutmeg tree first reached the Caribbean in 1824 on board a merchant ship returning to England from the East Indian Spice Islands. The ship had a small quantity of nutmeg trees on board and some were left behind, beginning the nutmeg industry in Grenada.

The industry in the Caribbean now supplies nearly forty percent of the world's annual crop. Most nutmegs are ground into powder or crushed for their oils. The nut is covered with a scarlet aril layer which, when dried, is known as the spice called mace.

Nutmeg even has medicinal uses. In the islands, some sufferers from strokes keep a small piece of nutmeg in their mouth to "prevent" further attacks. ✻

Coconut Crust
9-inch

1 coconut, freshly grated
or 1-1/2 cups packaged shredded coconut
2 tbsp. butter
Bake at 325°F

Prepare the coconut *page 24*. Melt the butter in a **9-inch pie pan**.

Press the grated coconut with fingertips firmly and evenly against the bottom and sides of the pan. Bake for 15 to 20-minutes.

Crumb Crust
9-inch

3/4 cup ground almonds
1 cup graham cracker crumbs
1/4 cup sugar
1/4 cup butter or margarine, melted
Bake at 325°F

Mix all ingredients together in a **small bowl**. Turn the mixture into a **9-inch pie pan** patting onto the bottom and 1-1/2-inches up sides of the pan. Bake for 10-minutes.

No Need to Knead Piecrust
9-inch

1-1/2 cups all purpose flour
1 tsp. salt
1/4 tsp. baking powder
1 tsp. sugar
1/2 cup vegetable oil
3 tbsp. milk
Bake at 400°F

Sift the dry ingredients into a **9-inch pie pan**. In a **small bowl**, mix together the milk and oil. Combine with the dry ingredients in the pie pan mixing well. Pat out in the bottom and up the sides of the pan.

Bake for 10 to 12-minutes or fill the unbaked crust and follow your favourite recipe.

Pie Shell
9-inch

1 cup all purpose flour
1/2 tsp. salt
1/3 cup vegetable shortening
2 tsp. ice water

Sift together the flour and salt in a **small bowl**. Cut in the shortening with a **pastry cuter** until the mixture is the consistency of rice grains. While mixing with a fork, sprinkle with the ice water pressing the dough into a ball.

To avoid the dough cracking when handling, place the ball between 2 sheets of **wax paper** and with a **rolling pin**, roll out into a circle of 1/8-inch thickness. Remove one sheet of wax paper; fold the circle in half and carefully line a greased **9-inch pie pan**.

Pinch together any cracks, fold the under the edge and flute. Follow selected recipe for unbaked or baked crust.

Pie Shell Double
9-inch

2 cups all purpose flour
1 tsp. salt
2/3 cup vegetable shortening
1/4 cup ice water

Sift together the flour and the salt in a **medium-sized bowl**. Cut in the shortening with a **pastry cutter**, until the mixture is the consistency of rice grains.

While mixing with a fork, sprinkle with the ice water, 1-tablespoonful at a time pressing the dough into a ball. Divide the dough into two equal sized balls.

To avoid the dough cracking when handling, place each ball between 2 sheets of **wax paper** and with a **rolling pin**; roll out into 2 circles of 1/8-inch thickness. Remove one sheet of wax paper; fold the circle in half and carefully, line a greased **9-inch pie pan**. Pinch together any cracks.

Fill with selected filling; cover with the top crust. Trim, fold under and flute the edge making slits in the top for steam to escape. Follow selected recipe for baking.

Corn Meal Pastry

1-2/3 cups all purpose flour
1/3 cup Yellow Corn Meal
1/4 cup grated Parmesan cheese
1/4 tsp. salt
1/2 cup vegetable oil
3 tbsp. ice water

Bake at 375°F

Combine the flour, corn meal, cheese and salt in a **medium-sized bowl**. Add the oil and stir with a fork until moistened. Add the water, mixing well, and press into a ball.

Place the ball onto a floured **board** and, with a floured **rolling pin**, roll out to 1/8-inch thickness. With the **2-inch cutter** cut the dough into circles.

Place half of the circles on a greased **baking sheet**. Place 1-tablespoonful of selected meat filling on the bottom circle, top with another circle and press together with the tines of the fork.

Follow directions for baking of selected recipe.

Cassava Crust

1 cup grated cassava
1 cup all purpose flour
1-1/2 tsp. baking powder
1/2 tsp. salt
2 tsp. sugar
1 tsp. vegetable oil
3 to 4 tbsp. water

Peel and grate the cassava *page 30*.

In a **medium-sized bowl**, sift together the flour, baking powder and salt. Stir in the grated cassava, mixing well. Add the water one tablespoonful at a time to make a firm but soft dough.

Turn onto a floured **board**, knead lightly and roll out.

Seasoned Crust for Meat Pies
9-inch

1 cup unsalted mashed potato
1 cup all purpose flour
1/2 tsp. salt
1/2 tsp. curry powder
1/2 tsp. sugar
1/3 cup plus 1 tbsp. vegetable shortening
1 tsp. water
1 egg white
1 tbsp. water

Bake at 400°F

Place the cooled, unsalted mashed potato into a **large bowl**.

Sift together the flour, salt, curry powder and sugar into a **medium-sized bowl**. Add to the mashed potato and, with a **pastry cutter** *or fork*, mix to the consistency of corn meal.

Add the shortening, cutting to the consistency of rice grains. Press the dough into a ball. Wrap in **wax paper** and chill for 1/2-hour.

Place the pastry ball onto a floured **board** and with a floured **rolling pin**, roll out to 1/8-inch thickness. Roll into a 10-inch circle to cover top of prepared casserole.

Pizza Crust

1/4 pkg. active dry yeast (1/2 tsp.)
3/4 cup plus 2 tbsp. warm water (not hot)
3 to 3-1/4 cups all purpose flour
1 tsp. garlic powder
1 tsp. onion powder
1/2 tsp. ground oregano
1 tsp. parsley flakes

Bake at 425°F

In a **small bowl**, dissolve the yeast in the warm water. In a **large bowl**, sift together the flour and seasonings; make a well in the middle of the mixture and stir in the dissolved yeast, mixing well.

Turn onto a flat surface and knead lightly; cover and let rise in a warm place until double in size, 1-1/2 to 2-hours. Roll out for one large pizza or divide in half for two 14-inch pizzas. Place on **pizza pan**, roll edges and using a fork, pierce holes in the bottom of the crust.

Bake for 10 to 12-minutes; add toppings and continue to bake according to recipe.

Peach Turnovers
Fried Pies

Crust

1 lb. all purpose flour
1 lb. butter, room temperature
1 lb. cottage cheese, small curd, room temperature

Filling

2 pkgs. (8 oz. each) dried peaches
4 cups water
2 to 3 cups sugar (or to taste)
1 tsp. ground cinnamon
Confectioners' sugar for dusting

Bake at 425°F

Crust

Sift the flour into a **medium sized bowl**; cut in the butter with a **pastry cutter**. Add the cottage cheese mixing thoroughly to form smooth dough *(or place the ingredients into the bowl of a food processor and mix for about 1-minute).*

Press into a ball, return to the bowl, cover and refrigerate over-night or for at least six hours.

Filling

Chop the fruit into 1/2-inch chunks and place into a **medium-sized bowl with a cover**. Add the water, cover and soak until plump (overnight or for at least 4-hours).

Turn the fruit and water mixture into a **2-quart sized saucepan**, adding the sugar and cinnamon, and bring to a boil.

Reduce the heat and simmer over medium low heat, stirring occasionally using a **wooden spoon**. Cook until the fruit is tender, about 45-minutes. Taste-test, adding sugar if needed, and let cool.

(Filling may be prepared ahead and placed into refrigerator overnight, same as crust).

When ready to make the pies, divide the dough into sections for a few pies at a time. Place onto a floured **board** and using a floured **rolling pin**, roll out to 1/8-inch thickness. Using a **Pocket Gourmet** *or saucer,* cut into 6 inch circles.

Place about 2-tablespoonfuls of the filling into the center of each circle and fold over pressing the edges together with the cutter or with the tines of a fork. Make small decorative slits in the tops.

Gently place the turnovers onto a greased **baking sheet** and bake just until brown, 12 to 15-minutes. Remove to a **cooling rack** and dust with Confectioners' sugar. Serve warm or cold.

Apricot Turnovers

Prepare same as *Peach Turnovers* except *substitute 2 packages of dried apricots* for the peaches.

Apple Turnovers

Prepare same as *Peach Turnovers* except *substitute 2 packages of dried apples* for the peaches.

Mincemeat Turnovers

Prepare same as *Peach Turnovers* except substitute *1-16 oz. can mincemeat for the peaches.*

Rum Raisin Nut Turnovers

Prepare same as *Peach Turnovers* except substitute *Rum Raisin Nut Filling page 275* for the peaches.

• Tropical Fruit Fillings for the Turnovers below are found on *page 333 to 335.*

Guava Filling • *Pineapple Filling* • *Coconut Filling* • *Sapodilla Filling*

Bananas In Blankets

Firm ripe bananas
Freshly squeezed lemon juice
Sugar
Slices of bacon or ham
Bake at 350°F

Peel and cut large bananas into quarters or medium-sized bananas into halves lengthwise.

Dip the bananas into the lemon juice and sprinkle lightly with sugar. Wrap in bacon slices or very thin slices of ham. Secure with **toothpicks**.

Sauté in an **un-greased skillet** *or bake* until the bacon is crisp, turning frequently. When using ham, grease the skillet lightly.

Coconut

Most people's idea of a tropical island includes white sandy beaches fringed with coconut palms. The islands of the Caribbean certainly live up to this dream. They have coconut palms in abundance. The origin of these tall, graceful palms is lost in history. What is certain is that they are now spread widely through the tropics and they are one of the first sights to greet visitors.

The fruit of the coconut consists of a green or yellowish-brown husk inside which the coconut itself is found. The fibrous husk is waterproof and the protection it gives the nut has resulted in the seeds floating around the world to establish the palms on most tropical beaches.

The nut itself has a hard outer shell with a kernel inside. In young 'green' coconuts, the kernel is soft and jelly-like and the central cavity is filled with coconut 'milk'. As the coconut matures, the kernel becomes harder and the amount of milk decreases. The dried kernel is used in all kinds of cooking and baking. A by-product is coconut oil, widely used in the manufacture of various products including soap. Even the leaves are not wasted. They are used in the production of straw products and, in many islands, they are still used for thatching of roofs. ✹

Coconut Tart
9x12-inch

Crust

2 cups all purpose flour
3 tsp. baking powder
3 tbsp. sugar
1/2 tsp. salt
1/3 cup vegetable shortening
1/2 cup milk
1 egg, well beaten

Filling

2 freshly grated coconut to yield 4 cups
2 cups water
2 cups sugar
1/2 tsp. ground nutmeg
1/2 tsp. ground allspice

Bake at 350°F

Crust

In a **medium sized bowl**, sift together the flour, baking powder, sugar and salt. With a **pastry cutter**, cut in the shortening until the mixture resembles coarse crumbs. Make a well in the middle of the mixture; mix in the milk and beaten egg to form a firm dough.

Place onto a floured **board**; with a floured **rolling pin**, roll out to 1/4-inch thickness, and line a greased **9x12-inch-baking pan**. Trim the edges and roll excess dough into 1-inch wide strips for lattice top decoration.

Prepare the fresh coconut *page 24*. In a **2-quart sized saucepan**, combine the water and sugar with the coconut. Over medium heat, cook for 20 minutes, stirring continuously using a **large wooden spoon**.

Remove from the heat and let cool. Turn the filling into the lined pan and create the lattice top by overlapping the strips. Press the strips into the sides of the dough and flute the edges. Bake for 40 to 45-minutes or until crust is golden brown. Serve warm or cold.

Pineapple Tart

Substitute 4 cups *Pineapple Filling page 334* for the coconut.

Sapodilla Tart

Substitute 4 cups *Sapodilla Filling page 335* for the coconut.

Green Mango Tart

Substitute 4 cups *Green Mango Filling page 334* for the coconut.

277

Tartlets

To make Tartlets, choose fillings and dough for *Turnovers (Fried Pies), Tarts* or tropical fruit fillings *page 333 to 335*. Line **muffin cups** with dough; fill to 2/3 full with filling, flute the edges and create the lattice top by overlapping thin strips of dough. Press the strips into the sides of the dough and flute the edges and bake for 12 to 15-minutes or until the crust is golden brown.

Fruit Puffs

Crust

2 tsp. active dry yeast
1/2 cup warm not hot water
2 to 2-3/4 cups all purpose flour
1/2 cup sugar
1 tsp. salt
2 tbsp. vegetable oil
1 egg
2 tsp. Confectioners' sugar

Fruit Fillings page 333 to 335

Bake at 350°F

In a **small bowl**, dissolve the yeast in the warm water. In a **large bowl**, mix together 1-1/2 cups of the flour, sugar and salt; make a well in the centre and pour in dissolved yeast. Add the oil and egg mixing thoroughly. *(If a food processor or bread maker is used, combine ingredients and mix according to manufacturer's directions)*.

Place the dough onto a lightly floured **board** and knead for several minutes, adding more flour as necessary. Form into a ball, coat with oil, place into the bowl, cover and let rise until doubled in size, about 1-1/2 to 2-hours.

Fillings

Meanwhile, prepare one of the *Fruit Fillings*.

Punch down the dough, place onto the floured board, divide into half and with a floured **rolling pin**, roll out each section to 1/8-inch thickness. With a **2-inch cutter**, cut into circles.

Place half of circles onto a greased **baking sheet** and place 1-teaspoon of filling in centers. Brush the edges with water; place another circle on top and press together with the tines of a fork.

Cover and allow rising in a warm place until doubled in size, 1-1/2 to 2 hours. Bake for 10 to 12-minutes remove to cooling rack and dust with Confectioners' sugar.

Crispy Sapodilla Roll-ups

Crust for *Peach Turnovers page 274*
6 medium to large sapodillas (firm-ripe)
1/2 to 1 cup filling
1 tbsp. butter

Bake at 350°F

Prepare the crust, chill for about 30-minutes. Place onto a floured **board** and, with a floured **rolling pin**, roll out to 1/4-inch thickness. Cut into squares large enough to wrap around the varying sizes of sapodillas.

Wash the sapodillas thoroughly and with a **small paring knife**, cut around the tops of the dillies about 1-1/2-inches. With a teaspoon, scoop out the centre membrane and all seeds, forming a cavity.

Place the sapodillas in the centre of the squares. Draw up the sides, overlapping at the top; press together securely and flute.

Grease a **baking sheet** with butter; arrange the rolled up sapodillas on the sheet and bake for 20 to 25-minutes until the crust is golden brown.

Gently remove to a **cooling rack** and let cool. Serve warm with *Soka Hard Rum Sauce page 315* or ice cream of your choice.

Avocado Lime Pie

1 Baked 9-inch Pie Shell page 271
1 large ripe avocado for 1 cup purée
1 can (8 oz.) sweetened condensed milk
1 tsp. grated lime rind
1/2 cup lime juice
2 egg yolks, lightly beaten
Dash of salt

Prepare and bake the pie shell.

Cut the avocado in half and, with a **melon baller**; scoop out about 8 balls for garnish. With a spoon, remove remaining pulp to the bowl of a **blender** and purée. Measure out 1-cup.

In a **medium-sized bowl**, combine the purée, milk, lime rind and juice. Add the lightly beaten egg yolks and salt, stirring until the mixture thickens. Fold in the rest of the avocado purée.

Turn into the baked pie shell and place in refrigerator chilling thoroughly. Garnish with mint leaves and the avocado balls.

Paradise Pie
Green Mango

Crust

2 cups all purpose flour
3 tsp. baking powder
3 tbsp. sugar
1/2 tsp. salt
1/3 cup vegetable shortening
1/2 cup milk
1 egg, well beaten

Filling

4 large green mangoes (4 to 5 cups)
1 cup sugar
2 tbsp. all purpose flour
1 tsp. ground cinnamon
1 tsp. ground nutmeg
1-1/2 tbsp. butter, softened
2 eggs, slightly beaten
1/4 cup canned coconut milk

Bake at 325ºF

Crust

In a **medium sized bowl**, sift together the flour, baking powder, sugar and salt. With a **pastry cutter**, cut in the shortening until the mixture resembles coarse crumbs.

Make a well in the middle of the mixture; mix in the milk and beaten egg to form firm dough. Divide the dough into two equal sized balls.

Place one of the balls onto a floured **board** and, with a floured **rolling pin,** roll out to1/4-inch thickness. Line a greased **9-inch pie pan**. Roll out the second ball and set aside for the top

Filling

Peel the mangoes, cut the flesh away from the seed, cut into thin slices and place into a **large bowl**.

In **another bowl**, mix together the flour, sugar, cinnamon and nutmeg and combine with the mango slices. Add the butter, eggs and coconut milk mixing well.

Turn the mixture into the lined pie pan and cover with the top crust. Press the edges together and flute. Cut decorative slots in the top and bake for 45 to 50-minutes.

Paradise Pie à la Mode

Serve warm *Paradise Pie* with *Rum Raisin Ice Cream page 346.*

Cocoa Rum Pie

9-inch" Coconut Crust page 270

Filling

1/2 cup sugar
1 envelope unflavoured gelatin
1/2 tsp. salt
1-1/4 cups milk
3 eggs, separated
3 tbsp. Ole Nassau Jack Malantan Rum
1/2 cup heavy cream, whipped
2 tbsp. powdered cocoa
3 tbsp. hot water
1/2 cup finely chopped almonds
Whipped cream for topping

Prepare the crust. Bake and chill for about 30 minutes.

In a **2-quart sized saucepan**, combine 1/4-cup of the sugar, the gelatin, salt and milk. Beat the egg yolks lightly and stir into the mixture.

Over very low heat, cook, stirring constantly with a large **wooden spoon**, until thickened. Remove from heat, stirring in the rum.

Refrigerate the mixture, chilling until it starts to thicken.

In a **small mixing bowl**, with **electric mixer**, beat the egg whites, gradually adding remaining sugar until stiff.

Mix the cocoa with the hot water in a **small bowl** and allow to cool. Remove the chilled mixture; fold in the egg whites, whipped cream and mixed cocoa. Return to refrigerator and chill until mixture starts to set.

Turn into the pie crust and chill until firm at least 4-hours, overnight is best. Top with whipped cream (optional).

Caribbean Sweet Potato Pie

Unbaked *9-inch Double Pie Shell* page 271
1 cocount freshly grated to produce 2 cups
4 medium-sized yams or red sweet potatoes
1/2 tsp. salt
3/4 cup sugar
1 grated lemon rind
1 tsp. freshly grated nutmeg
1 tsp. ground cinnamon
2 eggs, well beaten
2 tbsp. Ole Nassau Coconut Rum
2 tbsp. melted butter

Bake at 350°F

Prepare the pie shell and prepare the 1-inch wide strips of dough for the lattice top. Prepare the fresh coconut *page 24*.

Pour water enough to cover potatoes into a **3-quart sized saucepan**, add the salt and bring to a boil. Place the peeled potatoes into the boiling water and cook until soft when tested with a sharp knife. Turn into a **food mill** *or colander* placed over a **large bowl**, drain and mash using the food mill.

Add the coconut and remaining ingredients to the large bowl mixing together thoroughly. Turn into the unbaked pie shell and decorate the top by overlapping the strips of dough.

Bake for 45-minutes or until a knife inserted into the centre comes out clean. Allow to cool and serve with whipped cream if desired.

Rum Pineapple Custard Pie

Unbaked *9-inch Coconut Crust* page 270
Custard

2 eggs
1/3 cup sugar
2 tbsp. all purpose flour
3/4 cup heavy cream
4 tbsp. Ole Nassau Pineapple Rum

Topping

1 cup pineapple chunks (drained)
Bake at 350°F

Prepare crust and set aside. In a **small mixing bowl** with **electric mixer**, beat the eggs and sugar until light and fluffy. Continue mixing adding the flour until the mixture is smooth. Add the cream and rum. Turn into the pie shell and bake for 40 to 45-minutes until centre is set. Allow to cool and decorate top with drained pineapple chunks.

Bahamian Pumpkin Pie

9-inch Pie Shell page 271

1 envelope unflavoured gelatin
3/4 cup sugar
1/2 tsp. ground cinnamon
1/2 tsp. ground nutmeg
1/4 tsp. salt
1/2 cup milk
3 slightly beaten egg yolks
1 can (16 oz.) pumpkin
1/4 cup Makers Mark Bourbon
3 egg whites
2 tbsp. sugar
Whipped cream

Prepare the pie crust and allow to cool.

In a **2-quart sized saucepan**, combine the gelatin, sugar, cinnamon, nutmeg and salt. Stir in the milk, beaten egg yolks and canned pumpkin. Cook over medium heat stirring with a **wooden spoon** until the mixture thickens and just begins to boil.

Remove the saucepan from the heat stirring in the bourbon. Chill the mixture until partially set.

In a **small mixing bowl** with **electric mixer**, beat the egg whites gradually adding the sugar until stiff peaks are formed. Gently fold into the pumpkin mixture.

Pile into the pie crust and refrigerate for several hours or until the mixture is set. Cut into wedges and serve topped with whipped cream sprinkled with a little nutmeg if desired.

Soursop

Like the sugar apple and the pomegranate, the soursop is a member of the "Segmented Fruit" family. The fruit is large and green, filled with "cottony" snow-white pulp and deliciously flavoured juice. It has fleshy, curved spines, may be oval or conical or oddly irregular and misshapen and is often curved or knobbed at the smaller end. It is picked from the tree when still firm and kept at room temperature until it gradually ripens and softens.

When slightly soft to the touch, the fruit is ready to be eaten. At this stage, it must be handled with especial care, for the skin, while leathery in appearance, is thin and tender and easily punctured.

Although the less acid fruits may be cut melon-style, in lengthwise portions, or the pulp may be removed from the skin, seeded and sweetened, the real fame of the soursop is based on the use of the pulp, pureed, blended with milk or brandy as a beverage or added to ice cream mix just prior to freezing. ❋

284

Soursop Pie

9-inch Coconut Crust page 270

Filling

1 medium-sized ripe soursop for 4 cups puree page 27
1 can (8 oz.) sweetened condensed milk
2 envelopes unflavoured gelatin
1/2 cup cold water
1/2 cup coconut milk
1 tsp. vanilla extract

Prepare and bake the crust. Place the soursop pulp into a **large mixing bowl** and stir in the sweet milk. Turn the mixture into the bowl of a **food processor** fitted with the knife blade and process for 2-minutes. Turn the purée back into the large mixing bowl.

In a **1-quart saucepan**, sprinkle the gelatin over the 1/2-cup of water and let stand 1-minute. Stir over low heat until the gelatin is completely dissolved.

With **electric mixer**, gradually beat the gelatin mixture with the soursop mixture adding the coconut milk and vanilla extract beating until smooth. Place the bowl into refrigerator and chill for 1-hour. Turn into the prepared crust; place into refrigerator and chill until firm.

Sapodilla Pie

Unbaked 9-inch Pie Shell page 271

Filling

4 large ripe sapodillas
1/4 cup milk
1/4 cup sugar
1/4 tsp. ground cinnamon
1/4 tsp. ground nutmeg
1/4 tsp. salt
2 eggs, slightly beaten

Topping
Whipped Cream (optional)

Prepare the crust and set aside. Peel the sapodillas, mash three with a fork and thinly slice the fourth (horizontally). In a **medium-sized bowl**, beat the eggs. Using a **large wooden spoon**, gently mix in the mashed sapodilla, milk, sugar, cinnamon, nutmeg and salt.

In a **medium-sized bowl**, beat the eggs. Using the wooden spoon, gently mix in the mashed sapodilla, milk, sugar, cinnamon, nutmeg and salt. Turn the mixture into the piecrust, smooth out and place the sapodilla slices in a decorative pattern. Bake for 45-minutes, serve warm or cold with whipped or ice cream.

Sugar Apple Pie

9-inch Coconut Crust page 270

Filling

4 medium-sized ripe sugar apples for 4 cups purée page 27
2 envelopes unflavoured gelatin
1/2 cup cold water
1/2 cup canned coconut milk
1 tsp. vanilla extract

Prepare the crust and set aside.

Place the pulp into the bowl of a **food processor** fitted with the knife blade and process for 2-minutes. Turn back into the large mixing bowl.

In a **1-quart saucepan**, sprinkle the gelatin over 1/2-cup of the cold water and let stand 1-minute. Stir over low heat until the gelatin is completely dissolved.

With **electric mixer**, gradually beat the gelatin mixture with the sugar apple mixture adding the coconut milk and vanilla extract, beating until smooth.

Place the bowl into refrigerator and chill for 1-hour. Turn into the prepared crust; place into refrigerator and chill until firm.

Sugar & Spice

Europeans of the fifteenth century wanted routes to the Orient, the Spice Islands, in large part to obtain the spices that enabled them to preserve their usually spoilt meat and other food making it in some way palatable. However, they landed in the west where there were no spices, but found that the climate in this part of the world was also conducive to growing spices and many Old World crops. Sugar-cane (Saccharin) originally from southeastern Asia thrived in the warm humid lowlands, and once Europeans had a taste of it, their lust for the sugar of the Americas became an addiction - and a major reason for much of the colonization.

Sugar Apple

Originally from South America, the sugar apple or sweet sop is a cousin of the soursop and pomegranate which are know as "Segmented Fruit". Like the pomegranate, it is packed with seeds with a thin layer of pulp covering each seed.

Sugar apple contains dextrose, 18% sugar, and is usually "eaten out of hand".

The outer layer of the fist-sized fruit appears leathery and is green even when ripe. The delicate, delicious, white, sweet pulp is described as tasting like "strawberries and cream". ❀

Tequilime Pie

9-inch Crumb Crust page 270
Grated rind of 2 fresh limes
1/2 cup freshly squeezed lime juice
3 eggs, separated
4 tbsp. all purpose flour
5 tbsp. cornstarch
1-3/4 cups sugar
1/2 tsp. salt
1-1/2 cups boiling water
1/2 cup Tequila Sauza Commemorative
1/4 tsp. cream of tartar

Bake at 425°F

Prepare the crust and allow to cool.

In a **2-quart sized saucepan**, combine the flour, cornstarch, salt and 1-1/2-cups of the sugar and the Tequila Sauza. Using a wire **whisk**, whisk thoroughly.

In a **separate saucepan** *or kettle*, bring the water to a boil and, while whisking, gradually add the boiling water to the saucepan. Continue to a boil, stirring constantly, for about 5-minutes or until the mixture is thickened. Remove from the heat.

In a **small mixing bowl** with **electric mixer**, beat the egg yolks until very light. Spoon a little of the hot mixture into the yolks, then stir the yolk mixture into the sauce. Cook, stirring, for 2-minutes over low heat. Stir in the lime rind and lime juice, mixing well. Pour into the baked pie shell and allow to cool.

Meringue

In the **small mixing bowl**, with **electric mixer**, beat the egg whites until frothy, adding the cream of tartar while beating. Add the remaining 1/4-cup of the sugar gradually until the whites form stiff peaks.

Spread on top of the pie filling, forming peaks. Bake for 10 to 15-minutes or until meringue is brown.

Tropical Yogurt Pie

9-inch Coconut Crust page 270

Filling

2 cups puréed fruit (listed below)
2 cups plain yogurt
1/2 to 1 can (8 oz.) sweetened condensed milk
2 envelopes unflavoured gelatin
1 cup cold water

Prepare the *Coconut Crust* bake and set aside.

In a **medium-sized mixing bowl** with **electric mixer** set at low speed, mix together the puréed fruit, yogurt and milk.

In a **1-quart saucepan**, sprinkle the gelatin in water and let sit for 1-minute. Over very low heat, cook, stirring constantly, until the gelatin is completely dissolved, about 5 or 6-minutes.

Set the mixer on medium speed; pour the gelatin slowly into the fruit mixture and beat for 3 or 4-minutes.

Remove the bowl to refrigerator and chill for 1 hour. Turn the chilled mixture into the coconut crust *(or other baked crust)*. Chill thoroughly, preferably overnight. Serve chilled.

Fruits

Mango • Pineapple • Papaya • Sugar Apple • Guava • Sapodilla

Key Lime Rum Pie

9-inch Crumb Crust page 270

Filling

2 pkgs. (8 oz. each) cream cheese, softened
1/3 cup freshly squeezed lime juice
2 envelopes unflavoured gelatin
1 tsp. grated lime rind
1-1/2 cups cold water
2 tbsp. Ole Nassau Chick Charney Rum
4 to 6 drops green food colouring
2/3 cup sugar

Topping

1/2 pint heavy cream
3 tbsp. Confectioners' sugar
1 tbsp. Ole Nassau Chick Charney Rum

Prepare crust and set aside.

Filling

In a **1-quart saucepan**, sprinkle the gelatin over 1/4-cup of cold water and let stand for 1-minute. Stir over low heat until the gelatin is completely dissolved. Remove from heat. Add remaining cold water.

In a **large mixing bowl** with **electric mixer**, beat the cream cheese, sugar and rum until blended. Gradually beat in the lime juice, rind and gelatin mixture. Add the food colouring.

Turn the mixture into the prepared crust.

Topping

In a **small mixing bowl** with the **electric mixer**, whip the cream, *Confectioners'* sugar and rum together until stiff. Spread on top of the pie and chill well.

Mango Pie

Unbaked No Need to Knead Pie Shell page 270

Filling

3 large half-ripe mangoes for 4 cups sliced
3/4 cup sugar
1/2 cup lemon juice
1/2 tsp. ground cinnamon
1/2 tsp. ground nutmeg
1/2 tsp. ground allspice

Topping

3/4 cup all purpose flour
1/2 cup sugar
1/3 cup butter

Bake at 350°F

Prepare the pie shell and set aside.

Filling

Peel the mangoes; slice the flesh from the seed and place into a **medium-sized bowl**. Using a **wooden spoon**, mix all ingredients together and turn into the pie shell.

Topping

Mix the flour, sugar and butter together until crumbly. Sprinkle on top of the pie.

Bake for about 55-minutes to 1-hour or until centre is firm. Cool and serve with whipped cream or ice cream.

Notes

Cakes
Cookies
Dessert
Sauces &
Icings

Recipes

❋ Pound Cakes

Pina Colada, Olga's Pound

Big Gramma's Pound

Big Gramma's Birthday

❋ Fruitcakes

Traditional, Banana, Miniature

❋ Cakes

Ole Nassau Rum, Mango Rum,

Guava Jam, Guava Upside Down

Sapodilla Bundt, Merdina Carrot

Guava Duff

❋ Cookies

Coconut Wafers, Coconut Crisps

High Tea Cookies

Slice & Bake Guava

Tortilla Sandwich, Calypso

Chic Charney Moca

Ginger Bread Collier Boys

Fruitcake, Coconut Brownies

❋ Frostings & Icings

Whipped Cream Frosting

Cocoa Whipped Frosting

Rum Whipped Cream Frosting

Creamy Frosting

Soka Hard Rum Sauce

Rum Runner Brown Sugar Sauce

❋ Glazes & Sauces

Pineapple Glaze, Mango Glaze

Guava Glaze, Sapodilla Glaze

Rum Glaze

Coconut Cream for Dessert

Lemon Sauce for Dessert

Tamarind Sauce

❋ Syrups

Sapodilla, Mango, Lemon

Piña Colada Cake

1 pkg. (18 oz.) White Cake Mix with pudding
4 eggs
1 cup water
1/4 cup vegetable oil
1/3 cup Ole Nassau Coconut Rum

Filling

1 fresh ripe pineapple, finely chopped
or 1 can (12 oz.) pineapple, drained & crushed
1 pkg. (4 servings) Coconut Cream Instant Pudding and Pie Filling mix
1/2 cup Ole Nassau Coconut Rum

Frosting

1 container (9 oz.) frozen whipped topping, thawed
1 cup flaked coconut

Bake at 350°F

Combine all of the cake ingredients in a **large mixing bowl** and with **electric mixer**; beat 4-minutes at medium speed.

Divide the batter between **two 9-inch layer cake pans**, greased and floured. Bake for 25 to 30-minutes and allow to cool.

Filling

Prepare the pineapple *page 25*, drain off the juice and place into a **medium-sized mixing bowl**. With electric mixer, beat together remaining filling ingredients, until well blended. Spread between the layers.

Frosting

In a **small bowl**, fold together the whipped topping and coconut. Frost the sides and top of the cake. Sprinkle with additional coconut if desired.

Olga's Pound Cake

1 pkg. (18 oz.) Yellow Cake Mix
1 pkg. (4 oz.) Vanilla Pudding & Pie Filling Mix
1 cup (1/2 pt.) sour cream
4 eggs
1/3 cup Canola oil
1/4 tsp. ground mace
Bake at 350°F

Combine all ingredients in a **large mixing bowl** and with **electric mixer** blend at low speed just to moisten. Scrape the sides of the bowls.

With mixer at medium speed, beat for 3-minutes. Grease a **10-inch tube pan** and line the bottom with parchment or waxed paper. Turn the mixture into the pan and bake for 55-minutes.

Cool in the pan placed on a **wire rack** for 15-minutes. Loosen from the sides, remove from the pan and cool completely.

Big Gramma's Pound Cake

1 pound butter (2 cups)
1 pound sugar (2 cups)
9 eggs
1 tsp. vanilla extract
1 tsp. rum extract
1 tsp. brandy extract
4 cups Cake flour
1/2 tsp. cream of tarter
1/2 tsp. salt
Bake at 325°F

In a **large mixing bowl** with **electric mixer**, cream the butter thoroughly. Add the sugar one tablespoonful at a time and continue to cream the butter and sugar beating in the eggs one at a time. Continue to beat, adding the extracts one at a time.

Sift together the flour, cream of tarter and salt. With the mixer on low speed, blend in small amounts of the flour at a time. With the mixer set at medium speed, mix thoroughly.

Grease **two loaf pans** and line with parchment or waxed paper (allow paper to extend over the sides of the pans for easy removal of the cakes) and bake for about 1-hour. Remove to **cooling racks** and allow to cool.

Big Gramma's Birthday Cake

Prepare *Big Gramma's Pound Cake* recipe; remove 1/3 of batter to a **small bowl**.

❋ *Grandsons* - Stir 1-teaspoon blue food colouring into the 1/3 portion of batter until blended.

❋ *Granddaughters* - Stir 1-teaspoon red food colouring into the 1/3 portion of batter until blended.

Grease a **10-inch round cake pan** and line with parchment or waxed paper. Turn the 2/3 portion of the batter into the pan.

Drop tablespoonfuls of the coloured batter about 2-inches apart on top of the batter in the pan, and using a knife, swirl in the coloured batter.

Bake for about 1-hour on top rack of the oven. Remove to a **cooling rack**.

Big Gramma never topped her cakes with icing because they were carefully boxed and shipped to her grandchildren. Moms would prepare the icing, decorating the cakes with our children's names.

Lady Darling and her mum, Big Gramma,
decorate a birthday cake

Holiday Fruitcakes

Two 10-inch Cakes

1 lb. brown sugar
1 lb. butter
1 dozen eggs
4 cups Cake flour
4 tsp. baking powder
1 tbsp. ground cinnamon
1 tbsp. ground cloves
1 tbsp. ground allspice
1 tbsp. ground nutmeg
1/2 tsp. ground mace
1 cup Ole Nassau Jack Malantan Rum
1 lb. chopped dates
2-1/2 lbs. currants
2-1/2 lbs. raisins
1 lb. citron (chopped fruit)
1 lb. pecan, chopped
1 lb. walnuts, chopped

Bake at 300°F

TIP:
Drizzle the cooled Fruitcakes with rum and store in an airtight container or wrap tightly in heavy foil allowing 3 to 4 weeks before serving.

In a **large bowl with cover**, combine the fruit, currants, raisins, dates and nuts with the rum. Cover and "soak" for at least a few days, stirring occasionally. (No need to refrigerate).

Grease and flour **two 10-inch spring release tube pans** or line tube pans **with parchment or wax paper**.

In a **large bowl**, sift together the flour, salt, baking powder and spices.

In a **large mixing bowl** with **electric mixe**r, cream the butter, sugar and eggs. Gradually mix in the sifted dry ingredients.

With a **large wooden spoon**, stir the batter into the bowl with the fruit "soak", mixing thoroughly. Turn into the prepared pans and bake for 2-1/2-hours. Place a **pan of water** on the bottom rack of oven to keep the cakes from drying out.

Remove to **cooling racks** and sprinkle additional rum over cooled cakes.

Banana Fruitcake

3-1/2 cups Cake flour
4 tsp. baking powder
1 tsp. salt
1/2 tsp. baking soda
2 tsp. ground cinnamon
2 tsp. ground ginger
1/2 tsp. ground nutmeg
1/2 tsp. ground allspice
1 cup butter, softened
1-1/3 cups sugar
4 eggs
2 cups mashed banana (3 to 4 ripe bananas)
1 cup raisins
1 cup currants
1 cup chopped walnuts
1 cup chopped almonds
4 cups diced glazed fruit

Bake at 300°F

Peel and mash the bananas. Sift together the flour, baking powder and salt. Mix together the spices and baking soda, adding to the flour mix.

In a **large mixing bowl** with **electric mixer**, beat together the butter and sugar. Beat in the eggs one at a time adding the flour mixture alternately with the banana pulp.

Combine the raisins, currants, nuts and glazed fruit. Stir into the batter, using a **wooden spoon**.

Turn the batter into a greased and floured **10-inch Bundt pan** and place on the centre rack of the oven. Bake for 1-1/2 to 2-hours or until a knife comes out clean when inserted in the centre.

Miniature Fruitcakes

1/2 cup currants
1/2 cup raisins
1/2 lb. candied pineapple, chopped
1/4 lb. candied orange, chopped
1/4 lb. candied citron, chopped
1/4 lb. glazed cherries, quartered
1/4 lb. candied lemon, chopped
3 cups pecans, walnuts or almonds
1/2 cup Ole Nassau Jack Malantan Rum
1/4 cup butter
3/4 cup light brown sugar
2 eggs
2 cups Cake flour
1/2 tsp. ground cloves
1/2 tsp. ground nutmeg
1/2 tsp. ground allspice
1/2 tsp. salt
1/2 tsp. baking soda

Bake at 325°F

In a **large bowl with cover**, combine the fruit, currants, raisins, dates and nuts with the rum. Cover and "soak" for at least a few days, stirring occasionally. (No need to refrigerate).

In a **large mixing bowl** with **electric mixer**, cream together the butter and brown sugar, beating in the eggs.

In a **separate bowl**, sift together the flour, cloves, nutmeg, allspice, salt and baking soda. Fold into the batter and beat for 2-minutes.

Using a **wooden spoon**, fold in the rum-soaked fruit and nuts and the remaining ingredients into the flour mixture.

Grease the **muffing tins** or insert **paper bake cups**. Drop 2-tablespoonfuls of batter into each cup and bake for about 25 to 30-minutes.

Carefully remove the mini cakes to a cooling rack and sprinkle with rum or brandy. Cool completely, serve or store in an **airtight container**.

Ole Nassau Rum Cake

3 cups all purpose flour
2 tsp. baking powder
1/2 cup packed light brown sugar
1/2 tsp. salt
8 oz. unsalted butter
1-1/2 cups milk
1/3 cup Ole Nassau Chick Charney Rum
3 eggs
2 cups chopped walnuts

Glaze

1-1/4 cups sugar
1/3 cup water
1/2 cup Ole Nassau Chick Charney Rum
1 oz. butter
4 cups Confectioners' sugar

Bake at 350°F

In a **bowl**, combine the flour, sugar, baking powder and salt. Using a **pastry cutter**, cut in the butter until mixture resembles rice grains.

In a **large mixing bowl**, combine the milk, rum and eggs and, with **electric mixer**, beat until blended.

Slowly add the flour mixture and beat well for about 3-minutes. Turn the batter into a greased and floured **tube pan** or *Bundt pan* and bake for 55-minutes to 1-hour or until the top of the cake springs back when touched.

Glaze

In a **saucepan**, combine the sugar and water and bring to a boil. Add the rum and turn off the heat. Add the butter and stir until melted. Pour 3/4-cup of this syrup into a **separate container** for soaking the cake.

Add 2-cups of the Confectioners' sugar to the remaining syrup and whisk until smooth. Add remaining sugar as needed to make a thick but pourable glaze. When the cake is done, cool for 15-minutes in the pan.

Invert the cake onto a **cooling rack** with a large plate underneath to catch drippings from the glaze. With a skewer or **toothpick**, pierce the cake all over and spoon reserved rum syrup over to soak. Transfer to a **serving plate** and pour the glaze over, then sprinkle with remaining walnuts.

Guava Jam Cake

1 pkg. (18 oz.) Yellow Cake Mix
2 eggs
1 cup Sawyer's Guava Jam
1/4 cup vegetable oil
1/2 cup canned coconut milk
3/4 cup water

Bake at 350ºF

In a **large mixing bowl**, combine the cake mix, eggs, guava jam, oil, coconut milk, and water. With **electric mixer** set at medium speed, beat for 2-minutes.

Grease and flour a **10-inch Bundt** *or tube pan*. Turn the batter into the pan and bake for 35 to 40-minutes or until a knife comes out clean when inserted into the centre.

Guava Upside Down Cake

10 to 12 large guavas
Maraschino cherries
2 tbsp. butter
2 tbsp. sugar
1 pkg. (18 oz.) Yellow Cake Mix
1-1/4 cup water
1/4 cup vegetable oil
3 eggs

Bake at 350°F

Melt the butter in a **large heavy iron skillet** or a 10-inch round baking pan. Sprinkle the sugar over the bottom of the pan and place the cherries a few inches apart around the pan.

Peel the guavas, cut into halves and using a teaspoon, scoop out the seeds. Place the guava halves over the cherries.

Combine the cake mix, water, oil and eggs in a **large mixing bowl** and with electric mixer, beat for 2-minutes. Pour over the guava halves and bake for 35 to 40-minutes or until a knife comes out clean when inserted into the centre.

Allow cake to cool in the pan for 10 to 15-minutes. Turn from the pan upside down onto a **cake plate**.

Sugarcane

Sugarcane that we eat originated in China and India and is a grass that can grow as tall as 15 feet, growing best in warm tropical climates. The sugarcane was brought to the New World on Columbus' second voyage and planted in Santo Domingo as early as 1493. Large sugar plantations were established on the islands of the Caribbean.

Of nearly 10 million slaves debarked in the New World, the majority was brought during the 18th century. Slaves were used for many different purposes in the Western Hemisphere. None were as important as in the sugar industry.

The growth in the scale of the sugar industry and the market for its products did much to expand the commerce in human beings. Large numbers of men and women were needed to work the plantations. It has been recorded that to run the smallest plantation required 250 persons.

The sugar is extracted from the mature crop by crushing the stems. Apart from sugar, by products of the industry include molasses from which rum is made. ✳

Sapodilla Bundt Cake

4 medium-sized sapodillas for 2 cups purée *page 27*
2 cups sugar
1/2 cup vegetable oil
4 eggs
3 cups all purpose flour
3 tsp. baking powder
2 tsp. baking soda
1 tsp. salt
2 tsp. ground cinnamon
1 cup chopped nuts
1 cup raisins

Creamy Frosting

1 pkgs. (8 oz.) cream cheese
2 cups Confectioners' sugar
1 cup shredded coconut

Prepare sapodillas.

In a **large mixing bowl** with **electric mixer**, mix together, sugar, oil and purée, beating well. Add the eggs, one at a time, beating well after each addition.

Sift together the flour, baking powder and baking soda, cinnamon and salt. Fold into the batter and fold in the nuts and raisins.

Turn the batter into a greased **10-inch Bundt pan** and bake for about 1-hour or until a knife comes out clean when inserted into the centre. Place onto a **cooling rack** and cool.

Frosting

In a **small bowl**, mix together the sugar and butter; blend in the softened cream cheese and shredded coconut. Spread over the top and side of cake.

Merdina Carrot Cake

2-1/4 cups all purpose flour
1-1/2 cups sugar
2 tsp. baking soda
1-1/2 tsp. ground cinnamon
1/2 tsp. salt
1 cup vegetable oil
3 eggs
1/2 cup milk
2 cups shredded carrot
1-1/2 cups flaked coconut
1/2 cup chopped nuts
1/2 cup currants or raisins

Frosting

1 pkg. (3 oz.) cream cheese, softened
2 tbsp. butter
2 tbsp. milk
1/4 tsp. vanilla extract
1/8 tsp. salt
2 to 2-1/4 cups Confectioners' sugar

Bake at 325°F

In a **large mixing bowl** of **electric mixer**, sift together the flour, sugar, baking soda, cinnamon, nutmeg and salt. Make a well in the centre and pour in the oil, add the eggs, milk and shredded carrot. With the mixer set on low speed, mix until ingredients are moistened, scraping the sides of the bowl constantly.

Beat at medium speed for 2-minutes and stir in remaining cake ingredients. Turn into a well-greased **13x9-inch pan** and bake for 55 to 60-minutes or until a knife inserted in the centre comes out clean. Place the cake on a **cooling rack** and cool completely.

Frosting

In a **small mixing bowl**, blend the cream cheese and butter mixing well. Mix in the milk, vanilla and salt. Stir in enough Confectioners' sugar for desired consistency. Spread on the cooled cake.

Coconut Wafers

1 large freshly grated coconut for 2 cups page 24
1 cup sugar
1/2 cup butter
1 cup all purpose flour
1 tsp. baking powder
Bake at 350°F

In a **small bowl**, mix together the sugar, butter and coconut.

Sift together the flour and baking powder. Combine with the coconut mixture, mixing well.

Place onto a floured **board** and, with a floured **rolling pin**, roll out very thin. Cut with a **cookie cutter** and place onto a greased **baking sheet**.

Bake for a few minutes only until the cookies are brown. Allow to cool on the baking sheet for a few minutes before removing to a **cooling rack**.

Coconut Crisps

1 cup freshly grated coconut page 24
1/2 cup all purpose flour
1 tsp. baking powder
1 oz. butter
2/3 cup milk
Bake at 350°F

Spread the grated coconut in a **baking pan** and toast in the oven for 10-minutes, stirring for even browning. Allow to cool.

In a **medium-sized bowl**, sift together the flour and baking powder. In a **1-quart saucepan**, heat the milk and melt the butter in the hot milk. Allow to cool and stir into the flour mixture. Add the coconut, mixing to a smooth paste.

Turn onto a well-greased **baking sheet** and flatten to 1/2-inch thickness. Cut into squares; return to the oven and bake for 15 to 20-minutes. Cool completely before serving.

Guava Duff Cake

Batter

2 cups all purpose flour
2 tsp. baking powder
1/2 tsp. salt
2 tbsp. sugar
1/3 cup vegetable shortening
1 cup milk

Filling

12 medium to large ripe guavas
1 cup guava purée
1 oz. sugar
1 oz. water
1 tsp. ground cinnamon
1 tsp. ground allspice
Soka Hard Rum Sauce page 315

Bake at 350°F

Filling

Prepare the guavas and the purée *page 26*. In a **1-quart saucepan**, combine the sugar and water; bring to a boil, stirring continuously. Lower the heat and cook for 20-minutes. Remove from the heat. Add the guava, purée and spices mixing well.

Batter

In a **large bowl**, sift together the flour, baking powder, salt and sugar. With a **pastry cutter**, cut in the shortening until the mixture is consistency of rice grains.

Mix in the milk to form a smooth batter. Spread half the batter in a well-greased **9x12-inch pan**. Spread the filling over the batter and spread remaining batter over the filling. Bake for 35 to 40-minutes.

Allow the cake to remain in the pan cooling, but not completely. Spread the *Soka Hard Rum Sauce* over the warm cake and serve.

Slice & Bake Guava Cookies

Yield 4 Dozen

1 cup softened butter
1 cup Confectioners' sugar
1/2 cup sugar
1 egg
2 tsp. rum extract
2-1/4 cups all purpose flour
1/2 tsp. baking soda
1 cup diced guava page 26

Bake at 350°F

In a **medium-sized mixing bowl** with **electric mixer**, cream the butter and sugar adding the egg and rum extract. Beat until light and fluffy.

Sift together the flour and baking soda. Add to the bowl mixing well. Shape into a 12-inch roll; cover and chill until firm. Slice into 1/4-inch slices.

Place on a **non-stick cookie sheet** and bake for 10 to 12-minutes. Remove to a **wire rack** and cool.

Fruitcake Cookies

Maraschino cherries
Batter for *Holiday Fruitcake page 298*
Confectioners' sugar

Bake at 400ºF

Prepare the batter and chill for about 30 minutes.

Drop one heaping tablespoonful of chilled batter onto greased **baking sheets** about 2-inches apart. Press a cherry into each cookie and bake for about 15-minutes.

Cool slightly on the baking sheets and, using a **pancake turner**, carefully remove to a **cooling rack**. Dust with Confectioners' sugar and store in **air-tight containers**.

High Tea Cookies

3-1/4 cups all purpose flour
3/4 tsp. baking powder
3/4 tsp. baking soda
1 tsp. ground cinnamon
1/4 tsp. ground cloves
1/4 tsp. ground nutmeg
1/4 tsp. salt
1-1/2 tsp. vegetable oil
7 tbsp. frozen orange juice concentrate, thawed
1/3 cup sugar
1-1/2 tsp. grated orange peel
1-1/4 tsp. very finely chopped pecans, divided
1/4 cup honey

Bake at 350ºF

In a **medium-sized bowl**, mix together the flour, baking powder, baking soda, spices and salt. Set aside.

In a **large bowl with a cover**, combine 6-tablespoons of the orange juice concentrate, sugar and orange peel. Blend in the flour mixture and stir in 3/4-cup of the pecans. Cover and refrigerate for 2-hours.

Shape the chilled dough into 2-1/2-inch cookies and place about 2-inches apart on an ungreased **baking shee**t. Flatten to 1/2-inch thickness and bake for 12 to 16-minutes or until the edges are light brown. Gently remove to a **cooling rack** and cool completely.

In a **small bowl** blend together the honey and remaining 1-tablespoon of orange concentrate. Drizzle over the cooled cookies and sprinkle with remaining 1/2-cup of pecans.

Tortilla Sandwich Cookies

Yield about 2 Dozen

1/2 cup butter
1/2 cup light corn syrup
2/3 cup light brown sugar
1/2 teaspoon instant coffee powder
1 cup all purpose flour
4 teaspoons unsweetened cocoa
1/2 cup finely ground nuts

Kahlúa Filling

1-1/3 cups un-sifted Confectioners' sugar
6 tbsp. cocoa
4 tsp. hot water
3 tbsp. Kahlúa

Bake at 375ºF

In a **2-quart saucepan**, combine the butter, corn syrup and brown sugar; bring to boil. Remove from the heat.

In a **bowl**, combine remaining ingredients and stir into the hot mixture mixing well (consistency will be like thick syrup).

Drop by level measuring teaspoon about 2-inches apart onto greased **cookie sheets**. Bake for 5 to 6-minutes. Cool 2-minutes on the cookie sheet before removing with a **spatula** onto a **cooling rack**. Use the Kahlúa Filling to frost bottom of half the cookies. Join to another cookie to make a sandwich.

Kahlúa Filling

In a **small bowl**, mix together the sugar, cocoa and hot water until smooth. Add tablespoons of Kahlúa. Stir well until mixture becomes thick.

Chick Charney Mocha Cookies

4 oz. unsweetened chocolate, chopped
3 cups semisweet chocolate chips
4 oz. unsalted butter, cut into bits
3/4 cup all purpose flour
1/2 tsp. baking powder
1/2 tsp. salt
4 eggs
1-1/2 cups sugar
1-1/2 tsp. instant espresso powder
3 oz. Ole Nassau Chick Charney Rum

Bake at 350°F

In a **metal bowl** set over a **saucepan** of simmering water, melt the unsweetened chocolate, 1-1/2-cups of the chocolate chips and the butter, stirring until the mixture is smooth. Remove the bowl from the heat.

In a **small bowl**, stir together the flour, baking powder and the salt. In **another bowl**, beat the eggs with the sugar until the mixture is thick and pale. Beat in the espresso and the rum.

Fold the chocolate mixture into the egg mixture. Fold in the flour mixture and stir in the remaining 1-1/2-cups chocolate chips. Allow the batter to stand for a few minutes.

Drop the batter by tablespoonfuls onto **baking sheets** lined with **parchment paper** and bake for 8 to 10-minutes. Allow the cookies to cool on the baking sheet.

Calypso Cookies

1-1/4 cups all purpose flour
1/2 tsp. salt
1/2 tsp. baking soda
1 egg
1/2 tsp. vanilla extract
1 tsp. Ole Nassau Jack Malantan Rum
1/2 cup margarine
1/2 cup freshly grated coconut
3/4 cup brown sugar
2/3 cup chocolate chips

Bake at 375°F

Sift together the flour, salt and baking soda.

In a **large mixing bowl** with **electric mixer**, beat the margarine and sugar until fluffy. Add the egg, vanilla and rum, mixing well.

Add the sifted dry ingredients, beating well. Fold in the coconut and chocolate chips.

Drop tablespoonfuls of the mixture 2-inches apart onto a well-greased **baking sheet** and bake for 10 to 12-minutes.

Coconut Brownies

3/4 cup freshly grated coconut page 24
3/4 cup butter, melted
1 cup brown sugar
1 egg
1 tsp. rum extract
1/2 cup all purpose flour
1 tsp. baking powder

Bake at 350°F

In a **medium-sized mixing bowl** with **electric mixer**, beat together the melted butter, sugar, egg and rum extract mixing well.

In a **small bowl**, sift together the flour, baking powder and salt. Mix into the butter mixture.

Fold in the coconut and turn into a greased and floured **8x8-inch pan**. Bake for about 30-minutes. Cool and cut into bars.

Ginger Bread Collier Boys

6 cups all purpose flour
2 tsp. soda
1 tsp. salt
1 tsp. ground ginger
1 tsp. ground cloves
1 tsp. ground allspice
1 tsp. ground cinnamon
1/3 cup vegetable shortening
1 cup brown sugar (packed)
1-1/2 cups dark molasses
2/3 cup cold water

Bake at 350ºF

Sift together the flour, baking soda, salt and spices.

In a **large mixing bowl**, with **electric mixer**, cream the shortening, brown sugar and molasses until well blended. Mix in the water.

Stir in the mixture of dry ingredients. Chill.

Divide the dough into sections, enough to cut out a few boys at a time. Place onto a floured **board** and with a floured **rolling pin**, roll out to 1/2-inch thickness. Cut with a **gingerbread boy cutter** and, using a **pancake turner**, carefully transfer the boys to a greased **baking sheet**.

Press raisins into the dough for eyes, nose, mouth and shoe and cuff buttons. Other decorations can include bits of candied cherries and citrus for buttons and ties. Bake for about 15-minutes.

Cool slightly on the baking sheet and carefully remove to a **cooling rack** using the pancake turner.

Creamy Frosting page 314 (without nuts or coconut) can be used to make collars, belts and shoes.

Whipped Cream Frosting

2 cups Whipped Cream
1/2 cup Confectioners' sugar
1 tsp. vanilla extract

Place the Whipped Cream into a **small mixing bowl** and, with **electric mixer** set at high speed, gradually beat in the Confectioners' sugar and extract.

Cocoa Whipped Cream Frosting

2 cups Whipped Cream
1/2 cup Confectioners' sugar
3 tbsp. powdered cocoa
1 tsp. vanilla extract

Place the Whipped Cream into a **small mixing bowl** and, with **electric mixer** set at high speed, gradually beat in the Confectioners' sugar, cocoa and extract.

Rum Whipped Cream Frosting

2 cups Whipped Cream
1/2 cup Confectioners' sugar
1 tsp. Ole Nassau Chick Charney Rum

Place the Whipped Cream into a **small mixing bowl** and with **electric mixer** set at high speed, gradually beat in the Confectioners' sugar and rum.

Creamy Frosting

1 pkg. (4 oz.) cream cheese, softened
2 tbsp. butter, softened
2 tbsp. milk
1/4 tsp. vanilla extract
Dash of salt
2 to 2-1/4 cups Confectioners' sugar
1 cup shredded coconut (optional)
3/4 cup chopped nuts (optional)

Blend the softened cream cheese and butter in a **small bowl**. Add the milk, vanilla and salt, mixing well. Stir in the sugar mixing well. Mix in shredded coconut and chopped nuts. Spread on the cooled cake.

Soka Hard Rum Sauce

This sauce is personal to every Bahamian cook, so you have to stir it up to suit yourself. Some like it hot with lots of rum and some like it with granulated sugar as our grandmothers did. So add sugar and rum to make the sauce to your liking. I like Confectioners' sugar for a smoother sauce.

1/2 cup butter, softened
3 to 4 cups Confectioners' sugar
1/2 tsp. vanilla extract
2 tbsp. Ole Nassau Chick Charney Rum (approximately)

In a **small bowl**, using a wooden spoon, vigorously stir the softened butter adding the Confectioners' sugar, vanilla extract and rum according to consistency of your sauce.

Allow the sauce to set, even chill, and serve on hot or warm duffs, puddings or desserts.

Variation

Substitute other Ole Nassau flavoured rums, Coconut, Pineapple or Banana for Chick Charney Rum in the sauce, .

Rum Runner Brown Sugar Sauce

4 tbsp. dark brown sugar
2 oz. butter
4 tbsp. Ole Nassau Yer Ho Rum
Pinch nutmeg

In a **small mixing bowl** with **electric mixer**, cream the sugar and butter. Add the rum to the sugar and butter, beating well.

Turn the mixture into a **1-quart saucepan**. Over very low heat, stir continuously until well blended. Add the nutmeg just before serving.

Rum Glaze

1-1/4 cups sugar
1/3 cup water
1/2 cup Ole Nassau Chick Charney Rum
1 oz. butter
4 cups Confectioners' sugar

In a **1-quart saucepan**, combine the sugar and water and bring to a boil. Add the rum and turn off the heat. Add the butter and stir until melted.

Add 2 cups of the *Confectioners'* sugar and, with a **wire whisk**, whisk until smooth. Add remaining sugar as needed to make a thick but pourable glaze.

Pineapple Glaze

1/2 cup sugar
3 tbsp. cornstarch
3/4 cup fresh pineapple juice
1/2 tsp. salt
1 cup finely chopped pineapple, drained *page 25*

In a **1-quart saucepan**, mix together the sugar, cornstarch and salt. Stir in the juice and over low heat, stirring constantly, bring to a boil. Boil for 1-minute.

Remove from the heat and stir in the drained pineapple.

Mango Glaze

Substitute *1 cup mango juice and 1 cup mango purée page 27* for the pineapple.

Guava Glaze

Substitute *1 cup orange juice and 1 cup guava purée page 26* for the pineapple.

Sapodilla Glaze

Substitute *1 cup orange juice and 1 cup sapodilla purée page 27* for the pineapple.

Orange Glaze

1-1/4 cups sugar
1 cup freshly squeezed orange juice
1 tbsp. orange zest
1 oz. butter
4 cups Confectioners' sugar

In a **1-quart saucepan**, combine the sugar and orange juice and bring to a boil. Turn off the heat, add the butter and stir until melted.

Add 2-cups of the icing sugar and, with a **wire whisk**, whisk until smooth. Add remaining sugar as needed to make a thick but pourable glaze.

Coconut Cream for Desserts

1-1/2 cups freshly grated coconut *page 24*
1/2 cup coconut milk (fresh or canned)
1/2 cup light cream
Dash of salt
1 tbsp. sugar

Combine all ingredients in a **container**; close tightly and let stand in refrigerator for a few hours.

Turn into the bowl of a **blender** and purée. Serve over fresh or canned tropical fruits.

Lemon Sauce for Dessert

1/4 cup sugar
2 tbsp. cornstarch
1-1/4 cups boiling water
1/2 cup white corn syrup
Dash of salt
1/3 cup freshly squeezed lemon juice
1 tsp. grated lemon rind
1 tbsp. butter

Blend the sugar and cornstarch in a **1-quart saucepan**. Stir in the boiling water, mixing thoroughly for a smooth sauce.

Add the corn syrup and salt and cook over low heat, stirring until the mixture is thick and clear. Add the lemon juice and rind. Continue to cook until well blended. Cool.

Sapodilla Syrup

4 large ripe sapodillas, puréed page 27
1 cup brown sugar
1 cup apple juice

In a **2-quart sized saucepan**, combine the purée, sugar and juice and bring to a boil. Reduce the heat and simmer, stirring with a **wooden spoon** until the mixture is heavy syrup about 20 to 25-minutes. Serve over pancakes, ice cream or desserts.

Mango Syrup

1 large mango for 2 cups purée page 27
1 cup sugar
1 cup orange juice

In a **2-quart sized saucepan**, combine the purée, sugar and orange juice and bring to a boil. Reduce the heat and simmer, stirring with a **wooden spoon** until the mixture is heavy syrup about 20 to 25-minutes. Serve over pancakes, ice cream or desserts.

Lemon Syrup for Lemonade

Yield 5-1/2 cups

1-1/2 cup sugar
4 cups water
1-1/2 cups freshly squeezed lemon juice

Combine the sugar and water in a **2-quart sized saucepan** and bring to a boil. Boil briskly for 5-minutes; remove from the heat and cool.

Add the unstrained lemon juice, seeds removed, and stir thoroughly. Pour into a **large glass jar**, cover and store in refrigerator.

To prepare lemonade to suit your taste, stir syrup into tall glasses of water and add crushed ice.

Duffs, Puddings & Cheesecakes

Recipes

Avocado Dessert

Coco Coconut, Banana Alfredo

Baked Bananas in Tamarind Sauce

Bananas with Sherry & Cream

Honey Rum Baked Bananas

Rum Barbeque Bananas

❋ **Fritters**

Banana, Carrot, Sapodilla

Caribbean Guava Cobbler

Guava Surprise, Guava De-light

Mango & Pineapple Strudel

Mango Short Cakes, Fruit Drops

North Eleuthera Pineapple Fries

Stuffed Baked Sapodilla, Dillie Flambé

❋ **Jelly Rolls** Guava, Chocolate,

Guava, Pineapple

❋ **Puddings**

Banana, Rum Banana Bread

Coconut, Miniature Bread, Sapodilla

❋ **Tropical Fruit Fillings**

Guava, Coconut, Green Mango, Pineapple,
Sapodilla, Soursop, Green Mango

❋ **Traditional Duffs**

Guava, Coconut, Mango,

Pineapple, Dillie

❋ **Double Boiler Duffs**

Guava, Coconut, Mangoo, Dillie

❋ **Roly Polys**

Guava, Coconut, Mangoo, Pineapple, Dillie

No Bake Tropical Crunchies

❋ **Cheesecakes**

Yamacraw Guava, South Beach Mango,

South Eleuthera Pineapple,

Fox Hill Sapodilla

❋ **No Bake Cheesecakes**

Guava, Banana, Mango, Pineapple, Sapodilla

Cheesecake Mousse with Poached Plumbs

❋ **Frozen Desserts**

Tropical Fruit Sherbet, Frozen Fruit
Slushie, Fruity Yogurt Cups

❋ **Ice Creams**

Vanilla with Mango Syrup, Rum
Raisin, Coconut, Rum Raisin, Soursop

Banana or Mango Crêpes & Ice Cream

Dillie Ice Cream Cup, Banana Split

Tropical Cake & Ice Cream

Paradise Pie á la Mode

Mango & Pineapple Strudel

Dough

1-3/4 cups all purpose flour
1 oz. butter or margarine, melted
1 egg, slightly beaten
3/4 cup warm water
3/4 tsp. salt

Filling

4 large firm-ripe mangoes, chopped
1 fresh ripe pineapple, chopped
2 oz. brown sugar
2 oz. raisins
2 oz. ground almonds
2 oz. chopped, almonds
3/4 tsp. ground cinnamon
Freshly squeezed juice of 1 lemon
Confectioners' sugar
Whipped Cream (optional)

Bake at 350°F

Dough

Place the flour into a **small mixing bowl**. Make a well in the flour mixing in the water and butter. Add the egg and mix to a smooth and elastic dough. Cover and let rest.

Filling

Prepare the mangoes *page 27* and chop into small cubes.

Prepare the pineapple *page 25* and chop into small pieces.

Combine the fruit in a **large bowl**, adding the sugar, raisins, almonds, cinnamon and lemon juice, mixing well.

On a floured **board** with a floured **rolling pin**, roll out the dough into a rectangular shape 1/2-inch thick. Place onto a **tea towel**. Brush the dough all over with melted butter. When well lubricated, stretch by using the back of hands.

Spread the filling on the dough, leaving a little space at the edges. Roll up tightly.

Grease a **baking sheet**. Remove the roll from the tea towel and place onto the sheet, brush with melted butter. Bake for 35 to 40-minutes. Cut into 1/2-inch thick slices. Sprinkle with Confectioners' sugar and serve with Whipped Cream if desired.

Caribbean Guava Cobbler

2 doz. large guavas for 6 cups of slips page 26
1/2 cup coconut milk
1/2 cup brown sugar
3 tbsp. cornstarch
2 tsp. butter
1 cup chopped roasted coconut

Topping

1 cup Bisquick Baking Mix
1/2 cup rolled oats
1/2 cup brown sugar
4 tbsp. margarine
1/2 tsp. ground cinnamon

Bake at 350°F

Place the guava slices into a **large bowl**, and combine with the rum, brown sugar, cornstarch, lemon juice and coconut. Turn into a **10x10-inch casserole dish**, dot with margarine and set aside.

Topping

In a **small bowl**, combine the topping ingredients, working quickly with fingers, mix until it resembles coarse meal. Sprinkle over the guava and bake for 45-minutes. Serve warm topped with *Rum Raisin Ice Cream page 346.*

Guava Surprise

Sawyer's Jelly Roll Crust page 330
12 medium-sized fresh guavas or canned guava halves
6 oz. Guava Cheese page 366 or store-bought guava cheese
1/2 cup sugar
3/4 cup ground almonds
Confectioners' sugar for dusting

Bake at 350°F

Prepare the guavas shells *page 26*.

Cut the guava cheese into 1-inch chunks. Place one chunk into each guava halves and set aside. In a **small bowl** mix, together the sugar and almonds and set aside.

Prepare the jelly roll crust and cut off pieces to make 2-inch balls. On a floured **board** with a floured **rolling pin**, roll out the balls into 1/2-inch thick oblongs.

Spread the almond-sugar mixture on a sheet of **wax paper**. Press one side of the oblong into the mixture and transfer to the greased **baking sheet** with nut/sugar side up.

322

Place a filled guava half open end down covering the guava cheese on the oblong, pressing into the dough. Bake for 15 to 20-minutes. Transfer to a **cooling rack** and sprinkle with powered sugar. Allow to cool before serving.

Mango Shortcakes

3 to 4 ripe mangoes
1 cup sugar
Shortcakes page 90
Whipped Cream

Peel the mangoes, cut the meat from the seeds and cut into 1/2-inch chunks, reserving the juice. Place into a **bowl with a cover** and sprinkle with the sugar. Gently mix, cover and place into refrigerator to chill thoroughly.

Prepare the shortcakes, place on individual **serving dishes** and while hot, split. Spoon half the chilled mango over the bottom halves. Cover with top halves and spoon remaining mango and juice over the tops, topping with Whipped Cream.

Cocoa Coconut

1 large freshly grated coconut page 24
1 cup strong coffee
2 cups milk
2 cups stale bread chunks
4 eggs, separated
1/2 cup brown sugar
1/2 cup powdered cocoa
Soka Hard Rum Sauce page 315

Bake at 400°F

In a **large mixing bowl**, mix together the coffee and milk, adding the bread. Beat the egg yolks well and fold into the bread mixture along with the sugar, coconut and cocoa.

In a **small mixing bowl** with **electric mixer**, beat the egg whites until stiff and gently fold into the mixture.

Turn into a greased **8x10-inch-baking dish** and bake for 30-minutes. Serve warm with the *Soka Hard Rum Sauce.*

Avocado Dessert

2 medium-sized ripe avocados for 2 cups purée
Freshly squeezed juice of 1 lime
1 cup Confectioners' sugar
1/4 tsp. ground cloves
Whipped Cream (optional)

Peel and mash the avocados. Place into the bowl of a **blender** adding the lime juice, Confectioners' sugar and cloves.

Blend until fluffy, scraping the sides of the blender to mix thoroughly. Chill and serve in **long stemmed glasses** (top with Whipped Cream if desired).

Banana Alfredo

1 egg
1 cup ice cold water
1/2 cup all purpose flour
1/2 tsp. salt
1 banana, sliced
Vegetable oil 1/4" deep in skillet
Confectioners' sugar

In a **small bowl** with a **wire whisk**, whisk together the egg and ice water. Quickly whisk in the flour and salt. Fold the sliced banana into the batter.

Heat the oil in a **heavy skillet**. Drop the pancakes in the hot oil and fry until brown and crispy turning once. Drain on a **wire rack** and dust generously with Confectioners' sugar.

Honey & Rum Baked Bananas

6 hard-ripe bananas
2 tbsp. butter
3/4 cup honey
2 tbsp. freshly squeezed lemon juice
2 tbsp. Ole Nassau Banana Rum

Bake at 325°F

Peel the bananas and cut into halves lengthwise. Melt the butter mixing well with the honey and rum.

Arrange the bananas in a greased **baking dish**; sprinkle with the lemon juice and brush with the butter mixture. Bake for 15 to 20-minutes and serve immediately.

Rum-Barbecue Bananas

6 firm-ripe bananas
1/2 cup Ole Nassau Banana Rum
1/2 cup brown sugar
Lime slices

Slit the skins of bananas along one side. Arrange on a **barbecue grill** over hot coals *or on the grill of an oven.*

Grill in the skins until soft. Open, but do not remove the banana. Sprinkle with rum and sugar, garnish with lime slices and serve warm.

Bananas With Sherry & Cream

7 bananas
2 tbsp. Sawyer's Guava Jam
3 tbsp. Sherry
Whipped Cream

Peel 6 bananas and cut into halves lengthwise. Place into a **shallow pan**.

Mix the jam and sherry; spread over the bananas and let stand for 1-hour.

Top with the whipped cream and decorate with the remaining banana cut into thin slices. Gently scoop into **dessert dishes** and serve.

Baked Bananas in Tamarind Sauce

4 ripe bananas
1/4 cup Tamarind Paste page 366
1/4 cup grated coconut
1/4 cup grated almonds
1 tbsp. honey
2 tbsp. Ole Nassau Banana Rum
2 tbsp. butter, melted
Bake at 350°F

Peel the bananas, split lengthwise and arrange in a buttered **casserole dish**.

Spread the Tamarind Paste over the bananas and sprinkle with the coconut and almonds.

In a **small dish**, mix together the honey and rum with the butter and pour over top of bananas. Bake for 20-minutes and serve hot.

Sapodilla Fritters

Prepare *Sapodilla Pancake* batter *page 133*.

Pour vegetable oil into a **deep fat fryer** *or deep po*t, heat and drop the mixture by tablespoonfuls into the hot oil. Fry until brown.

Remove using a **large slotted spoon**; drain on a **wire rack**, dust with Confectioners' sugar and serve hot.

Banana Fritters

2 ripe bananas
2 tsp. freshly squeezed lemon juice
1/2 cup Confectioners' sugar
1 cup all purpose flour
1 tsp. baking powder
1/2 tsp. salt
3 tbsp. sugar
1 egg
1/3 cup milk
1 cup butter, melted
Vegetable oil for deep-frying

Peel the bananas; cut into 1/4-inch slices and cut the slices into 1/4-inch dice. Sprinkle with the lemon juice and Confectioners' sugar and set aside. In a **small bowl**, sift together the flour, baking powder, salt and sugar.

In a **medium-sized mixing** bowl with **electric mixer**, beat the egg adding in the milk and flour. Continue to beat until the batter is smooth. With a **wooden spoon**, fold the banana into the batter.

Heat the oil in a **deep-fat fryer** *or deep pot* and drop teapoonfuls of the batter into the hot fat. Fry until brown, drain on a **wire rack** and serve.

Carrot Fritters

3 medium-sized carrots
1/2 cup all purpose flour
1/2 tsp. baking powder
1/4 tsp. ground cinnamon
1/4 tsp. ground nutmeg
1/3 cup sugar
3 tbsp. milk (approximately)
Vegetable oil for deep-frying

Peel and grate the carrots using a **food processor** fitted with disc for grating *or with a hand-held grater*.

In a **medium-sized bowl**, sift together the flour, baking powder and spices. Add the sugar; mix in the carrots and milk a little at a time, stirring to a dropping consistency, making sure it is not too soft.

Heat the oil in a **deep-fat fryer** *or deep pot*. Drop tablespoonfuls of the mixture into the hot oil and fry until golden brown. Remove using a **large slotted spoon**, drain on a **wire rack** and serve hot.

Tropical Fruit Drops

2 bananas for 1 cup mashed
1-1/2 cups sugar
1-1/2 cups Whole Bran cereal
1/2 tsp. ground cinnamon
1/2 cup butter or margarine
2 eggs
1-1/2 tsp. Ole Nassau Coconut Rum
2-1/2 cups all purpose flour
2 tsp. salt
2-1/2 tsp. baking powder
1 cup chopped nuts

Bake at 425°F

Combine 1/2-cup of the sugar with the cereal and cinnamon. With a **rolling pin**, roll out on a sheet of **wax pape**r, blending until fine.

Place the remaining sugar and the butter into a **small mixing bowl** and, with **electric mixer**, beat the butter until light and creamy. Mix in the eggs and rum.

Sift together the flour, baking powder and salt. Mix the flour and mashed bananas alternately into the creamed mixture.

Using a teaspoon, drop the batter into the bran mixture coating completely and with fingers, form into 1-1/2-inch balls. Place on a greased **baking sheet** and bake for 10-minutes.

North Eleuthera Pineapple Fries

1 fresh pineapple, cut into 1/2" slices *page 25*

Batter

1/4 cup sugar
1/2 cup all purpose flour
1/2 tsp. salt
1 egg
1/2 cup milk
Vegetable oil 1/2" deep in pan
Confectioners' sugar for dusting

Sprinkle the pineapple slices with the sugar. Set aside.

Batter

Sift together the flour and salt. In a **small mixing bowl**, with **electric mixer**, beat the egg with half the milk. Continue to beat, adding the flour mixture, until thoroughly smooth. Mix in the balance of the milk and let sit for 1-hour.

Pour the oil into a **small non-stick frying pan**, and preheat. Dip each slice of pineapple into the batter and fry until golden brown. Dust with Confectioners' sugar and serve hot.

Stuffed Baked Sapodilla

A delicious tropical treat combing the exotic sapodilla with a variety of fruits, jams and rum sauces or ice cream. Choose firm-ripe sapodillas.

6 medium to large firm-ripe sapodilla
1/2 to 1 cup filling *page 333 to 335*
Coconut Filling • Guava Filling • Pineapple Filling • Soursop Filling • Guava Jam • Minced Meat • Diced Bananas with nuts
1-1/2 tbsp. butter

Bake at 350°F

Prepare your choice of filling. Set aside

Wash the sapodillas thoroughly and with a **small paring knife**, cut into the top of the dillies about 1-1/2-inches around. Using a teaspoon, scoop out the centre membrane and all seeds, forming a cavity for the filling.

Pare a thin slice at the bottom of the dillies so they will stand upright. Press about 2-tablespoons of filling into the cavity.

Melt the butter in a **9x12-inch-baking dish**, arrange the sapodillas and bake for 20-minutes. Allow to cool and serve with *Rum Raisin* or *Soursop Icecream* or *Mango Syrup page 345 to 347.*

Dillie Flambé

4 medium-sized firm ripe sapodillas
1/2 cup Ole Nassau Yer Ho Rum
1/2 cup sugar
2 tbsp. cornstarch
2 tbsp. grated orange rind
1-1/2 to 2 tbsp. water
Grated rind of 1 lemon
1/4 cup Caton Brandy
1 tsp. vanilla extract
4 large sugar cubes
4 scoops *Soursop Ice Cream* page 349

Peel the sapodillas, cut into 1/2-inch chunks and set aside. In a **2-quart sized saucepan**, mix together the sugar, orange and lemon rinds, vanilla and rum. Bring to a boil.

In a **1-quart saucepan**, stir together the cornstarch and water and using a **wire whisk**, whisk until well blended. Stir in the dillie chunks and cook for 5-minutes over medium heat. Remove from the heat.

Soak the sugar cubes in the brandy. Turn the dillie mixture into a heated chafing dish.

Scoop the *Soursop Ice Cream* into **individual serving dishes** and place in front of your guests. Arrange the rum-soaked sugar cubes over the dillie mixture and ignite. Allow burning for a few seconds and when the flame has gone out, spoon over the Ice Cream.

David's Peach Cobbler

2 - 29 oz. cans sliced peaches in light syrup
3/4 cups sugar
1/2 cup melted butter
Crust
1 cup all purpose flour
1 tsp. baking powder
1 cup sugar
1/2 cup freshly grated coconut (or packaged coconut)
3/4 cup coconut milk (or whole milk)

Bake at 350ºF

Place peaches into a **colander**, drain and rinse. In a **large bowl**, mix together the drained peaches, sugar and melted butter. Turn into an un-greased **11x14-inch baking pan**.
Crust
Sift together the sugar, flour and baking powder; mix in the coconut and add the coconut milk, blending well. Pour over the peaches and spread evenly over the top. Bake for 1-hour.

Sawyer's Guava Jelly Roll

Filling

1 cup Sawyer' Guava Jelly

Crust

1 cup all purpose flour
1/4 tsp. salt
3 eggs
1 cup sugar
1/3 cup coconut milk (fresh or canned)
1 tsp. rum extract

Bake at 375°F

Crust

Sift together the flour, baking powder and salt.

In a **medium-sized mixing bowl**, with **electric mixer**, beat the eggs, and, at low speed, gradually beat in the sugar, water and rum extract. Add the dry ingredients beating for two minutes at medium speed.

Grease a **baking sheet** and line with **foil wrap**. Turn the mixture onto the sheet spreading out evenly. Bake for 12 to 15-minutes.

Loosen the edges and immediately turn upside down on a **dish towel** sprinkled with Confectioners' sugar.

Remove the foil wrap and trim off the crisp edge of the Jelly Roll. While hot, roll up the cake in the towel from the narrow end. Place onto a **cooling rack**.

Unroll the cake and remove the towel. Spread with the Guava Jelly and roll up again. Place seam side down onto a **serving platter**, sprinkle with Confectioners' sugar and cut into 1-inch slices.

Chocolate Guava Jelly Roll

Prepare same as *Sawyer's Guava Jelly Roll* except blend in *1/4-cup of cocoa* with the dry ingredients.

Pineapple Jelly Roll

Prepare same as *Sawyer's Guava Jelly Roll* except substitute 1 cup *Pineapple Jelly page 361 for the* Guava Jelly.

Banana Pudding

2 cups mashed bananas
1 tbsp. butter
2 tbsp. all purpose flour
3 tbsp. brown sugar
3/4 cup milk
3/4 tsp. ground nutmeg

Bake at 350°F

In a **medium-sized mixing bowl** with **electric mixer**, beat the butter and sugar together until light and fluffy.

Add the banana, butter and sugar. Add the flour alternately with the milk.

Turn into a greased **9-inch Pyrex pie dish** and bake for 40 to 45-minutes. Serve hot with *Soka Hard Rum Sauce page 315*.

Rum & Banana Bread Pudding

1/2 loaf stale sliced bread
3 ripe bananas cut into 1" pieces
2 cups heavy cream
1 cup milk
3 egg yolks
3 whole eggs
1/4 cup sugar
1/2 cup Ole Nassau Jack Malantan Rum

Bake at 350°F

Butter an **8-inch square glass-baking dish**. Cut the bread slices into 3/4-inch squares.

In a heavy **2-quart sized saucepan**, bring the cream and milk to a boil. In a **large bowl**, beat together the yolks and eggs and sugar. Then using a **wire whisk**, whisk in the cream and milk mixture beating until combined well. Stir in the rum.

Arrange the bread and bananas in the baking dish, pour the cream mixture over and let stand in refrigerator for 1-hour pressing down the bread to coat evenly.

Place the baking dish into a **large baking pan** adding enough hot water in the larger pan to reach halfway up the sides of the smaller dish. Bake the pudding in middle of the oven for 45 to 50-minutes or until springy to the touch. Cool for 30-minutes before serving.

Coconut Pudding

1 cup freshly grated coconut page 24
2 cups stale bread chunks
2 cups milk
2 eggs, slightly beaten
1 cup raisins
1 tsp. almond extract
1/2 cup sugar

Bake at 325°F

In a **small saucepan**, bring the milk to a boil. Combine the coconut and bread chunks in a **large bowl** and pour the hot milk over the mixture.

Stir the eggs into the mixture, adding the sugar, almond extract and raisins. Turn into a greased **8x10-inch-baking dish** and bake for about 45-minutes or until set. Serve warm.

Miniature Bread Puddings

Yield 12 Mini Puddings

6 slices stale bread
1/2 tsp. ground nutmeg
1 cup canned coconut milk
1/2 tsp. ground cinnamon
1/2 cup grated coconut
3/4 cup sugar
1/2 cup raisin
1 tbsp. butter, softened
1/2 tsp. salt
1 egg, slightly beaten

Bake at 350°F

Break up the bread slices into chunks; place into a **medium-sized mixing bowl** and soak with the coconut milk. Add remaining ingredients to the bread, mixing gently.

Grease the **muffin pan** *or insert paper bake cups*. Spoon the mixture into the muffin cups to 2/3 full and bake for 35 to 40-minutes. Serve warm with *Soka Hard Rum Sauce page 315* or ice cream.

• Prepare a double batch, seal in plastic bags and freeze. When ready to serve, defrost and pop into the microwave to heat and serve warm.

Sapodilla Pudding

4 medium-sized ripe sapodillas
3 cups coarse bread chunks
1 cup milk
1 cup coconut milk (fresh or canned)
1/2 cup sugar
2 eggs, slightly beaten
1 tsp. rum extract
1/2 tsp. salt
1/2 tsp. ground nutmeg
Bake at 325°F

Peel the sapodillas, place into a **shallow dish** and mash with a fork, removing the seeds.

Place the bread chunks into a **large bowl**. Scald the milks and pour over the bread. Gently mix in the mashed sapodilla, eggs and remaining ingredients.

Turn into a greased **8-inch square baking dish** and bake for 45-minutes. Serve warm with *Sapodilla Syrup page 318*.

Guava Filling

12 medium to large sized ripe guavas
1 cup guava purée from the guavas
1 oz. sugar
1 oz. water
1 tsp. ground cinnamon
1 tsp. ground allspice

Prepare the guavas and purée *page 26*. In a **3-quart sized saucepan**, combine the sugar and water. Over low heat bring to a boil, stirring continuously with a **wooden spoon** until the mixture is syrupy and forms a ball when dropped into a **small dish** of cold water.

Remove from the heat; add the guava, purée and spices mixing well. Allow to cool and use in selected recipes.

Coconut Filling

1 large freshly grated coconut page 24
1 cup sugar
1 cup water
1/2 tsp. ground nutmeg
1/2 tsp. ground allspice

In a **1-quart saucepan**, combine the sugar, water and coconut. Bring to a boil. Reduce the heat and stirring continuously with a **wooden spoon**, cook for about 20-minutes or until the mixture is syrupy and forms a ball when dropped into a small dish of cold water.

Remove from the heat and stir in the spices. Allow to cool and use in selected recipes.

Green Mango Filling

3 large green mangoes
1/2 cup canned coconut milk
1 cup sugar
2 tbsp. all purpose flour
1 tsp. ground cinnamon
1 tsp. ground nutmeg
1-1/2 tbsp. butter, softened

Peel the mangoes; cut the flesh away from the seed, cut into 1/2-inch chunks.

In a **3-quart sized saucepan**, mix together the coconut milk and remaining ingredients and bring to a boil. Add the mango chunks and cook for 20-minutes. Allow to cool and use in selected recipes.

Pineapple Filling

1 medium-sized ripe pineapple
1 oz. water
1 oz. sugar
1/2 tsp. ground nutmeg
1/2 tsp. ground allspice

Prepare the fresh pineapple page 25 and chop into fine mince to measure 2-cups.

In a **1-quart saucepan**, combine the sugar and water; over low heat bring to a boil, stirring continuously with a **wooden spoon** until the mixture is syrupy and forms a ball when dropped into a small dish of cold water. Remove from the heat and mix in the pineapple and spices. Allow to cool and use in selected recipes.

Sapodilla Filling

4 to 5 large ripe sapodillas
1 oz. sugar
1 oz. water
1/2 tsp. ground cinnamon
1/2 tsp. ground allspice
1/2 cup raisins (optional)

Wash and peel the sapodillas; cut into halves, removing the seeds and centre membrane. Slice into thin slices horizontally. Using a fork, mash the slices into about 1/2-cup of pulp.

In a **1-quart saucepan**, combine the sugar and water. Bring to a boil over low heat, stirring continuously with a **wooden spoon** until the mixture is syrupy and forms a ball when dropped into a **small dish** of cold water.

Remove from the heat and mix in the dillie slices, pulp and spices. Allow to cool and use in selected recipes.

Soursop Filling

1 medium-sized ripe soursop
1 can (8 oz.) sweetened condensed milk
1 tsp. vanilla extract
1/2 tsp. freshly grated nutmeg

Prepare the soursop, removing all seeds *page 27*.

Stir in the condensed milk and place the mixture into the bowl of a **food processor** fitted with the knife blade and process for 2-minutes. Turn the purée back into the large mixing bowl and stir in the vanilla and nutmeg.

Sugar Apple Filling

3 or 4 ripe sugar apples
1 cup vanilla yogurt

Break open the sugar apples; remove the centre membranes and discard. Scoop the pulp into a **bowl** and remove the seeds *page 27*. Mix in the yogurt.

Guava

Guava is native to the warm regions of the Americas, stretching from Mexico to Peru. Although the guava plant was domesticated more than 2,000 years ago, it was not until 1526 that the first commercial cultivation of guava was reported in the Caribbean islands. Later, explorers into the Philippines and India that took the guava there and from there it quickly spread to most of the tropical and subtropical regions of the world where it has become naturalized.

Ripe guava fruit is an excellent source of vitamin C and dietary fiber. Reportedly, consumption of guava fruit reduces serum cholesterol levels, triglycerides and hypertension. Both ripe and green fruits, the roots, leaves and bark are used in local medicine throughout the guava-growing regions .

Guava can be eaten as fresh fruit when ripe, prepared into sauces, chutneys and desserts or cooked as a vegetable when green. It can be processed for jam, jelly, nectar and fruit juices as well as flavouring other foods.

There are fresh fruit or dessert varieties of guava with white, salmon red, or pink flesh and light green to yellow skin colours.

❀

Guava Duff

Guava Filling page 333

Dough

2 cups all purpose flour
3 tsp. baking powder
1 tsp. salt
1/4 cup vegetable shortening
3/4 cup milk
Soka Hard Rum Sauce page 315

Bake at 350°F (optional)

Prepare the *Guava Filling* and set aside.

Dough

In a **large bowl**, sift together the dry ingredients. With a **pastry cutter**, cut in the shortening until the mixture looks like meal. Stir in the milk making smooth dough.

Place onto a floured **board** and knead lightly adding more flour if necessary. With a floured **rolling pin**, roll out into a rectangle about 12x15-inches.

Spread the filling over the dough to 1-inch of the edges. Brush edges with water and roll up like a log pinching edges together securely. (see Story of the Duff *page 338 for boiling method*).

Spray **heavy foil wrap** with non-stick spray and wrap the duff securely, forming a dome. Place into a large **baking dish** and half fill the dish with water. Place on bottom rack of oven and bake for 1-1/2 hours adding more water if necessary while baking.

Carefully remove the foil packet from the dish and remove the duff from the foil onto a **serving platter**. Slice into 1/2-inch thick slices and serve warm with *Soka Hard Rum Sauce*.

Coconut Duff

Prepare same as *Guava Duff* substituting *Coconut Filling page 334*.

Mango Duff

Prepare same as *Guava Duff* substituting *Green Mango Filling page 334*.

Pineapple Duff

Prepare same as *Guava Duff* substituting *Pineapple Filling page 334*.

Dillie Duff

Prepare same as *Guava Duff* substituting *Sapodilla Filling page 335*.

The original method of cooking the duff was to wrap it in a piece of cheesecloth tied at both ends and placed on a saucer in a large pot of boiling water. Today it is more convenient to use foil wrap instead of the cheesecloth. Tear off a length of foil long enough to form an airtight dome-shape so that duff will be allowed to expand. Grease the foil with butter to prevent the duff from sticking. Place the duff onto the foil; fold the foil with a folded seam at the top and both s i d e s securing w e l l. Place a saucer or small plate in the bottom of the pot before adding the water. Place the foil packet into a large pot with water to cover and boil for about 2 hours. Alternatively, the duff may be boiled in the top of a double boiler (below).

Double Boiler Guava Duff

Batter

1/2 cup butter
1/2 cup sugar
3/4 cup milk
2 eggs
2 cups all purpose flour
2 tsp. baking powder
Guava Filling page 333
Soka Hard Rum Sauce page 315

Prepare the filling and set aside.

Batter

In a **small mixing bowl** with **electric mixer**, cream the butter and sugar. Add the eggs one at a time beating thoroughly.

Sift together the flour and baking powder. Add *alternately* with the milk to the creamed butter mixing until smooth.

Add the water to the bottom of a **double boiler** and bring to a boil. Grease the top of the boiler and spread in half the batter. Spread the guava filling over the batter and add remaining batter spreading evenly.

Cover tightly, lower the heat and boil the duff for 1-1/2 to 2-hours Add hot water to bottom of double boiler if necessary while cooking. Scoop out and serve hot with *Soka Hard Rum Sauce.*

Variations • Coconut • Mango & Sapodilla Duffs :-

Substitute one of the following fillings found beginning on *page 334 to 335*

Coconut Filling • Mango Filling • Sapodilla Filling

338

Guava Roly Poly

Guava Filling page 333

Crust

2 cups all purpose flour
2 tsp. baking powder
4 oz. butter
1/2 cup freshly grated coconut page 24
1/2 cup canned coconut milk
Granulated sugar for dusting

Egg Wash

1 egg
3 tbsp. water
Soka Hard Rum Sauce page 315
Bake at 350°F

Prepare *Guava Filling* and set aside.

Crust

In a **small bowl**, sift together the flour and baking powder; cut in the butter using a **pastry cutter**. Add the sugar and coconut, stirring in the coconut milk to form soft dough.

Turn onto a floured **board** kneading lightly. With a floured **rolling pin**, roll out into a rectangle approximately 12x10-inches. Spread the filling to within 1-inch of the edges.

Egg Wash: In a **small dish**, beat together the egg and water and brush edges. Roll up into a log pressing edges firmly together to seal.

Pour 1/2-cup water into a **baking dish**. Place the log into the dish seam side down; brush the top with egg wash and sprinkle with sugar.

Bake for 35 to 40-minutes. Remove to a **serving platter**; allow to cool. While still warm, slice into 1/2-inch thick slices. Serve with *Soka Hard Rum Sauce* or ice cream.

Coconut Roly Poly

Prepare same as *Guava Roly Poly* substituting *Coconut Filling page 334.*

Mango Roly Poly

Prepare same as *Guava Roly Poly* substituting *Green Mango Filling page 334.*

Pineapple Roly Poly

Prepare same as *Guava Roly Poly* substituting *Pineapple Filling page 334.*

Dillie Roly Poly

Prepare same as *Guava Roly Poly* substituting *Sapodilla Filling page 335.*

Mango

What's sweet, juicy and delicious to the last sticky bite? Mango, of course. The mango tree is native to North India, Burma and West Malaysia and has been cultivated for thousands of years in India, where 150 varieties are grown. The fruit varies in size from that of an apricots to some mangoes that weigh four or five pounds.

Its importance in the tropics has been likened to that of the apple in the Temperate Zone. They are u s u a l l y eaten in the raw fruit form. However, there are many, many different ways in which to use the delicious flesh, including desserts, jams, syrups and chutneys.

The mango tree thrives in The Bahamas and the islands of the Caribbean. A few varieties are planted in California and Southern Florida. ✺

South Beach Mango Cheesecake

9-inch Crust page 270

Filling

3 to 4 large ripe mangoes to yield 5 cups, chopped (3 cups for the Cheesecake and 2 cups for the Topping)
3 packages (8 oz. each) cream cheese, softened
3/4 cup sugar
3 eggs
1 tsp. vanilla extract

Topping

1 cup mango, chopped
1 cup mango purée
1/2 cup sugar
2 tbsp. cornstarch

Bake at 300ºF

Prepare the crust and set aside.

Peel the mangoes, slice the flesh from the seed, preserving the juice and chop into 3/4" chunks (5-cups total). Place 2-cups of the chunks along with the juice into the bowl of a **blender** and purée.

Filling

In a **medium-sized mixing bowl** with **electric mixer** set at medium speed, mix the softened cream cheese together with the sugar adding the eggs, one at a time.

With a **large wooden spoon**, fold in 2-cups of the chopped mango, 1-cup of the purée and the vanilla extract.

Turn the mixture into the crumb crust and bake for 55-minutes to one hour (until the centre is set). Leave in the oven to cool for 10-minutes after turning off, with the door ajar about 4-inches. Remove from the oven and cool completely. Refrigerate overnight.

Topping

Combine 1-cup of the mango purée, water, sugar and cornstarch in a **1-quart saucepan** and bring to a boil. Reduce the heat and cook over low heat stirring constantly with a **wooden spoon** until the mixture is smooth, about 3-minutes.

Remove from the heat; stir in the chopped mango and cool. Spread over the chilled cheesecake and refrigerate until set.

Yamacraw Guava Cheesecake

Prepare same as *South Beach Mango Cheesecake page 341* substituting *5 cups of fresh guava slips with purée page 27.*

South Eleuthera Pineapple Cheesecake

Prepare same as *South Beach Mango Cheesecake page 341* substituting *5 cups fresh pineapple chunks page 25.*

Fox Hill Sapodilla Cheesecake

Prepare same as *South Beach Mango Cheesecake page 341* substituting *5 cups finely chopped sapodilla page 27.*

No-Bake Tropical Crunches

1-1/2 cups crushed vanilla or chocolate wafers
1/2 cup soft butter
1 cup Confectioners' sugar
1 egg white
1 cup Coconut Filling page 334
1 cup Whipped Cream

Spread half the crumbs in the bottom of an **8-inch square pan**.

In a **small mixing bowl**, with **electric mixer**, beat the egg white, adding the sugar and butter, beating until light and fluffy. Spread over crumbs in the pan.

Prepare *Coconut Filling* and spread over the sugar mixture.

Spread the whipped cream over the fruit. Sprinkle with remaining crumbs. Chill overnight or at least 10-hours and cut into squares.

Variation

Substitute one of the fillings found beginning on *page 333 to 334*
• *Guava* • *Pineapple* • *Mango*

No-Bake Mango Cheesecake

9-inch Crumb Crust page 270
2 large ripe mangoes for 2 cups, finely chopped
1 envelope unflavoured gelatin
1 cup cold water
2 packages (8 oz. each) cream cheese, softened
1/2 cup sugar

Prepare the crust and set aside. Peel the mangoes, slice the meat from the seed and chop into 1/4-inch chunks.

In a **large mixing bowl** with **electric mixe**r, beat the cream cheese, sugar and mango until blended.

In a **1-quart saucepan**, sprinkle the gelatin over 1/4-cup cold water and let stand for 1-minute. Stir over low heat until the gelatin is completely d i s s o l v e d. Gradually beat the cream cheese mixture with remaining 3/4-cup water until smooth.

Turn into the crust and chill until firm. Serve with Whipped Cream if desired.

No-Bake Guava Cheesecake

Prepare same as *No-Bake Mango Cheesecake* substituting *2-cups finely chopped guava with purée* page 26.

No-Bake Banana Cheesecake

Prepare same as *No-Bake Mango Cheesecake* substituting *2-cups mashed bananas.*

No-Bake Pineapple Cheesecake

Prepare same as *No-Bake Mango Cheesecake* substituting *2-cups finely chopped pineapple* page 25.

No-Bake Sapodilla Cheesecake

Prepare same as *No-Bake Mango Cheesecake* substituting *2-cups finely chopped dillies with purée* page 27.

Cheesecake Mousse
With Rum Poached Plums

1 cup water
1/3 cup sugar
1/3 cup Ole Nassau Chick Charney Rum
2 plums
3 oz. cream cheese, softened
3 tbsp. Confectioners' sugar
1/2 tsp. vanilla extract
1/2 cup heavy cream

Have ready a **bowl** of ice and cold water. In a **1-quart saucepan**, simmer the water, sugar and rum for 10-minutes.

Pit the plums; cut each into 12 wedges and simmer in the syrup until t e n d e r 3 to 4-minutes. Transfer the mixture to a **bowl** and set in the bowl of ice water. Let stand until cold.

In a **bowl**, with a **wire whisk**, whisk together the cream cheese, Confectioners' sugar, vanilla and pinch of salt until smooth. In **another bowl**, beat the heavy cream until it holds soft peaks, then whisk into the cream cheese mixture.

Divide the cream cheese mixture between **2 goblets** and chill for 15-minutes. Serve topped with the plums and some of the syrup.

Tropical Fruit Sherbet

3 cups water
2 cups sugar
Grated rind of 2 lemons
1-1/2 cups lemon juice
1 tsp. vanilla extract

In a **3-quart sized saucepan**, combine all ingredients and bring to a boil. Reduce to low heat and cook for 5-minutes.

Allow to cool completely and chill in refrigerator overnight. Turn into an **ice cream maker** and freeze according to manufacturer's directions. Pour into a **container with cover** for freezing and freeze overnight.

Serve with mint garnish or a scoop in half of lemon with membrane removed.

Variation

Substitute grated rind and juice of limes; or 1-1/2-cups of finely chopped pineapple and juice; or mango purée; or guava purée; or soursop purée.

Frozen Fruit Slusby

Peel one of the following ripe fruit:

Mango, Pineapple, Papaya, Sapodilla, Soursop, Banana or Guava

1 cup fruit
1 tbsp. sugar or 2 to 3 tbsp. sweetened condensed milk (if using soursop)

Peel the fruit, remove the seeds and centre membrane and cut into chunks. Place into the bowl of a **blender** and purée. Add the sugar or condensed milk.

Pour into an **ice cube tray** and freeze to slush (about 1-hour). Spoon into dessert dishes and serve immediately.

Fruity Yogurt Cups

Prepare the filling for *Tropical Yogurt Pie page 289* except use 1 envelope of unflavoured gelatin and spoon the mixture into **custard cups or dessert glasses** and chill thoroughly. Serve cold.

Vanilla Ice Cream with Mango Syrup

Yield 1 Gallon

2 cups sugar
2 eggs
1/8 tsp. salt
2 tbsp. all purpose flour
4 cups milk, scalded
2 cups heavy cream
2 tsp. vanilla
Mango Syrup page 318

In a **medium-sized mixing bowl** with **electric mixer**, beat the sugar well with the eggs, salt and flour. Add 2-cups of the milk (cool the remaining milk).

Pour the mixture into a **2-quart sized saucepan** and heat, stirring until the mixture it thickens. Remove from the heat and cool.

Add the cream and vanilla and pour into the can of an **ice cream freezer**. Add enough of the remaining cooled milk to fill the can within 1-inch of the top and freeze according to manufacturer's direction. Serve with *Mango Syrup*.

Rum Raisin Ice Cream

Yield 1 Gallon

1 cup dark raisins
1/2 cup Ole Nassau Chick Charney Rum
2 eggs
2 cups sugar
1/8 tsp. salt
2 tbsp. all purpose flour
3-1/2 cups milk, scalded
2 cups heavy cream

In a **small container with a cover**, soak the raisins in the rum overnight.

In a **medium-sized mixing bowl** with **electric mixer**, beat together the eggs sugar, salt and flour, blending well. Add 2-cups of the scalded milk (cool remaining milk).

Pour into a **2-quart sized saucepan** and heat, stirring until the mixture thickens. Cool.

Stir in the cream, rum/raisin mix and pour into the can of an **ice cream freezer**. Add enough of the remaining cooled milk to fill the can within 1-inch of the top. Freeze according to manufacturer's directions.

Coconut-Rum Raisin Ice Cream

2 cups canned coconut milk, scalded
1/8 tsp. salt
1/2 cup Ole Nassau Coconut Rum
2 tbsp. all purpose flour
2 cups sugar
1-1/2 cups whole milk, scalded
2 eggs
2 cups heavy cream
1 cup raisins

In a **medium-sized mixing bowl** with **electric mixer**, beat the sugar well with eggs, salt and flour.

In a **small bowl**, mix together the scalded coconut and whole milks. Add 2-cups of the combined milks (cool remaining milk) mixing well.

Turn the mixture into a **2-quart sized saucepan** and heat, stirring until the mixture thickens. Cool.

Add the cream, rum and raisins; turn into the can of an **ice cream freezer**. Add enough of the remaining cooled milk to fill the can to within 1-inch of the top. Freeze according to manufacturer's direction.

Banana Crêpes & Ice Cream

Crêpes

1 cup milk
2 eggs
1/2 cup mashed banana
1 tbsp. vegetable oil
3/4 cup all purpose flour
1/2 tsp. salt
1/8 tsp. ground nutmeg

Filling

2 or 3 ripe bananas (1/2 cup for crêpes)
1/4 cup honey
2 tbsp. freshly squeezed lemon juice
2 tbsp. Ole Nassau Banana Rum
Butter for frying

Peel the bananas; mash enough for 1/2-cup for the crêpes; cut remainder into 1/4-inch slices and the slices into 1/4-inch dice.

Crêpes

In a **small mixing bowl** with **electric mixer**, beat the egg, milk, oil and mashed banana, mixing well. Add the flour and continue to mix, but do not over mix. Chill for 1-hour.

Filling

In a **shallow bowl**, combine the honey, lemon juice, and rum; add the diced banana and marinate for 30-minutes.

Heat the butter in a **large skillet** and, with a slotted spoon, place the banana into the skillet (reserving the marinade) and fry for 5 or 6-minutes. Pour the marinade over the cooked banana, and, stirring, cook for 2 or 3-minutes. Remove the skillet from the heat and set aside.

Remove the crêpe mix from refrigerator. Place 1-tablespoon of butter into a **6-inch non-stick skillet** and heat. Pour in enough mix to cover the bottom of the pan with a thin coating. Keep the pan moving and after 1-minute, turn the crêpe and turn again until brown on both sides.

Place 2 to 3-tablespoonfuls of the banana filling into the centre and fold the crêpe over each end to the centre. Gently remove to **individual serving dishes** and top with Ice Cream *page 345 to 349*.

Mango Crêpes & Ice Cream

Crêpes

3/4 cup all purpose flour
2 tbsp. Confectioners' sugar
1/4 tsp. salt
1 cup milk
2 eggs, slightly beaten
2 tbsp. vegetable oil

Filing

2 ripe mangoes, finely chopped
1 cup plain yogurt
3 tbsp. honey
1/2 cup chopped Maraschino cherries

Crêpes

In a **small mixing bowl**, mix together the flour, sugar and salt. Add the milk, eggs and oil, stirring until smooth. Cover and refrigerate for 1-hour.

Lightly grease a **6-inch non-stick skillet** and heat over medium heat. Pour in 2-tablespoons of batter, tilting the skillet to make the crepe. Keep the pan moving for 60-seconds or until the bottom is brown. Turn the crêpe over and cook for 30 to 45-seconds longer. Cool on a **wire rack**.

Lightly oil the skillet if necessary and repeat with remaining batter.

Filling

In a **small bowl**, blend together the yogurt and honey. Remove 1/2-cup and place into **another bowl**, stir in the mango chunks and cherries.

Spread about 2 to 3-tablespoonfuls of the fruit mixture down the centre of each crêpe. Fold opposite edges of crêpe over the fruit mixture and arrange 2 crêpes on **each serving dish**. Top with remaining yogurt mixture.

Sapodilla Ice Cream Cup

Ripe sapodillas
Soursop Ice Cream page 349, or *Rum Raisin Ice Cream page 346*

Peel the sapodillas; using a teaspoon, scoop out the centre membrane with the seeds and some of the pulp making a deep cavity.

Cut a thin slice from the bottom so that the dillies stand upright. Place into a **flat pan** and chill. When ready to serve, place dillies into **ice-cream cups** *or dessert dishes*. Fill the cavity with ice cream; sprinkle with nuts or dessert sauce and serve.

Tropical Banana Split

1 ripe banana
2 scoops (1/4 cup) *Vanilla Ice Cream page 345*
1 scoop *Coconut Rum Raisin Ice Cream page 346*
2 tbsp. chocolate sauce
1 tbsp. *Mango Syrup page 318*
3 cherries
1 tbsp. grated nuts

Peel and slice the banana in half lengthwise. Place in **oval dessert dish**. Arrange the scoop of *Coconut Rum Raisin Ice Cream* in centre of banana and scoops of vanilla ice cream on each side.

Decorate with cherries and pour on chocolate sauce and *Mango Syrup*. Sprinkle with nuts.

Tropical Cake & Ice Cream Roll

Crust for *Sawyer's Guava Jelly Roll page 330*
1 quart *Soursop Ice Cream (below)*

Prepare the crust and spread with the ice cream. Roll up; cut into 1-inch slices and serve.

Soursop Ice Cream

2 cups whole milk
2 cups sugar
1-1/2 cups heavy cream
1-1/2 cups sweetened condensed milk
1-1/2 cups soursop purée *page 27*
1/2 tsp. freshly ground nutmeg

In a **2-quart sized saucepan**, heat the milk and dissolve the sugar in it. Add the cream and the condensed milk. Pour into an **ice cream freezer** to within 1-inch of the top and freeze according to manufacturer's instructions until partly frozen.

Add the soursop purée mixed with the nutmeg and continue to freeze until firm.

Place in freezer for 2 hours to "set" and serve.

Notes

Confections,
Jams,
Jellies &
Chutneys

Recipes

Fudges

Fabulous, Butterscotch,

Peanut Butter, Coconut,

Divine Rum

❋ Cakes

Coconut, Creamy Coconut Squares

Benné, Nell's Peanut, Almond,

Carmel Popcorn Balls

Peanut Popcorn Balls

Roasted Guinep Seeds

❋❋ Jams, Jellies & Chutneys

❋ Jellies

Guava, Pineapple, Mango,

Hog Plum, Sea Grape,

Scarlet Plum Jelly

Jelly Bag

Spice Bag

❋ Jams

Guava, Pineapple, Mango

Hog Plum, Sea Grape

❋ Chutneys & Pickles

Mango, Tamarind,

Mango Tamarind, Pineapple

Pickled Guava Peel

Pickled Tropical Almond Meats

Tamarind Puree

Tamarind Paste

Tamarind Guava Paste

Guava Puree

Guava Cheese

Fabulous Fudge

2-1/4 cups sugar
3/4 cup evaporated milk
1 cup Marshmallow Crème or 16 large marshmallows
1/4 cup butter or margarine
1/4 tsp. salt
1 pkg. (6 oz.) Semi-sweet Chocolate Morsels
1 tsp. vanilla extract
1 cup chopped nuts

In a heavy **2-quart sized saucepan**, mix together the sugar, evaporated milk, marshmallow crème or marshmallows, butter and salt.

Cook, stirring constantly, over medium heat to a boil (mixture will be bubbling all over the top). Boil and stir until the mixture registers 236°F on a **candy thermometer** or about 4 to 5-minutes. Remove from heat.

Stir in the chocolate morsels until completely melted. Stir in the extract and the nuts. Spread in a buttered **8-inch square pan**. Cool and cut into 30 pieces.

Butterscotch Fudge

Prepare same as *Fabulous Fudge* (above) except use one package (6 oz.) of *Butterscotch Morsels* in place of the Chocolate Morsels.

Peanut Butter Fudge

2 cups white sugar
1 cup canned coconut milk
2 tbsp. white Karo Syrup
2 tbsp. butter
1 cup smooth peanut butter

In a heavy **3-quart sized saucepan**, combine the sugar, coconut milk and syrup; bring to a boil.

Reduce the heat and cook over medium heat stirring constantly until the mixture forms a soft ball when dropped into a **small dish** of cold water.

Remove from the heat. Add the butter and peanut butter and, with a large **wooden spoon**, beat vigorously until thick. Turn into a **9-inch square pan** greased with butter.

Allow to cool and cut into 1-inch squares before fudge is completely cold.

Coconut Fudge

3/4 cup canned coconut milk
2 tbsp. butter
1-3/4 cups Marshmallow Crème or 2 cups miniature marshmallows
2 cups sugar
1 cup packaged coconut flakes
2 cups Semi-sweet Chocolate Chips

Grease a **9-inch square pan** with butter.

In a heavy **3-quart sized saucepan**, combine the coconut milk, butter, sugar and marshmallow cream (or marshmallows). Bring to a rolling boil over medium heat, stirring constantly with a **large wooden spoon**. Continue to boil and stir for 4 to 5-minutes.

Remove from the heat. Immediately add the chips, stirring until smooth. Stir in the coconut. Pour into the greased pan and Cool. Cut into 1-inch squares before fudge is completely cold.

Divine Rum Fudge

2-1/4 cups sugar
1/2 cup evaporated milk
1/4 cup Ole Nassau Chick Charney Rum
1 cup Marshmallow Crème or 16 large marshmallows
1/4 cup butter or margarine
1/4 tsp. salt
1 pkg. (6 oz.) Semi-sweet White Chocolate Morsels
1 cup chopped nuts

Grease a **9-inch square pan** with butter. In a heavy **2 quart-sized saucepan**, mix together the sugar, evaporated milk, rum, Marshmallow Crème or large marshmallows, butter and salt.

Over medium heat stirring constantly with a **large wooden spoon**, bring to a boil (mixture will be bubbling all over the top). Boil and stir about 4 to 5-minutes more; remove from the heat.

Stir in the chocolate morsels until completely melted. Stir in the extract and the nuts. Spread in the buttered pan. Cool and cut into 30-pieces.

Roasted Guinep Seeds

Remove pulp from guinep seeds; place into a **heavy iron skillet** and over medium-high heat, stirring, roast until dark brown. Or place seeds directly into hot coals and roast like our ancestors did. Cool and enjoy much like "chestnuts roasted on an open fire".

Coconut Cakes

1 large freshly grated coconut page 24
3 to 4 slices fresh ginger, crushed
3 cups water
4 cups sugar

In a **3-quart sized heavy saucepan**, combine the grated coconut with remaining ingredients and bring to a boil.

Reduce the heat and cook, stirring constantly with a **wooden spoon**, until the mixture is thick and forms a ball when dropped into a **small dish** of cold water.

Drop by tablespoonfuls onto a greased **baking sheet**. Allow to cool completely. To store, place in an **airtight container**.

Creamy Coconut Squares

2 cups freshly grated coconut page 24
2 cups white sugar
1 cup canned coconut milk
1/4 tsp. salt
1 tbsp. butter
1/2 tsp. baking soda
1 tsp. vanilla extract
1 tsp. red food colouring (or to desired colouring)

In a **heavy 2-quart sized saucepan**, combine the sugar, coconut milk, salt, butter and baking soda, mixing thoroughly. Bring to a boil and continue to boil without stirring until the mixture registers 236°F on a **candy thermometer** *or a little of the mixture forms a ball when dropped into a small dish of cold water.*

Remove from the heat and cool slightly (about 15-minutes). Add the coconut and vanilla. Beat vigorously with a **large wooden spoon** until light and creamy.

Divide mixture in half between **two separate bowls**. Add the food colouring to half the mixture stirring for even colouring. Spread the white half of mixture in a buttered **8-inch square pan** and press down. Spread the white half over the red and press down. Cool.

Just before the mixture is completely cooled, cut into 2-inch squares.

Sesame Seeds

Sesame seeds have a nutty, slightly sweet flavour, enhanced by toasting and are believed to be one of the first condiments, as well as one of the first plants to be used for edible oil. The annual herb can grow as high as seven feet, though most plants range two to four feet. Usage dates back to 3000 BC. Over 5000 years ago, the Chinese burned sesame oil not only as a light source but also to make soot for their ink blocks. "Open Sesame", the magic words used by Ali Baba to open the treasure cave in the classic Arabian tale "The Thousand and One Nights", suggests the phrase comes from the manner in which the sesame seeds burst open with a pop much like the sudden pop of a lock springing open. Since this process scatters the seeds, the pods are often harvested by hand before they are fully ripe. Through the ages, the seeds have been a source of food and oil and sesame seed oil is still the main source of fat used in cooking in the Near and Far East. African slaves brought sesame seeds, which they called "benné seeds" to the New World.

In the Caribbean, influenced by our African ancestors, the seeds are called benné seeds and are used in flavouring a variety of dishes but most popular with all ages is the confection - Benné Cakes. ✽

356

Benné Cakes

2 cups benné seeds (sesame seeds)
1 cup brown sugar
1 cup white sugar
1 cup water

In a **large**, dry **skillet**, parch the benné seeds over medium heat, stirring constantly until the seeds are golden.

In a **heavy 2-quart sized saucepan**, combine the ingredients. Bring to a rolling boil over medium heat and cook, stirring constantly with a **large wooden spoon**, until the mixture forms a soft ball when dropped into a **small dish** of cold water.

Remove from the heat and drop by tablespoonfuls onto a greased **baking sheet**. Cooling completely and serve as a candy treat.

Nell's Peanut Cakes

Traditional Peanut Cakes are made using two methods, each with a distinct taste. Cooks have their favourite, believing that the method of "boiling" the peanuts makes them more tender. The "parching" method gives the cakes a "nuttier" taste. Try both and make your choice.

Boiled Method

2 quarts raw peanuts, unshelled
3 to 4 cups white or brown sugar
1 tsp. grated fresh ginger or orange zest
Water

Shell the peanuts but do not remove the skins. Place into a **large heavy pot** with water to cover and bring to a boil. Boil for about 30-minutes and test if the peanuts are tender (you will taste when they are done).

When the peanuts are done, drain off the hot water and place them into cold water. Cool and slip off the skins. You may also break the nuts into halves.

Place the peanuts back into the pot with just enough water to cover and bring to a boil. Add sugar to taste. Add the zest and cook until the mixture thickens and forms a ball when dropped into a **small dish** of cold water. Remove from the heat and drop by tablespoonfuls onto greased **baking sheets**. Allow to cool completely.

Parched Method • *Bake at 350°F*

Spread unshelled peanuts in a **large baking pan** (sprinkle with about 2-tbsp. salt if desired), place into the oven and "parch" stirring a few times. Bake for 25 to 30-minutes and test (you will smell when they are done). Shell the peanuts and prepare same as **Boiled Method** except do not add ginger or orange zest.

Caramel Popcorn Balls

3 qts. popped corn
1/3 cup evaporated milk
3/4 cup white corn syrup
1/2 cup sugar
2 tsp. vinegar
1/4 tsp. salt
1 tsp. vanilla extract
2 tbsp. butter

In a **2 quart-sized saucepan**, mix together all ingredients except popped corn. Stir over low heat until the sugar is dissolved. Increase the heat without stirring and put a **candy thermometer** in place. Cook until the mixture reaches 280°F (remove from the heat while testing).

When temperature has reached 280°F, add the evaporated milk gradually (so that the mixture does not stop boiling), while stirring constantly with a **large wooden spoon**. Bring caramel mixture to 280°F again, stirring constantly.

Remove from the heat and remove the thermometer. Stir in the vanilla extract.

Gradually pour the hot caramel syrup into the centre of the warm popped corn. With a **long handle fork**, quickly blend to coat the corn with the syrup and dot with the butter. With buttered hands, gather and press into firm balls.

Peanut Popcorn Balls

Prepare same as *Caramel Popcorn Balls* above except add *1-cup warm, salted, roasted peanuts* with popped corn before pouring on the caramel syrup.

Jelly Bag

The following jelly recipes are prepared using the traditional method. To make clear jelly, the juice would be strained through a "Jelly Bag".

To make the bag: cut a double thickness of cheesecloth about 36-inches long and fold in half. Put a **large strainer** or colander over a **bowl** and lay the cloth in the strainer or colander.

Pour the cooled cooked fruit carefully into the cheesecloth. Gather the four corners of the cloth together and tie firmly. Allow the juice to drip through the cheesecloth and through the colander into a **bowl**. Speed up the process by pressing the bag against the colander using a **wooden spoon**.

Guava Jelly

Fresh ripe guavas
Sugar
Water

Wash the guavas, peel and cut into halves *page 26* (do not remove the seeds) place into a **large stockpot** with water to cover. Bring to a boil and cook until the guavas are soft. Cool.

Place the *Jelly Bag* into a **colander** *or a strainer* and carefully pour the cooled guava into the bag and follow method above for clear juice.

After the juice is drained from the guava, measure and pour into the stockpot (preserve the cooked guava to make purée for jam). Measure 3/4-cup of sugar for each cup of juice and bring to a boil.

Reduce the heat and stirring with a **large wooden spoon**, cook until the mixture thickens and forms a ball when dropped into a **small dish** of cold water.

Stir in Liquid Fruit Pectin per packaged instructions; pour the jelly into **sterilized jars** and seal.

Mango Jelly

Peel ripe mangos and chop into chunks *page 27*. Prepare same as *Guava Jelly* (above) except substitute the *mango juice for the guava juice.*

Sea Grape Jelly

Wash the sea grapes, place into a **large stockpot** and boil until the grapes are soft *page 28*. Prepare same as *Guava Jelly* (above) except substitute the *sea grape juice for the guava juice.*

Hog Plum Jelly

Wash the hog plums, place into a **large stockpot** and boil until the plums are soft *page 28*. Prepare same as *Guava Jelly* (above) except substitute the *hog plum juice for the guava juice.*

Scarlet Plum Jelly

Wash the scarlet plums place into a **large stockpot** and boil until the plums are soft *page28*. Prepare same as *Guava Jelly* (above) except substitute the scarlet plum juice *for the guava juice.*

Pineapple

In ancient world, the Pineapple was used as a symbol of generous hospality and wealth. The first encounter between Europeans and a pineapple occurred in 1493, when Christopher Columbus went ashore on the Caribbean island of Guadeloupe. The sailors ate and enjoyed the curious new fruit and Columbus brought some back to Queen Isabella. Spanish explorers thought they looked like pine cones and called them "Pina" and the English added apple to associate it with fruit.

The pineapple became a celebrity fruit. Its rarity, expense, reputation and attractiveness make it the ultimate exotic food item. Into the 1600s, it remained uncommon and so coveted that King Charles II posed for an official portrait in which he is receiving a pineapple as a gift. Sculptured pineapples appeared as gateposts, door lintels and were stencilled on walls and other household items.

It was nearly two centuries before they were able to perfect a hothouse method for growing a pineapple plant. It has been an important fruit in The Bahamas for more than two hundred years and was exported to England by the early settlers. The story is told that a ship "put in" at Eleuthera and pineapple slips were taken to Hawaii.

Pineapple Jelly

Peel and core fresh ripe pineapples *page 25* and chop into chunks. Prepare same as *Guava Jelly page 359* except substitute the *pineapple juice for the guava juice.*

Guinep Jelly

Using a paring knife, peel the guineps. Place into a large stockpot and boil for about 30-minutes. Prepare same as *Guava Jelly page 359* except substitute the *guinep juice for the guava juice.*

Guava Jam

Fresh guavas
Sugar, 3/4-cup for each cup of purée (or to taste)

Was the guavas, peel and cut into halves (do not remove the seeds). Place into a **large stockpot** with water to cover. Bring to a boil and cook until the guavas are soft; Cool.

Turn the cooled guavas into a **food mill** *or colander* placed over a **large bowl** and drain (liquid can be used for making *Guava Jelly page 359*). Using the food mill, purée the guava removing and discarding the seeds.

(Alternatively, turn the guava into a colander and using a sieve, press out the pulp, discarding the seeds).

Measure purée; add sugar to taste, return to the stockpot and bring to a boil. Reduce the heat and stirring with a **large wooden spoon**, cook until the mixture thickens and stays in place when dropped from a teaspoon onto a cold plate. (The mixture will bubble and splatter while cooking; it will also stick to the bottom of the pot and burn very easily, so be careful and diligent for best results).

Stir in Liquid Fruit Pectin per packaged instructions; pour the jam into sterilized jars and seal.

Pineapple Jam

4 cups fresh pineapple (about 2 pineapples)
3 cups sugar
1 tsp. grated lemon peel

Prepare the fresh pineapples *page 25*; chop into fine pieces, reserving the natural juices.

Combine the pineapple, sugar, lemon peel and natural juices in a **heavy stockpot**. Bring to a boil over medium heat, stirring constantly with a **large wooden spoon**.

Lower the heat and simmer, uncovered, stirring, until the jam thickens, about 30 to 45-minutes. Cool. Pour into **sterilized jars** and seal.

Mango Jam

Mango purée page 27
Sugar
Water

Measure equal amounts of purée and sugar, adding enough water to cover. Place into a **large heavy stockpot**.

Bring to a boil; reduce the heat and simmer, uncovered, stirring with a **large wooden spoon** until the mixture is thick about 45-minutes to 1-hour. Cool. Pour into **sterilized jars** and seal.

Sea Grape Jam

4 quarts ripe sea grapes
Water to cover
8 cups sugar (approximately)
1 tbsp. freshly squeezed lime juice

Wash the grapes and place into a **large stockpot** with water to cover. Boil for 20-minutes and let cool. Pour off the water (preserve for jelly or a delicious drink or punch).

Using fingers, remove the seeds and discard, preserving as much pulp and skin as possible. Place into a **food processor** *or blender* and purée.

Place the purée, sugar and lime juice back into the pot and simmer, uncovered, stirring with a **large wooden spoon** until the mixture is thick about 45-minutes to 1-hour.

Cool. Pour into **sterilized jars** and seal.

Mango Chutney

10 large firm-ripe mangoes
1 cup raisins
1 cup vinegar
1 cup freshly squeezed lime juice
1-1/2 cups brown sugar
2 to 4 bird peppers
2 cloves garlic, grated
1 medium-sized onion, finely chopped
1 tbsp. mustard seed
1 tbsp. celery seed
2 tbsp. chopped fresh gingerroot or 2 tsp. ground ginger
1-1/2 tbsp. salt

Peel the mangoes, slice the flesh from the seeds and cut into small pieces. Combine all ingredients in a **large bowl** mixing well. Cover and let stand overnight (no need to refrigerate).

After the overnight soak, place the mixture into a **large stockpot** and cook over low heat for 45-minutes to 1-hour.

Pour into **sterilized jars** and seal. Serve with meat dishes.

Tamarind Chutney

About 2 lbs. of tamarinds in the pods for 6 cups pulp without seeds
1 cup raisins
1 cup Dry White Wine
1 cup water
3 cups sugar
1 large onion, finely chopped
2 cloves garlic, finely chopped
1 tbsp. finely chopped ginger
1 tsp. mustard seeds or dry mustard
1 tsp. celery seeds or flakes
1 tsp. ground white pepper
1 tsp. salt

Shuck the shell from the tamarind and cut the fruit into sections. Using a **paring knife**, remove the seeds.

Combine all of the ingredients in a **large bowl**, mixing well. Cover and let stand overnight (no need to refrigerate).

After the overnight soak, place the mixture into a **large stockpot** and cook over low heat for 45-minutes to 1-hour.

Pour into **sterilized jars** and seal. Serve with meat dishes.

Tamarind Mango Chutney

4 cups seeded tamarind *page 26*
6 cups 3/4" chopped mango
1 cup raisins
1 cup vinegar
1 cup Dry White Wine
2 cups brown sugar
2 to 4 bird peppers
2 cloves garlic, grated
1 medium-sized onion, finely chopped
1 tbsp. mustard seed
1 tbsp. celery seed
2 tbsp. chopped fresh gingerroot
or 2 tsp. ground ginger
1-1/2 tbsp. salt

Combine all of the ingredients in a **large bowl** mixing well. Cover and let stand overnight (no need to refrigerate).

After the overnight soak, place the mixture into a **large stockpot** and cook over low heat for 45-minutes to 1-hour.

Pour into **sterilized jars** and seal. Serve with meat dishes.

Pineapple Chutney

Prepare same as *Mango Chutney page 363* except substitute *4 large fresh ripe pineapples, peeled, cored and chopped into 1/4-inch chunks page 25* for the mango.

Tamarind Purée

1 lb. peeled ripe tamarind *page 26*
Water to cover
1 cup liquid from cooking tamarinds

Prepare tamarind and cool.

Turn the tamarinds into a **colander** placed over a **large bowl** and drain. Measure out 1-cup of the liquid. (Remaining liquid may be sweetened and used as a punch).

Remove all of the seeds and place the tamarinds into the bowl of a **food processor** fitted with the knife blade with 1-cup of the liquid and process for about 1-minute.

Tamarind

Native to Tropical East Africa and possibly Southern Asia, the tamarind was first introduced into Europe from India during the Middle Ages. Europeans at first thought the brown pods to be the fruit of the palm tree. Transported to Tropical America long ago, it has become naturalized and is now common in the Caribbean.

The tamarind is used in many ways and is the key ingredient in Worcestershire sauce, so you have tasted it. The young tender fruit are cooked in rice and used for seasoning fish and meat.

The fully-grown and ripe, but undried fruits, their pulp much like apple butter in appearance, are shelled and eaten out of hand. The young tender and very acid fruits can be "as sour as a lime".

The tree-dried fruits are shelled and preserved in sugar or strained to a thick sauce for use as a refreshing healthful cold drink. The native children of the tropics, too, have their own way of eating the full grown but not yet ripe fruits, called "swells", picked right off the tree and sprinkled with salt. ✱

Tamarind Paste

1 cup Tamarind Purée page 26
1-1/2 cups sugar (or to taste)

Prepare the *Tamarind Purée* place into a **2-quart sized saucepan**, add the sugar and water. Bring to a boil over medium heat.

Reduce the heat and, stirring with a **wooden spoon**, cook for at least 20 minutes or until the mixture is very thick. If the fruit is tart, add more sugar for desired taste.

Tamarind Guava Paste

1 cup Tamarind Purée page 26
1 cup Guava Purée page 26
1-1/2 cups sugar, or to taste

In a **2-quart sized saucepan**, combine the purées and sugar and bring to a boil over medium heat. Reduce the heat and stirring with a **large wooden spoon**, cook for about 20-minutes until the mixture is very thick. If the tamarind is tart, add more sugar for desired taste.

Guava Cheese

4 cups Guava Purée page 26
4 cups sugar

Measure equal amounts of *Guava Purée* and sugar mixing together in a **heavy stockpot**.

Bring to a boil, reduce the heat and simmer uncovered, stirring with a **large wooden spoon** until the mixture forms a hard ball when dropped into a **small dish** of cold water.

Cool slightly, and pour into a greased **pan** to a depth of 1-inch; allow to cool and cut into 2-inch squares.

Spice Bag

To make a spice bag, cut cheesecloth into an 8-inch square. Place whole spices and peppers in the centre and tie securely with a string and place into the pot with chutneys or soups etc. The spice bag can be used over and over.

Pickled Guava Peels

2 cinnamon sticks
2 tsp. whole allspice
2 tsp. whole cloves
1 cup water
2 cups sugar
1/2 cup vinegar
1 tsp. salt
6 cups guava peel

Break the cinnamon stick into pieces; combine with the spice seeds and cloves and place into a spice bag (above).

Combine the water, sugar, vinegar, and salt in a **3-quart sized saucepan**. Add the spice bag and bring to a boil over high heat. Boil for about 5-minutes

Place the guava peels into a **large glass bowl** *or enamel bowl*. Remove the mixture from the heat and pour over the guava peel. Cover and let "steep" over-night. Return to the saucepan and boil for about 10-minutes. Cool. Place into **sterilized glass jars**, cover and store.

Pickled Almond Meats

4 or 5 dozen ripe tropical almonds

Wash the almonds thoroughly and gently remove the ripe outside meat from the almond seeds to measure 6-cups. Prepare same as *Pickled Guava Peels* above, except substitute the almond meats.

Almond Cakes

2 quarts tropical almond
3 to 4 cups white or brown sugar to taste
Almond extract

Collect dried almonds, place on a flat surface and using a hammer, break open or "bark" the almonds to remove the centre kernel (see following page); place into a **large heavy pot** with water to cover; boil for about 30-minutes and prepare same as *Nell's Peanut Cakes,* **Boiled Method**, *page 357.*

367

Almond

Part of the plum family, the almond tree is native to North Africa, West Asia and the Mediterranean. Ancient Romans also referred to almonds as "Greek Nuts," since they were first cultivated in Greece. Almonds date back in print to the Bible.

The bitter almond growing in the islands, is cousin to the sweet almond and in the Caribbean, the beautiful, stately, spreading trees grow in abundance. On the tree, the fruit looks like a small elongated peach and during the summer months they fall to the ground, usually ignored except by the children who enjoy the tart outside meat.

Left on the ground, the outer meat will dry out leaving a hard husk-like bark similar to the coconut. Using a hammer, you can "bark" or break open this outer bark, revealing the inner shell containing the nut.

Traditionally, Bahamians use the nuts (kernels) to make a confection, Almond Cakes, and on the preceding page is a recipe for Pickled Almond Meats.

Party
Drinks &
Punches

Recipes

Independence Swizzle

Hurricane Jack

Rum Pineapple Fizz

Rum Rickey

Tropical Rum Shakes

Cappuccino Rum Shakes

Banana Sunset

Zombie

Blue Dolphin

Ocean Breeze

Midnight Mango

Moonlight Mango

Soursop Coconut

Guava De-light

Tia Shake

❋ **Punches**

John Canoe Punch

Rum Pineapple Fizz

Gin & Coconut Water

Anguilla Punch

La Roma Cola

Solar Rum Punch

Cocktails

Ole Nassau Rum Cocktails

Independence Swizzle

2 oz. Chic Charney Gold Rum
1/2 oz. Simple Syrup
1/2 oz. lemon juice
1/4 oz. egg white
3 dashes Angostura Bitters

Shake well with crushed ice. Serve in a **12-oz. glass**.

John Canoe Punch

1-1/2 oz. Chick Charney Gold Rum
1/2 oz. Bardinet Grenadine
1/2 oz. Curacao
1/2 oz. Simple Syrup
2 oz. orange juice
2 oz. pineapple juice
2 dashes Angostura Bitters

Shake well with crushed ice. Serve in a **12-oz. glass**.

Hurricane Jack

1 oz. Jack Malantan Dark Rum
1 oz. Chick Charney Gold Rum
1 oz. Chick Charney Light Rum
1/2 oz. Coconut Liqueur
1/2 oz. Pineapple Liqueur
1 oz. Bardinet Grenadine

Shake well. Serve over ice in a **tall glass**. Garnish with orange slice & cherry.

Rum Rickey

1-1/2 oz. Chick Charney Rum
1/2 oz. Cointreau or Triple Sec
1-1/2 tbsp. freshly squeezed lime juice
Superfine sugar to taste
Chilled Club Soda
Orange wedge
Strip of orange zest

In a **tall glass** filled with ice, combine rum, Cointreau, lime juice, sugar and top off with soda. Stir the drink well and garnish with orange wedge and zest.

Famous Rums
Made and Distributed
by Burns House, Bahamas

These **"Bahamian-Style" Rums** are of the highest and finest quality made with special ingredients which can only be found in The Bahamas. After considerable aging in oak barrels, 7 years for the Yer Ho' and 5 years for our Jack Malantan Special Reserve, our Rums are of an exceptional high quality, perfect for making delicious punches. Our premium white spirits also represent the finest in perfectly mixable rums for any special event or for august occasion. *Pick up a bottle in The Bahamas!*

"Bahamian-Style" Rums: Chick Charney,
Jack Malantan, Yer Ho', Ole Nassau Liqueurs

Tropical Rum Shakes

1 pint softened *Vanilla Ice Cream page 345*
1 oz. Chick Charney Rum
1/2 Crème De Cacao
1 tbsp. chopped crystallized gingerroot

In a **blender**, blend all ingredients until smooth. Pour into **2 long stemmed glasses**.

Cappuccino Rum Shakes

1 pint softened Coffee Ice Cream
3 oz. Chick Charney Rum
1/4 tsp. ground cinnamon
1/2 cup Whipped Cream
Unsweetened Cocoa Powder
Cinnamon stick

In a **blender**, blend the ice cream, rum and ground cinnamon until smooth but still thick. Pour into **2 long stemmed glasses**. Top drinks with whipped cream and garnish with cocoa powder and cinnamon stick.

Banana Sunset

2 oz. Chick Charney Rum
2 oz. pineapple juice
1 oz. fresh orange juice
1-1/2 oz. Liquid Sweet & Sour Mix
1/2 tbsp. Grenadine Syrup
2 Maraschino cherries

In a **cocktail shaker** half filled with ice cubes, combine the rum, pineapple juice, orange juice, sweet & sour mix and Grenadine syrup. Shake for 30-seconds. Strain into **2 tall glasses** filled with ice. Garnish with cherries.

Zombie

1-1/2 oz. Chick Charney Rum
1-1/2 oz. Jack Malantan Rum
1-1/2 oz. Yer Ho Rum
1 tbsp. Apricot Liqueur
2 tbsp. freshly squeezed lime juice
2 tbsp. Unsweetened pineapple juice
Cracked ice
Orange & lime slices

In a **cocktail shaker** filled with ice cubes, combine the rums, apricot liqueur and the juices. Shake the mixture well and strain into a **tall glass** filled with cracked ice. Garnish with the orange and lime slices.

Blue Dolphin

1 oz. Vodka
1 oz. Dry Vermouth
1/2 oz. Blue Curacao
1/2 oz. Coconut Rum
1 Orange slice

In a **cocktail shake**r, combine all ingredients with 3 ice cubes. Shake the mixture and strain into a **martini glass**. Garnish with orange slice.

Midnight Mango

2 oz. Jack Malantan Rum
1/2 teaspoon Triple Sec
1/2 oz mango purée *page 27*
Garnish with a slice of lime

In a **cocktail shaker** filled with ice cubes, combine the ingredients. Shake and strain into **cocktail glasses** and garnish with the slice of fresh lime.

Moonlight Mango

2 oz. Chick Charney Rum
1/2 teaspoon Triple Sec
1/2 oz. mango purée page 27
Garnish with a slice of lemon

In a **cocktail shaker** filled with ice cubes, combine the ingredients. Shake and strain into **cocktail glasses** and garnish with the slice of fresh lemon.

Guava De-light

1-1/2 oz. Chick Charney Rum
1/2 oz. fresh guava purée page 26
1/2 oz. pineapple juice
1/2 oz. Grenadine syrup
1 oz. canned coconut milk
Garnish with a slice of guava

Place the ingredients with crushed ice into the bowl of a **blender** and blend. Pour into a **chilled glass** and garnish with the guava slice.

Ocean Breeze

1-1/2 oz Chick Charney Rum
1 oz. Scarlet Plum Juice
1 oz. fresh coconut water

Combine all of the ingredients in a **cocktail shaker** mixing well. Pour over rocks in a **tall glass** and top with a thin slice of coconut.

Soursop Coconut

1 cup soursop pulp page 27
1/2 cup coconut milk or cream
Sweetened condensed milk to taste
1/2 cup Chick Charney Rum

Remove the seeds from the soursop pulp and combine all of the ingredients into the bowl of a **blender**. Blend, chill and serve in **long stemmed glasses**.

Solar Rum Punch

Serves 6

6 to 8 cups Tropical Solar Ice Tea *page 43*
2 cups Yer Ho Rum
1/2 to 3/4 cups sugar
1 orange, sliced
4 limes, sliced
4 lemons, sliced

Prepare the tea; thinly slice the fruits and chill.

Stir the sugar into the tea, until dissolved. Add the rum and slices of the chilled fruit. Pour the mixture into a **punch bowl** filled with ice cubes, dip and serve in **punch cups**.

Rum & Pineapple Fizz

9 oz. Chick Charney Rum
3 cups chilled unsweetened pineapple juice
1/4 cup freshly squeezed lime juice
5 Club Sodas or Seltzers
Lime slices for garnish

In a **large pitcher**, combine the rum, pineapple juice and lime juice. Fill **six tall glasses** with ice; divide the rum mixture among them and add the club soda. Garnish the drinks with the lime slices.

Famous Liquors
Made and Distributed
by Allied Domecq
Spirits & Wines

Canadian Club.

Tequila Sauza.

ALLIED DOMECQ
Spirits & Wine

Gin & Coconut Water

1-1/2 oz. Beefeater Gin
5 oz. Water from a freshly picked coconut

Mix together, chill or serve over rocks in a **tall glass**.

Gin & Sin

1 1/2 oz. of Beefeater
3/4 oz. lemon juice
3/4 oz. orange juice
Dash of Grenadine
1 teaspoon of sugar
Stemmed cherry

Shake well over ice cubes in a cocktail shaker, strain into cocktail glass or serve over ice in a tumbler and add cherry for garnish.

Anguilla Punch

3 cups orange juice
1 cup lemon juice
1 cup sugar
2 lemons thinly sliced
1 quart iced Club Soda
One 25 oz. bottle Canadian Club
Ice Ball page 52

Combine the fruit juices and sugar in a **punch bowl**. Stir until the sugar dissolves. Add the lemon slices and refrigerate 1-hour.

Stir in the club soda and whisky. Add a large *Ice Balls*.

Margarita

1-1/2 oz. Hornitos Tequila
1 oz. Cointreau
1-1/2 oz. lemon (or lime) juice, freshly squeezed (approximately 1 juicy
lemon or lime)
1/2 cup shaved or crushed ice
Salt
1 lemon or lime wedge

Salt rim of **glass** *(this is optional).

Place Tequila, Cointreau, juice and ice in **cocktail shaker**. Shake
vigorously. Strain or serve with ice.

To make a frozen Hornitos Margarita, use 1-cup crushed ice and blend in
a **blender** until liquid resembles a slush drink.

Tia Shake

2 parts Tia Maria
1 part light rum
2 scoops chocolate or *Vanilla Ice Cream page 345*

Place into the bowl of a blender and blend together. Serve in a **tall glass**.

La Romana Cooler

1-1/4 cups Courvoisier Cognac
1-1/4 cups soda water
1-1/2 cups orange juice
Juice of 1 lime
3/4 cup pineapple juice

Combine all ingredients a **large pitcher** *or thermos* and serve over ice.
Makes 6 to 8 servings.

Island Breezes

1 oz. Canadian Club
1/2 oz. lemon juice
2 oz. pineapple juice
3 oz. orange juice

Blend ingredients and pour over ice in a tall glass. Garnish with a pineapple
wedge.

Montego Bay Colada

2 oz. Kahlúa
1 oz. Sugar Bay Rum
2 oz. cream of coconut syrup
4 oz. pineapple juice
2 cups crushed ice

In a **blender**, combine all ingredients and blend. Garnish with maraschino cherry and pineapple wedge, if desired.

If you prefer, substitute Pina colada mix for coconut crème and pineapple juice.

San Juan Colada

1 1/2 oz. Canadian Club
3 oz. Pina colada mix
4 oz. pineapple juice
3 ice cubes

Blend until smooth. Serve in a **tall glass** garnished with a pineapple wedge.

Maker's Mark Manhattans

2 oz. Maker's Mark Whisky
1/2 oz. Sweet Vermouth
 (For a Sweet Manhattan) or
1/2 oz. Dry Vermouth
(Dry Manhattan) or
1/2 oz. Sweet and Dry Vermouth (Perfect Manhattan)

Shake over ice and serve in a **Manhattan glass**. Garnish with a cherry, olive, orange or onion.

Maker's Mark Sour

1 oz. Maker's Mark Whisky
2 oz. sweet/sour mix or
2 oz. lemon juice and 1 teaspoon fine sugar

Shake over ice and serve in a **sour** *or rocks glass,* garnished with a cherry and/or orange slice.

Plantation Sour

1 dash of sugar cane Syrup
2/3 Courvoisier VS
1/3 green lemon juice
Cherry
1/2 Courvoisier cognac
1/4 Curaao
1/4 pineapple juice

Island Boy

3/4 Courvoisier cognac
1/8 Curaao orange
1/8 pineapple juice
1 dash bitters

Shaker
Decorate with a twist of lemon peel on top.

Island Girl

1 1/2 oz. Courvoisier cognac
1/2 oz. Tia Maria
3 oz. orange juice
1 drop of Grenadine

Darkest Night

1 Courvoisier cognac
1/2 Drambuie
1/2 Blue Curaao
1 orange
1/2 sweet and sour grenadine syrup over ice

C.C. Manhattan

1 large measure Canadian Club
1/3 measure Sweet Vermouth
1 dash Angostura bitters
Maraschino cherry

Stir ingredients with ice and strain into a chilled cocktail glass. Garnish with a cherry.

Whisky Sour

2 measures of Canadian Club
Juice of half a lemon
1/2 teaspoon sugar
Maraschino cherry

Shake the ingredients with ice and strain into a **sour glass**. Garnish with lemon or orange.

Rye & Dry

2 measures of Canadian Club
Dry Ginger Ale

Stir ingredients and pour into a chilled glass. Add ice. Alternatively, add your favourite mixer e.g. cola, orange or lemonade instead of ginger ale.

Legacy of Christopher Columbus

Seeking riches, Christopher Columbus made four voyages to the "New World", the first in 1492 and the last in 1502; he died in 1506 still with the illusion of having found India. Within a half century of the first voyage of Columbus, Spain had conquered the Aztec, Maya and Inca empire. The Spanish conquest did not completely destroy the pre-Columbian agrarian system, instead it introduced Old World plants.

The cuisines of today's world are typically post-Columbian. What would many of the Mediterranean's gastronomic delights be without the tomato or her rich desserts without chocolate, Ireland's shepherds' pie or England's fish and "chips" without potatoes, Hungary without paprika, Italy's polenta without corn, India's curries, Thai or China's Sichuan dishes without the ubiquitous chile, an American hamburger without onions or Mexican carnitas without beef or pork.

The Spanish and other Europeans who followed them to the "New World" attempted to recreate the Old World agricultural system with which they were familiar. They introduced cattle, horses, donkeys, pigs, goats, sheep and chickens to their colonies. Desiring familiar foods, these immigrants brought with them a full compliment of Old World crops including sugarcane, rice and bananas which thrived in the warm and humid lowlands and wheat, barley and European broadbeans, coffee and winegrapes. They gradually learned to eat maize, monioc, (cassava) potatoes, sweet potatoes, peanuts, and other American foods.

The importance of ox, horse and donkey was momentous. It revolutionized transport and travel and encouraged long-distance trade. Livestock thrived on the vast plains and generated an important source of food for the New World. Indians recognized the superiority of European iron and steel axes, knives, hoes and other tools and before long, stone was virtually eliminated as a material for toolmaking. The post-Columbian exchange of plants and animals, tools and methods of production between the Old World and New vastly altered the agricultural patterns of both hemispheres and benefitted all mankind.

His discoveries redefined traditions and changed the course of history. While Columbus did not find extraordinary cities of gold, fine silks, precious stones and spices, certainly he and his followers succeeded in bringing vast gastronomic riches to both worlds.

Index

Original Bahama Mama doll created by Lady Darling

Abaco Baked Grouper, 160

Akara, African Bean Cakes, 252

❋ **African Dishes**

Stews

   Beef, 119

   Chicken, 119

Akara

  Bean Cakes, 252

  Description & History, 253

  African Culinary Influences, 185

❋ **Akee**

 How to prepare, 25

 Illustration & History, 158

 Salt Fish & Akee, 159

❋ **Almond**

 Cakes, 367

 Description & History,

  Tropical Pickled Meats, 367

Andros Stuffed Baked Crab, 200

Anguilla Punch, 377

❋❋ **APPETIZERS & DIPS, 53 - 66**

 Avocado

  Bacon Rings, 59

  Stuffed Celery, 55

 Balls

  Rum, 63

   Tamarind Guava Rum, 63

 Barbeque Party Drummetts, 62

 Cânapés

   Avocado Bacon Rings, 59

Conch Nips, 57

Corned Beef, 58

Pizza Bites, 60

Sardine, 58

Shrimp & Avocado, 56

Smoked Fish Roe, 58

Tuna Pinwheels, 59

Zippy Cheese, 58

Cheese Pinwheels, 58

Conch Fritters, 60

Chips & Crisps

   Breadfruit Chips, 56

   Plantain Chips, 55

   Plantain Crisps, 56

Dips

 Avocado Bacon, 66

 Clam, 65

 Cream Cheese, 65

 Guacamole, 65

 Mango, 66

 Mango Salsa, 66

Fish Roe Stuffed Eggs, 62

Fried Chicken Rissoles, 62

Guinep Royale, 63

Party Drummetts, 62

Sardine Stuffed Eggs, 61

Sherry Beef Bites, 61

Summer Fruit Kabobs, 55

Tia Maria Cheese Straws, 57

Anguilla Punch, 377

Apple Turnovers, 275

Apricot Turnovers, 275

Au Gratin See Potato Au Gratin

❋ **Avocado**

 & Eggs & Ham, 131

Bacon Dip, 66

Bacon Rings, 59

Baked with Seafood, 142

Dessert, 324

Guacamole, 65

How to prepare, 29

Illustration & History, 72

Lime Pie, 279

Orange/Grapefruit Salad, 71

Salad, 70

Salad Dressing, 80

Seafood Sauce, 257

Shrimp Canapés, 56

Soup, 104

Stuffed Celery, 55

With Seafood Salad, 141

❋ **Bacon**

 Avocado & Bacon Rings, 59

 Avocado Dip, 66

 Coconut Quiche, 145

 Skillet Slaw with Top, 243

 Sliced Breadfruit with Top, 249

❋ **Bahamian**

 Conch Chowder, 108

 Pigeon Peas & Rice, 206

 Pigeon Peas & Grits, 221

 Pumpkin Pie, 283

 Switcher "Limeade", 43

❋ **Baked**

 Avocado Seafood, 142

384

Bananas in Tamarind Sauce, 325

Canned Corned Beef, 195

Rice

   Black-eyed Peas & Rice, 208

   Pigeon Peas & Rice, 208
   With:

    Chicken, 209

    Shrimp, 209

    Crab, 209

❋ **Balls**

Peanut Popcorn, 358

Rum, 63

Tamarind Guava Rum, 63

❋ **Banana(s)**

Alfredo, 324

Baked in Tamarind Sauce, 325

Biscuits, 86

Bran Bread, 93

Crêpes & Ice-cream, 347

Daiquiri, 47

Doughnuts, 85

Fritters, 326

Fruitcake, 299

Green Polenta, 136

Green Sauté, 245

Grouper Filets in Batter, 164

Guava Daiquiri, 47

Honey Rum Baked, 324

Illustration & History, 132

In Blankets, 275

Laura's Pancakes, 133

Peanut Butter Sandwiches, 140

Pineapple & Bacon, 134

Pudding, 331

Rum Barbecue, 325

Rum Bread Pudding, 331

Shake, 47

Sunset, 373

Tropical Split, 349

Whole-wheat Muffins, 87

With Sherry & Cream, 325

❋ **Barbecue**

Jerk Beef or Pork Ribs, 193

Party Drummets, 62

Pineapple Turkey Roll, 188

Poultry Sauce, 261

Rum Barbecue Bananas, 325

Sesame Beef Strips, 190

Sauces

   Poultry, 261

   Kaklua Zesty Barbecue, 261

❋ **Barefoot**

Grits, 220

Rice, 206

❋ **Beef**

African Beef Stew, 119

Barbecue Sesame Beef Strips, 190

Corned See Corned Beef

Fried Rice, 213

Guyana Pepperpot, 115

Jamaican Beef Patties, 152

Jerk Barbecue Beef Ribs, 193

Jerk Roast Beef, 192

Tej's Guyanese Metagee, 114

Mock Drumsticks, 189

Party Drummetts, 62

Sherry Beef Bites, 61

English Steak & Kidney Pie, 191

With Oriental Vegetable, 194

❋ **Beer**

Battered Shrimp, 176

Cheese Cornbread, 91

Cheese Soup, 105

Conch & Beer Casserole, 231

Crawfish in Beer Sauce, 174

Marinade, 264

❋ **Benné** (see also Sesame Seed)

Benné Cakes, 357

Bread Sticks, 97

❋ **Beet(s)**

Salad, 71

Spicy Harvard, 240

❋ ❋ **BEVERAGES, 41 - 52**

Daiquiris

   Banana, 47

   Banana Guava, 47

   Papaya, 49

   Pineapple, 49

   Soursop, 49

   Sugar Apple, 49

Ginger Beer, 46

Ginger Limeade, 45

Juices

   Papaya, 46

   Papaya Orange, 46

   Scarlet Plum, 28

   Sea Grape, 28

Punches

   Hog Plum, 51

   Mango, 50

   Scarlet Plum, 51

   Sea Grape, 50

   Soursop, 51

   Tamarind, 52

Tropical Fruit, 50

Tropical Plum, 50

Lemonade, 43

Mock Pink Champagne, 46

Shakes

Banana, 47

Mango, 47

Switcher "Limeade", 43

Tamarind Cooler, 45

Tropical Solar Iced Tea, 43

Big Gramma's Birthday Cake, 297

Big Gramma's Pound Cake, 296

Biscuits See Banana Biscuits

❁ **Black-eyed Peas**

Akara (African Bean Cakes), 252

Baked & Rice, 208

Peas & Grits, 221

Peas & Rice, 208

Blue Dolphin, 374

Boiled Fish, 128

Bran See Banana Bran Bread

Bread Cups for Salads, 85

❁ **Breadfruit**

& Cheese Casserole, 230

Chips, 56

French Fries, 142

How to prepare, 29

Illustration & History, 248

Salad, 75

Sliced with Bacon Top, 249

Stuffed, 249

Akara (African Bean Cakes), 252

❁❁ **BREADS & ROLLS, 83 - 100**

Quick Breads

Banana Bran, 93

Corn, 90

Mango, 92

Pineapple Loaf-a-Bread, 92

Tia Maria Jamaican Bread, 94

Banana Biscuits, 86

Beer Cheese Cornbread, 91

Banana Doughnuts, 85

Cassava & Coconut Pone, 91

Bread Cups for Salads, 85

Muffins

Banana Whole Wheat, 87

Guava, 86

Molasses, 87

Johnny Cakes

Coconut, 89

Deluxe, 88

Traditional, 88

Rum Raisin Scones, 89

Short Cakes, 90

Yeast Breads

Coconut Bread Sticks, 97

Coconut Raisin Bread, 93

Guava Swirls, 98

Sesame (Benné) Bread Sticks, 97

Whole Wheat Bread, 95

Rolls

Clover Leaf, 97

Dillie Dinner, 97

❁❁ **BREAKFAST & LUNCH, 125 - 152**

❁ **BREAKFAST**

Banana Pineapple Bacon, 134

Corned Beef

& Egg Mounds, 129

Saute & Grits, 129

Carib Potato Pancakes, 134

Eggs

Deep Fried in Curry Sauce, 130

Avocado & Eggs & Ham, 140

Tomatoes Stuffed with Eggs, 131

Family Breakfast Pie, 135

Fish

Boiled Fish & Grits, 128

Mock Boiled Fish, 128

Sardines & Grits, 130

Kalik Junkanoo Rarebit, 134

Pancakes

Carib Potato, 134

Laura's Banana, 133

Sapodilla, 133

Polenta

Coconut, 226

Green Banana, 136

Sapodilla

Pancakes, 133

Waffles, 133

❁ **LUNCHES**

Seafood & Meat Salads in Avocado Halves, Tomato Stars & Breadcups, 141

Baked Avocado Seafood, 142

Burgers

Jerk Burgers, 150

Conch Burgers, 149

Corned Beef Baked Potato, 143

Conch Chili, 150

Conch Chili Baked Potato, 147

Conch Pockets, 151

French Fried Breadfruit, 247

Fritters

Cassava, 138

386

Conch, 60

Corn, 139

Fish, 139

Fish Roe Cassava, 138

Jamaican Beef Patties, 152

Pizzas

Conch Pizza, 147

Individual Pizzas, 149

Quiches

Bacon Coconut Quiche, 145

Curried Seafood Quiche, 144

Quick Stove Top Tuna Casserole, 141

Sandwiches

Banana Peanut Butter Spread, 140

Chicken Salad, 77

Corned Beef, 141

Egg Salad, 140

Avocado & Eggs & Ham, 140

Holiday Turkey, 141

Spicy Tuna, 141

Zippy Cheese, 140

Smoked Oyster Stuffed Potatoes, 144

Tofu

Chicken Sautéed, 146

Fried, 145

Chili, 146

With Crab Meat, 145

Broiled

Crawfish, 171

Fish,157

Grouper Cutlets, 162

Brown

Flour Stew, 266

Gravy, 265

Rice Croquettes, 219

Browned Rice, 215

Brownies See Coconut Brownies

Burgers

Conch Burgers, 149

Jerk Burgers, 150

Butter See Seafood Tamarind Butter

Butterscotch Fudge, 353

Cabbage

& Rice, 217

Chinese, 242

Skillet Slaw with Bacon Top, 243

Slaw, 73

Charline Soup, 110

Stuffed Rolls, 242

❋ ❋ **CAKES, COOKIES, ICINGS & DESSERT SAUCES, 293 -318**

Fruitcakes

Banana, 299

Holiday, 298

Miniature, 300

Guava

Duff Cake, 307

Jam Cake. 302

Upside Down Cake, 302

Mango Shortcakes, 323

Merdina Carrot Cake, 303

Pound

Big Gramma's, 296

Birthday Cake, 297

Olga's Pound Cake, 296

Piña Colada Cake, 295

Rum

Ole Nassau, 301

Sapodilla Bundt Cake, 304

Tropical Cake & Ice Cream Roll, 349

Coconut Brownies, 312

Cookies

Calypso, 312

Chick Charney Moca, 311

Coconut Crisps, 306

Coconut Wafers, 306

Fruitcake, 308

Ginger Bread Collier Boys, 313

High Tea, 309

Slice & Bake Guava, 308

Tortilla Sandwich Cookies, 310

Dessert Glazes & Sauces

Coconut Cream for Dessert, 317

Guava Glaze, 316

Lemon Sauce for Dessert, 317

Mango Glaze, 316

Pineapple Glaze, 316

Rum Glaze, 316

Rum Runner Brown Sugar Sauce, 315

Sapodilla Glaze, 316

Soka Hard Rum Sauce, 315

Icings & Frostings

Cocoa Whipped Cream, 314

Creamy, 314

Rum Whipped Cream, 314

Whipped Cream, 314

Syrups

Lemon for Lemonade, 318

Sapodilla, 318

Mango, 318

Tamarind Guava Paste, 366

❁ **Canapés**

Avocado Bacon Rings, 59

Conch Nips, 57

Corned Beef, 58

Pizza Bites, 60

Sardine, 58

Shrimp & Avocado, 56

Smoked Fish Roe, 58

Tuna Pinwheels, 59

Zippy Cheese, 57

❁ **Cakes (confection)**

Almond, 367

Bennié, 357

Coconut, 355

Nell's Peanut, 357

❁ **Cakes (savoury)**

Salmon, 167

Corned Beef, 195

Crab, 199

Cakes (vegetable)

Akara, 252

Plantain, 244

Wild Rice, 219

Calypso Cookies, 312

Cappuccino Rum Shake, 373

Carib Fried Shrimps, 174

Carib Potato Pancakes, 134

❁ **Caribbean**

Chicken Salad, 78

Guava Cobbler, 322

Sweet Potato Pie, 282

Carmel Popcorn Balls, 358

❁ **Carrot**

Fritters, 326

Merdina Carrot Cake, 305

Potato Carrot Mash, 246

❁ **Cassava**

Casserole, 230

Coconut Pone, 91

Creamy Soup, 106

Crust 9", 272

Fish Roe Cassava Fritters, 138

Fritters, 326

How to prepare, 30

Illustration & History, 107

❁ **Casseroles**

Breadfruit & Cheese, 230

Cassava, 230

Conch & Beer with Cassava Crust, 231

Sauté Macaroni Bake with Seafood, 228

Quick Stove Top Tuna, 141

Rice, 218

Savoury Macaroni & Cheese, 228

Seafood, 179

Cat Island Corn Grits & Crab, 222

Celery See Avocado Stuffed

Charline Cabbage Soup, 110

❁ **Cheese**

Beer Cheese Cornbread, 91

Beer Cheese Soup, 105

Breadfruit & Cheese Casserole, 230

Guava Cheese, 366

Kalik Junkanoo Rarebit, 134

Polenta with Cheese Sauce 227

Sauce, 257

Savoury Macaroni & Cheese, 228

Tia Maria Cheese Straws, 57

Zippy Cheese Canapés, 57

Zippy Cheese Pinwheels, 58

Zippy Cheese Sandwiches, 140

❁ **Cheesecakes**

Fox Hill Sapodilla, 342

Mousse with Poached Plums, 344

South Beach Mango, 341

South Eleuthera Pineapple, 342

Yamacraw Guava, 342

No Bake

Banana, 343

Guava, 333

Mango, 343

Pineapple, 343

Sapodilla, 343

Chick Charney Moca Cookies, 311

❁ **Chicken**

African Stew , 119

Azaleta's Mango, 185

Caribbean Salad, 78

Curried, 121

Party Drummetts, 62

Fried Rice, 213

George's & Dumplin', 116

Ginger Sautéed Tofu, 146

Grilled Tamarind Guava, 185

In Coconut Batter, 184

Jerk, 192

Jerk Wings, 192

Mock Drumsticks, 189

Oven Fried Bites, 184

Party Drummetts, 62

Pie with Cassava Crust, 187

Pineapple, 185

Rissoles

    Fried, 62

    In Mushroom Sauce, 188

    Savoury, 188

    Rotisserie Jerk, 192

    Salad, 77

    Smudder (Steamed), 123

    Souse, 122

    Vegetable Stir Fry, 186

❈ **Chilies**

Conch , 150

Tofu, 146

Conch Chili Baked Potatoes, 147

❈ **Chips**

    Breadfruit, 56

    Breadfruit Fries, 142,

    Plantain, 55

Chinese Cabbage, 242

❈ **Chocolate**

    Guava Jelly Roll, 330

    Jelly Roll Crust, 330

❈ **Chowder(s)**

    Bahamian Conch, 108

    Clam, 108

❈ **Chutney(s)**

    Pineapple, 364

    Mango, 363

    Tamarind Mango, 364

    Tamarind, 363

❈ **Clam**

    Chowder, 108

    Dip, 65

Clover Leaf Rolls, 97

❈ **Cobbler**

    Caribbean Guava Cobbler, 322

    David's Peach, 329

❈ **Cocktails**

    Margarita, 378

    Tia Shake, 378

    Banana Sunset, 373

    Blue Dolphin, 374

    Cappuccino Rum Shakes, 373

    Guava De-light, 374

    Hurricane Jack, 371

    Independence Swizzle, 371

    Midnight Mango, 374

    Moonlight Mango, 374

    Ocean Breeze, 374

    Rum Pineapple Fizz, 375

    Rum Rickey, 371

    Soursop Coconut, 375

    Tropical Rum Shakes, 373

    Zombie, 373

Punches

    Anguilla, 377

    Gin & Coconut Water, 377

    John Canoe, 371

    La Roma Cola, 378

    Rum Pineapple Fizz, 375

    Solar Rum, 375

Cocktail Sauce, 260

❈ **Cocoa**

    Coconut, 323

    Rum Pie, 281

    Whipped Cream Frosting, 314

❈ **Coconut**

    Bacon Coconut Quiche, 145

    Bread Sticks, 97

Brownies, 312

Cakes,355

Cassava Coconut Pone, 91

Chicken in Coconut Batter, 184

Cocoa Coconut, 323

Cream for Desserts, 317

Creamy Squares, 355

Crisps, 306

Crust 9", 270

David's Peach Cobbler, 329

Double Boiler Duff, 338

Duff, 337

Fudge, 354

Filling, 334

Gin & Coconut Water, 376

How to prepare, 24

Illustration & History, 276

Johnny Cake, 89

Polenta, 136

Pudding, 332

Raisin Bread, 93

Roly Poly, 339

Rum Raisin Ice-cream, 346

Soursop Coconut, 375

Tart, 277

Turnovers (Fried Pies), 275

Wafers, 306

❈ **Conch**

    & Beer Casserole, 231

    & Peas & Rice, 208

    Au Vin, 116

    Bahamian Chowder, 108

    Burgers, 149

    Chili, 150

    Chili Baked Potatoes, 147

Cracked Conch, 168

Curried, 121

Dumphries Créole, 170

Fried Rice, 213

Fritters, 60

Ginger, 169

Guanahani, 168

How to prepare, 31

Illustration & History, 148

Hurricane Ham Stew, 118

Individual Pizzas, 149

Nips, 57

Pepper Conch & Rice, 212

Pizza, 147

Pockets, 151

Spicy Rissoles, 170

Rissoles In Shrimp Sauce, 171

On Spaghetti, 171

Salads

Sir Clifford's, 75

Quick Sliced, 76

Sauce, 263

Souse, 122

Spaghetti & Rissoles, 171

Spicy, 169

Smudder (Steamed), 123

Stewed, 120

Cookies – See Cakes &Cookies

Cooler See Tamarind Cooler

❀❀ CONFECTIONS, JAMS,
JELLIES & CHUTNEYS, 351 - 368

Cakes

Almond, 367

Bennié, 357

Coconut, 355

Coconut Squares, 355

Nell's Peanut, 357

Chutneys

Mango, 363

Pineapple, 364

Tamarind, 363

Tamarind Mango, 364

Fudges

Butterscotch, 353

Coconut, 354

Divine Rum, 354

Fabulous, 353

Peanut Butter, 353

Guava Cheese, 366

Jams

Guava, 361

Mango, 362

Pineapple, 362

Sea Grape, 362

Jellies

Guava, 359

Hog Plum, 359

Mango, 359

Pineapple, 361

Scarlet Plum, 359

Sea Grape, 359

Pickles

Guava Peel, 367

Almond Meats, 367

Popcorn

Carmel Popcorn Balls, 358

Peanut Popcorn Balls, 358

Purées

Guava, 26

Tamarind, 26

Tamarind Guava Balls, 63

Tamarind Paste, 366

Roasted Guinep Seeds, 354

❀ Corn

Bread, 90

Bread & Oyster Stuffing, 235

Fritters, 139

Polenta Spicy Corn Cups, 227

Grits, 220

Cat Island & Crab, 222

Island Grits Stuffing, 233

Corn Meal Pastry, 272

Beer Cheese Corn Bread, 91

See Polenta Dishes

❀ Corned Beef,

& Egg Mounds, 129

Sauté & Grits, 129

& Rice Loaf, 218

Baked Canned, 195

Baked Potatoes, 143

Cakes, 195

Canâpes, 58

Salad, 79

Sandwiches, 141

❀ Cornish Hens

Stove Top Baked, 189

Glazed, 190

❀ Crab(s)

& Cat Island Corn Grits, 222

& Peas & Rice, 210

Andros Stuffed Baked, 200

Cakes, 199

Heritage Crab & Dough, 201

How to prepare, 32

Meat Salad, 77

Soufflé, 223

Tofu with Crab Meat, 146

Zesty Boiled, 200

Cream of Potato Soup, 109

❀ **Crawfish**

Avocado With Crawfish Salad, 141

Broiled, 171

Fried Rice, 213

How to prepare, 32

Illustration & Description, 172

In Beer Sauce, 174

Minced, 173

Mixed Mince, 173

Salad, 76

❀ **Creamy**

Cassava Soup, 106

Coconut Squares, 355

Icing, 314

Créole Sauce, 259

❀ **Crisps**

Plantain, 56

Coconut, 306

❀ **Crêpes**

Banana & Ice Cream, 347

Mango & Ice Cream, 348

Crispy Sapodilla Rollups, 279

❀ **Croquettes**

Brown Rice, 219

Potato, 247

Rice & Fish, 220

Crunchie See No Bake Tropical Crunchies

Crown Roast of Lamb, 198

❀ **Crust(s)**

9-inch Coconut, 270

9-inch Crumb, 270

9-inch Pie Shell, 271

9-inch Cassava, 272

Corn Meal Pastry, 272

No Need to Knead, 270

Seasoned for Meat Pies, 273

Crust for Tarts (Fried Pies), 274

Cassava, 272

9-inch Coconut, 270

Cucumber Salad Dressing, 81

❀ **Cups**

Fruity Yogurt, 345

Bread Cups for Salads, 85

Sapodilla Ice Cream, 348

Polenta Spicy Corn, 227

❀ **Curry**

Deep Fried Eggs in Curry Sauce, 130

Deluxe Sauce, 258

Fried Green Tomatoes, 240

Sauce, 257

Seafood with Curry Sauce, 260

Shrimp Curry in a Hurry, 175

❀ **Curried**

Chicken, 121

Conch, 121

Goat, 121

Grouper, 121

Quick Shrimp, 176

Rice, 211

Seafood Quiche, 144

❀ **Cutlets**

Grouper, 163

Broiled Grouper, 162

❀ **Daiquiris**

Banana, 47

Banana Guava, 47

Papaya, 49

Pineapple, 49

Soursop, 49

Sugar Apple, 49

Darkest Night, 380

David's Peach Cobbler

Deep Fried Eggs in Curry Sauce, 130

Deluxe Curry Sauce, 258

❀❀ **DUFFS, PUDDINGS & CHEESECAKES, 319 - 350**

Avocado Dessert, 324

Banana

Alfredo, 324

Baked in Tamarind Sauce, 325

Fritters, 326

Honey Rum Baked, 324

Rum Barbeque, 325

with Sherry & Cream, 325

Caribbean Guava Cobbler, 322

Coco Coconut, 323

David's Peach Cobbler, 329

Cheesecakes

Fox Hill Sapodilla, 342

Mousse with Poached Plums, 344

South Beach Mango, 341

South Eleuthera Pineapple, 342

Yamacraw Guava, 342

Dillie Flambé, 329

Duffs (Traditional)

Coconut, 337

Dillie, 337

Guava, 337

Mango, 337

Pineapple, 337

Double Boiler Duffs

Guava, 338

Coconut, 338

Mango, 338

Dillie, 338

Fritters

Banana, 326

Carrot, 326

Sapodilla, 326

Frozen Desserts & Ice Creams

Banana Crêpes & Ice Cream, 347

Coconut Rum Raisin Ice Cream, 346

Frozen Fruit Slushie, 345

Fruity Yogurt Cups, 345

Mango Crêpes & Ice Cream, 348

Paradise Pie à la Mode, 280

Rum Barbecue Bananas, 325

Rum Raisin Ice Cream, 346

Soursop, 349

Tropical Banana Split, 349

Tropical Cake & Ice Cream Roll, 349

Tropical Fruit Sherbet, 344

Vanilla Ice Cream with Mango Syrup, 345

Jelly Rolls

Chocolate Guava, 330

Pineapple, 330

Sawyer's Guava, 330

No Bake Cheesecakes

Banana, 343

Guava, 333

Mango, 343

Mousse with Poached Plums, 344

Pineapple, 343

Sapodilla, 343

No Bake Tropical Crunchies, 342

Puddings

Banana, 331

Coconut, 332

Miniature Bread, 332

Rum Banana Bread, 331

Sapodilla, 333

Roly Polys

Guava, 339

Coconut, 339

Mango, 339

Pineapple, 339

Dillie, 339

Tropical Fruit Fillings

Coconut, 334

Green Mango, 334

Guava, 333

Pineapple, 334

Sapodilla, 335

Soursop, 335

Fritters

Banana, 326

Carrot, 326

Sapodilla, 326

Guava Surprise, 322

Guava De-light, 374

Mango & Pineapple Strudel, 321

Mango Shortcakes, 323

North Eleuthera Pineapple Fries, 328

Stuffed Baked Sapodilla, 328

Tropical Fruit Drops, 327

Dillie (See also Sapodilla)

Double Boiler Duff, 338

Duff, 337

Flambé, 329

Ice Cream Cup, 348

❋ **Dips**

Avocado Bacon, 66

Clam, 65

Mango, 66

Guacamole, 65

Divine Rum Fudge, 354

Dolphin See Mahi Mahi

❋ **Double Boiler Duffs**

Coconut, 338

Guava, 338

Mango, 338

Sapodilla, 338

Doughnuts See Banana Doughnuts

❋ **Dressings (Stuffings)**

Corn Bread & Oyster, 235

Island Corn Grits, 233

Mashed Potato, 233

Stuffing for Fish, 234

Wild Rice, 235

Rice, 234

❋ **Dressings (Salads)**

Avocado Salad, 80

Hot Benné Seed, 81

Cucumber, 81

Mint, 80

Piña Colada Fruit Dressing, 80

Slaw, 81

❋ **Drummetts**

Barbecue Party, 62

Party, 62

❀ **Duffs (Traditional)**

Coconut, 337

Dillie, 337

Guava, 337

Mango, 337

Pineapple, 337

Dumphries Conch Creole, 170

❀ **Eggs**

Corned Beef & Mounds, 129

Deep Fried with Curry Sauce, 130

Fish Roe Stuffed, 62

Avocado Eggs & Ham, 131

Avocado Eggs & Ham Sandwiches, 140

Salad, 79

Sardine Stuffed, 61

Tomato Stuffed with, 131

❀ **English**

Steak & Kidney Pie, 191

Rum Raisin Scones, 89

Fabulous Fudge, 353

Family Breakfast Pie, 135

❀ **Fillets**

Grouper in Burnt Orange, 166

Grouper in Banana Batter, 164

Filling See Tropical Fruit

❀ **Fingers**

Grouper, 163

Tamarind Guava Grouper, 164

Fire Engine See Corn Beef & Grits

❀ ❀ **FISH & SEAFOOD**

Boiled

Boiled Grouper, 128

Mock Boiled, 128

Conch

& Beer Casserole with Cassava Top, 231

Cracked, 168

Dumphries Créole, 170

Ginger, 169

Guanahani, 168

Rissoles, 170

Rissoles in Shrimp Sauce, 171

Spicy, 169

Crawfish

Avocado with Salad, 141

Broiled, 171

Fried Rice, 213

In Beer Sauce, 174

Minced, 173

Mixed Mince, 173

Salad, 76

Fish Roe

Cassava Fritters, 138

Fish Sauce, 262

Fried Large Roe, 162

Fried Small Roe, 161

Sauce, 262

Smoked Canapés, 58

Stuffed Eggs, 62

Fried Fish

Barbados Flying, 156

Fish (Traditional), 157

Fritters

Conch, 60

Fish, 139

Grouper

Abaco Baked with Stuffing, 160

Boiled, 128

Broiled Cutlets, 162

Curried, 121

Cutlets, 163

Fillets with Banana Batter, 164

Fillets in Burnt Orange, 166

Fingers

Grouper, 163

Tamarind Guava, 164

Ginger Fish Sauce, 261

Mahi Mahi (Dolphin), 161

Oven Fried Scallops, 160

Oven Fried Swordfish, 159

Rice & Fish Croquettes, 220

Salt Fish & Akee, 159

Samana Baked Red Snapper, 156

Sardine

Stuffed Eggs, 61

Paté, 58

Salmon

Oven Fried Steaks, 166

Cakes, 167

Stuffed Tomatoes, 167

Shrimps

Beer Battered, 176

Carib Fried, 174

Quick Curried, 176

Curry in a Hurry, 175

Spiced Ginger Scampi, 177

Turtle

  Grilled Steaks, 177

  Pie, 178

Flambé See Dillie Flambé

Fox Hill Sapodilla Cheesecake, 342

French Fries, Breadfruit, 247

❋ **Fried Dishes**

  Chicken Rissoles, 62

  Fish (Traditional), 157

  Roe (large), 162

  Roe (small), 161

  Barbados Flying Fish, 156

  Ginger Plantain, 244

  Pies See Turnovers

  Plantain, 244

Rice

  Beef, Chicken, Conch, Crawfish, Pork, Shrimp, 212

Tofu, 145

❋ **Fritters**

Dessert

  Banana, 326

  Carrot, 326

  Sapodilla, 326

Savoury

  Cassava, 326

  Conch, 60

  Corn, 139

  Fish, 139

  Fish Roe Cassava, 138

❋ **Frosting(s)**

  Cocoa Whipped Cream, 314

  Creamy, 314

  Rum Whipped Cream, 314

  Whipped Cream, 314

❋ **Fruit**

  Frozen Slushie, 345

  Fruity Yogurt Cups, 345

  Tropical Yogurt Pie, 289

  Glazes, 316 -317

  Goombay Fruit Salad, 70

  Puffs, 278

  Summer Kabobs, 55

  Drops, 327

  Plum Punch, 50

  Tropical Punch, 50

  Sherbet, 344

❋ **Fruitcake(s)**

  Banana, 299

  Cookies, 308

  Miniature, 300

  Holiday, 298

Fu Fu, 251

❋ **Fudge(s)**

  Butterscotch, 353

  Coconut, 354

  Divine Rum, 354

  Fabulous, 353

  Peanut Butter, 353

George's Chicken & Dumplin', 116

Gin & Coconut Water, 377

Gin & Sin, 377

❋ **Ginger**

  Beer, 46

  Bread Collier Boys, 313

Conch, 169

Fish Sauce, 261

Fried Plantain, 244

Limeade, 45

Mashed Potatoes, 246

Seafood Sauce, 262

Spicy Ginger Scampi, 177

Glazed Cornish Hens, 190

❋ **Glazes**

Fruit

  Pineapple, Mango, Guava, Sapodilla, 316

  Orange, 317

  Rum, 316

  Tamarind Honey, 264

Goat - See Curried Goat

Golden Gravy, 266

Goombay Fruit Salad, 70

Avocado, Orange, Grapefruit, Salad, 71

❋ **Gravy(ies)**

  Brown, 265

  Golden, 266

  Roux, 265

❋ **Green Banana**

  Polenta, 136

  Sauté, 245

Green Mango Filling, 334

Green Mango Tart, 277

❋ **Green Pepper**

  Stuffed, 243

Green Pigeon Peas Soup, 112

Green Plantain Sauté, 245

Green Tomatoes See Curry Fried

❋ **Grilled**

  Polenta Squares, 226

394

Tamarind Guava Chicken, 185

Turtle Steaks, 177

❀ **Grits** *(See also Corn Grits)*

Bahamian Pigeon Peas &, 221

Barefoot, 221

Black-eyed Peas &, 208

Cat Island Corn & Crab, 222

Corned Beef Saute & Grits, 129

Croquetts, 222

Seasoned, 221

❀ **Grouper**

Abaco Baked with Stuffing, 160

Boiled, 128

Broiled Cutlets, 162

Cutlets, 163

Curried, 121

Fillets in Burnt Orange, 166

Fillets with Banana Batter, 164

Fingers, 163

Tamarind Guava Fingers, 164

Guacamole, 65

❀ **Guanahani**

Conch, 168

Tomato Sauce, 259

❀ **Guava**

Caribbean Cobbler, 322

Cheese, 366

Chocolate Jelly Roll, 330

De-light, 374

Double Boiler Duff, 338

Duff, 337

Duff Cake, 307

Filling, 333

Grilled Tamarind Chicken, 185

How to prepare, 26

Illustration & History, 336

Jam, 361

Jam Cake, 302

Jelly, 359

Muffins, 86

No Bake Cheesecake, 343

Petit Duffs, 99

Pickled Guava Peel, 367

Purée, 26

Roly Poly, 339

Sawyer's Guava Jelly Roll, 330

Slice & Bake Cookies, 308

Surprise, 322

Swirls, 98

Tamarind Grouper Fingers, 164

Tamarind Paste, 366

Tamarind Rum Balls, 63

Turnovers (Fried Pies), 275

Upside Down Cake, 302

Yamacraw Cheesecake, 342

❀ **Guinep**

Jelly, 361

Juice, 26

Punch, 52

How to prepare, 26

Illustration & History, 64

Roasted Seeds, 354

Royale, 63

❀ **Guyanese Dishes**

Tej's Metagee

Pepperpot, 115

❀ **Ham**

Avocado Eggs &, 131

Avocado Egg Sandwiches, 140

Harvey's Marinade, 264

Hatchet Bay Rice (Dirty Rice), 214

Heritage Crab & Dough, 201

High Tea Cookies, 309

❀ **Hog Plum**

Jelly, 359

Juice, 28

Punch, 51

❀ **Holiday**

Fruit Cakes, 298

Turkey Salad, 79

Holiday Turkey Sandwiches, 141

Turkey Soup, 110

❀ **Honey**

Rum Baked Bananas, 324

Tamarind Glaze, 264

❀ **Hurricane**

Ham Stew, 118

Jack, 371

Ice Tea See Tropical Solar Ice Tea

Independence Swizzle, 371

Individual Conch Pizzas, 149

Island

Corn Grits, 220

Corn Grits Stuffing, 233

Boy, 380

Breezes, 378

Girl, 380

Ice Balls, 52

❋ **Ice Cream(s)**

Banana Créps & Icecream, 347

Coconut Rum Raisin, 346

Sapodilla Cup, 348

Mango Crêpes &, 348

Rum Raisin, 346

Soursop, 348

Tropical Banana Split, 349

Tropical Cake Roll, 349

Vanilla with Mango Syrup, 345

Independence Swizzle, 371

Individual Conch Pizzas, 149

Island Boy, 380

Island Breezes, 378

Island Corn Grits, 220

Island Corn Grits Stuffing, 233

Island Girl, 380

❋ **Jamaican Dishes**

Beef Patties, 152

Peas & Rice, 209

Salt Fish & Akee, 159

Tia Maria Bread, 94

❋ **Jam(s)**

Guava, 361

Mango, 362

Pineapple, 362

Sea Grape, 362

❋ **Jellies**

Guava, 359

Guinep, 361

Hog Plum, 359

Mango, 359

Pineapple, 361

Scarlet Plum, 359

Sea Grape, 359

Jelly Bag, 358

❋ **Jelly Rolls**

Sawyer's Guava, 330

Chocolate Roll, 330

Pineapple, 330

❋ **Jerk**

Burgers, 150

Chicken, 192

Chicken Wings, 192

Pork Chops, 193

Beef Ribs or Pork Roast, 193

Beef or Pork Ribs, 193

Rotisserie Chicken, 192

John Canoe Punch, 371

❋ **Johnny Cake(s)**

Coconut, 89

Deluxe, 88

Traditional, 88

❋ **Juices**

Hog Plum, 28

Papaya, 46

Papaya Orange, 46

Scarlet Plum, 28

Sea Grape, 28

Kahlúa Zesty Barbeque Sauce, 261

Kalik Junkanoo Rarebit, 134

Key Lime Rum Pie, 290

Kidney See Steak & Kidney Pie

LaRoma Cola, 378

Laura's Banana Pancakes, 133

❋ **Lamb**

Crown Roast, 198

Lemon & Garlic Lamb Chops, 199

Lemon Sauce for Desserts, 317

Lemon Syrup for Lemonade, 318

Lemonade, 43

❋ **Lime**

Avocado Lime Pie, 279

Ginger Limeade, 45

Key Lime Pie, 290

Switcher (Limeade), 43

Tequilime Pie, 288

❋ **Lunch Dishes**

Avocado, Tomato Stars & Bread Cups with Salads:

Chicken, Crawfish, Egg,

Shrimp, Spicy, Turkey, 141

Baked Avocado Seafood, 142

Baked Potatoes

Conch Chili, 147

Corned Beef Baked, 143

Smoked Oyster Baked, 144

Breadfruit French Fries, 142

Burgers

  Jerk Burgers, 150

  Conch Burgers, 149

Conch

  Chili, 150

  Chili Baked Potato, 147

  Pockets, 151

Fritters

  Cassava, 326

  Corn, 139

  Fish, 139

  Fish Roe Cassava, 138

Jamaican Beef Patties, 152

Pizzas

  Conch Pizza, 147

  Individual Pizzas, 149

Quiches

  Bacon Coconut, 145

  Curried Seafood, 144

  Quick Stove Top Tuna Casserole, 141

Sandwiches

  Banana Peanut Butter Spread, 140

  Chicken Salad, 141

  Corned Beef, 141

  Egg Salad, 140

  Avocado Eggs & Ham, 140

  Holiday Turkey, 141

  Spicy Tuna, 141

  Zippy Cheese, 140

Tofu

  Fried, 145

  Chili,

  Ginger Sautéed with Pork, Beef, Chicken, Shrimp or Crab Meat, 146

✽ **Macaroni**

  Quick Stove Top Tuna Casserole, 142

  Salad, 74

  Savoury Macaroni & Cheese, 228

  Sauté Macaroni Bake, 228

Mahi Mahi (Dolphin), 161

✽ **Mango**

  & Pineapple Strudel, 321

  Bread, 92

  Azaleta's Chicken, 185

  Chutney, 363

  Crêpes & Ice Cream, 348

  Dip, 66

  Double Boiler Duff, 338

  Duff, 337

  Glaze, 316

  Salsa, 66

  Syrup & Vanilla Ice Cream, 345

  Tamarind Mango Chutney, 364

Green Mango

    Filling, 334

    Paradise Pie, 280

    Tart, 277

  How to prepare, 27

  Illustration & History, 340

  Jam, 362

  Jelly, 359

  Midnight, 374

  No Bake Cheesecake, 343

  Pie, 291

  Punch, 50

Roly Poly, 339

  salsa, 66

  Shake, 47

  Short Cakes, 323

  South Beach Cheesecake, 341

  Syrup, 318

Margarita, 378

✽ **Marinade(s)**

  Beer for Meat, 264

  Harvey's, 264

✽ **Mashed Potato**

  Potato Dressing, 233

  Potato Salad, 73

  Potato Carrot, 246

✽ **Meat Pie(s)**

  Chicken Pie with Cassava Crust, 187

  Conch Pockets, 151

  Family Breakfast Pie, 135

  Jamaican Beef Patties, 152

  Steak & Kidney Pie, 191

  Turtle, 178

Crust(s)

  Crust for 9-inch Meat Pie, 272

  Seasoned Crusts for Meat Pies, 273

✽ **MEAT DISHES**

Cakes

  Corned Beef, 195

  Crab, 200

  Salmon, 167

Poultry Dishes

  Oven Fried Chicken Bites, 184

  Chicken in Coconut Batter, 184

  Grilled Tamarind Guava Chicken, 185

  Jerk Chicken, 192

Jerk Chicken Wings, 192

Chicken Vegetable Stir Fry, 186

Chicken Pie with Cassava Crust, 187

Rotisserie Jerk Chicken, 192

Savoury Chicken Rissoles, 188

Chicken Rissoles in Mushroom Sauce, 188

Mock Drumsticks, 189

Stove Top Baked Cornish Hens, 189

Glazed Cornish Hens, 190

Barbeque Pineapple Turkey Roll, 188

Beef

Baked Canned Corned Beef, 195

Barbeque Sesame Beef Strips, 190

Beef with Oriental Vegetables, 194

Corned Beef Cakes, 195

Jerk Beef or Pork Ribs, 193

Jerk Beef or Pork Roast, 193

Sherry Beef Bites, 61

Lamb

Crown Roast, 198

Lemon & Garlic Lamb Chops, 199

Steak & Kidney Pie, 191

Pork

Jerk Pork Chops, 193

Jerk Barbecue Ribs, 193

Stir Fry Pork in Garlic Sauce, 196

Roast Pork Calypso, 197

Jerk Roast, 192

❀ **Land Crabs**

Andros Stuffed Baked, 200

Cakes, 199

Soufflé, 223

Heritage Crab & Dough, 201

Zesty Boiled, 200

❀❀ **MEAT SAUCES & GRAVIES, 255 - 266**

Barbecue Poultry Sauce, 261

Cheese Sauce, 257

Cocktail Sauce, 260

Créole Sauce, 259

Curry Sauce, 257

Deluxe Curry Sauce, 258

Guanahani Sauce, 259

Kahlúa Barbecue Sauce, 261

Mint Sauce, 258

Nut Sauce, 258

Pizza Sauce, 260

Tarter Sauce, 258

White Sauce, 257

Seafood Sauces

Avocado Seafood Sauce, 257

Ginger Fish Sauce, 261

Fish Roe Sauce, 262

Seafood Sauce, 260

Ginger Seafood Sauce, 262

Seafood Tamarind Butter, 263

Conch Sauce, 263

Marinades & Glazes

Beer Marinade, 264

Harvey's Marinade, 264

Tamarind Honey Glaze, 264

Gravies

Brown Flour Stew, 266

Brown Gravy, 265

Golden Gravy, 266

Roux, 265

Midnight Mango, 374

Moonlight Mango, 374

Merdina Carrot Cake, 305

Metagee See Tej's Guyanese

Mince Meat Turnovers (Fried Pies), 275

❀ **Mince(s)**

Minced Crawfish, 173

Mixed Mince, 173

❀ **Miniature**

Bread Puddings, 332

Fruitcakes, 300

❀ **Mint**

Sauce, 258

Salad Dressing, 80

❀ **Mock**

Boiled Fish, 128

Drumsticks, 189

Pink Champagne, 46

Molasses Muffins, 87

Montego Bay Colada, 379

Mousse See Cheesecake with Poached Plums

❀ **Muffins**

Banana Whole Wheat, 87

Guava, 86

Molasses, 87

❀ **Mutton**

Stew, 120

Smudder (Steamed), 123

❀ **Mushroom**

Onion Soup, 105

Polenta Squares, 226

Chicken Rissoles in Sauce, 188

No Bake Cheesecakes
Banana, 343
Guava, 333
Mango, 343
Pineapple, 343
Sapodilla, 343
Nell's Peanut Cakes, 357
No Bake Tropical Crunches, 342
No Need to Knead Pie Crust, 270
North Eleuthera Pineapple Fries, 328
Nut Sauce, 258

Ocean Breeze, 374
Okra
& Rice, 217
Soup, 113
Ole Nassau Rum Cake, 301
Olga's Pound Cake, 296
Onion Mushroom Soup, 105
Oven Fried
Chicken Bites, 184
Salmon Steaks, 167
Scallops, 160
Sword Fish, 159
Orange
Avocado Grapefruit Salad, 71
Grouper Fillets in Burnt Orange, 166
Papaya Juice, 46

Sweet Potato in Shells, 250
Sweet Potato with Peel, 251
Oyster See Corn Bread & Oyster Stuffing

Paella (Spanish Rice), 215
Pancakes
Carib Potato, 134
Laura's Banana, 133
Sapodilla, 133
Papaya
Daiquiri, 49
How to prepare, 28
Illustration & History, 48
Juice, 46
Orange Juice, 46
Paradise Pie (Green Mango), 280
Paradise Pie à la Mode, 280
Party Drummetts, 62
Pasta
Chicken Rissoles on, 188
Macaroni Salad, 74
Sauté Macaroni Bake, 228
Savoury Macaroni & Cheese, 228
Seafood Stuffed Shells, 229
Paste See Tamarind Paste
PASTRIES, PIES & TARTS, 267 - 292
Bananas in Blankets, 275
Crispy Sapodilla Rollups, 279
Crusts & Pie Shells
Cassava Crust, 272

Coconut Crust, 270
Corn Meal Pastry, 272
Crumb Crust, 270
Crust for Turnovers, 274
No Need to Knead Crust, 270
Pie Shell 9-inch, 271
Pie Shell 9-inch Double, 271
Pizza, 273
Seasoned Crust for Meat Pies, 273
Fruit Puffs, 278
Pies
Avocado Lime, 279
Bahamian Pumpkin, 283
Caribbean Sweet Potato, 282
Cocoa Rum, 281
Key Lime Rum, 290
Mango, 291
Paradise (Green Mango), 280
Rum Pineapple Custard, 282
Sapodilla, 285
Soursop, 285
Sugar Apple, 286
Tequilime, 288
Tropical Yogurt, 289
Pâté
Smoked Fish Roe, 58
Patties See Jamaican Beef Patties
Peach
Coconut Cobbler, 329
Peach Turnovers (Fried Pies), 274
Peanut
Nell's Cakes, 357
Popcorn Balls, 358
Peanut Butter Fudge, 353
Butter Guava Sandwich Spread, 140

Pepper Conch & Rice, 212

Peppers See Green Stuffed

Pepperpot See Guyana Pepperpot

Petits Guava Duffs, 99

❀ **Pickles**

Almond Meats, 367

Guava Peel, 367

Pies & Shells See Pastries Pies & Tarts

❀ **Pigeon Peas**

Bahamian Peas & Grits, 221

Baked Pigeon Peas & Rice, 206

Conch & Peas & Rice, 208

Crab & Peas & Rice, 210

Green Soup, 112

How to prepare, 31

Jamaican Peas & Rice, 209

Soup & Dumplin', 111

Piña Colada Cake, 295

Fruit Salad Dressing, 80

❀ **Pineapple**

Banana & Bacon, 134

Barbecue Turkey Roll, 188

Chicken, 185

Chutney, 364

Daiquiri, 49

Duff, 337

Filling, 334

Glaze, 316

Jam, 362

Jelly, 361

Jelly Roll, 330

Loaf-a-Bread, 92

Mango Strudel, 321

North Eleuthera Fries, 328

Roly Poly, 339

Rum Custard Pie, 282

Rum Fizz, 375

South Eleuthera Cheesecake, 342

Sweet Potato Drops, 250

Tart, 277

Pinwheels See Tuna Pinwheels

❀ **Pizza**

Bites, 60

Conch, 147

Crust, 273

Individual Conch, 149

Sauce, 260

❀ **Plantain**

Cakes, 244

Chips, 55

Crisps, 56

Drops, 245

Fried, 244

Ginger Fried, 244

Green Plantain Sauté, 245

Santa Maria, 225

Plantation Sour, 380

Pockets See Conch Pockets

❀ **Polenta**

Coconut, 136

Green Banana, 136

Grilled Squares, 226

Polenta (Plain), 226

Slices, 226

Spicy Corn Cups, 227

Squares, 226

Squares with Mushrooms, 226

With Cheese Sauce, 227

❀ **Popcorn**

Carmel Balls, 358

Peanut Balls, 358

❀ **Pork**

Fried Rice, 213

Guyana Pepperpot, 115

Jerk Pork Chops, 193

Jerk Barbecue Ribs, 193

Roast Calypso, 197

Smudder Pork Chops, 123

Stir Fry in Garlic Sauce, 196

❀ **Potato**

Au Gratin, 232

Carib Pancakes, 134

Carrot Mash, 246

Conch Chili Baked, 147

Corned Beef Baked, 143

Cream Soup, 109

Croquets, 247

Ginger Mashed, 246

Mashed Dressing, 233

Mashed Salad, 74

Savoury Salad, 73

Smoked Oyster Stuffed, 144

See also Sweet Potato

❀ **Pound Cakes**

Big Gramma's, 296

Big Gramma's Marble Birthday, 297

Olga's, 296

Piña Colada, 295

❀ **Poultry**

Chicken

George's & Dumplin', 116

Caribbean Salad, 78

Grilled Tamarind/Guava, 185

Hatchet Bay Rice, 214

In Coconut Batter, 184

Jerk, 192

Azaleta's Mango, 185

Mock Benné, 189

Oven Fried Bites, 184

Party Drummetts, 62

Pie with Cassava Crust, 187

Pineapple, 185

Rissoles in Mushroom Sauce, 188

Rissoles on Pasta, 188

Rotisserie Jerk, 192

Salad, 77

Savoury Rissoles, 188

Souse, 122

Vegetable Stir Fry, 186

Cornish Hens

Glazed, 190

Stove Top Baked, 189

Turkey

Barbecue Pineapple Roll, 188

Holiday Salad, 79

Holiday Soup, 110

Souse, 122

❋ **Pudding(s)**

Banana, 331

Banana Rum Bread, 331

Coconut, 332

Miniature Bread, 332

Sapodilla, 333

❋ **Pumpkin**

& Rice, 217

Bahamian Pie, 283

Soup, 104

Puffs See Fruit Puffs

❋ **Punch(es)**

Anguilla, 377

Hog Plum, 51

John Canoe, 371

La Roma Cola, 378

Mango, 50

Rum Pineapple Fizz, 377

Scarlet Plum, 51

Sea Grape, 50

Solar Rum, 375

Soursop, 51

Tamarind, 52

Tropical Fruit, 50

Tropical Plum, 50

❋ **Purée(s)**

Guava, 26

Tamarind, 26

❋ **Quiche(s)**

Bacon Coconut, 145

Curried Seafood, 144

❋ **Quick Dishes**

Curried Shrimp, 176

Sliced Conch Salad, 76

Stove Top Tuna Casserole, 141

❋ **Raisin**

Coconut Bread, 93

Rum Ice Cream, 346

Nut Turnovers (Fried Pies), 275

Rum Rice, 214

Scones, 89

Rarebit See Kalik Junkanoo

Red Snapper See Samana Baked

❋ **Ribs**

Jerk Beef, 193

Jerk Pork, 193

❋ **Rice**

& Fish Croquetts, 220

Bahamian Pigeon Peas &, 206

Baked Black-eyed Peas, 208

Baked Pigeon Peas, 208

Barefoot, 206

Beef Fried, 213

Black-eyed Peas &, 208

Brown Rice Croquettes, 219

Browned Rice, 215

Cabbage &, 217

Casserole, 218

Chicken Fried, 213

Conch & Peas &, 208

Conch Fried, 213

Corned Beef Loaf, 218

Crab & Peas &, 210

Crawfish Fried, 213

Curried, 211

Dressing, 234

Hatchet Bay (Dirty Rice), 214

Jamaican Peas &, 209

Okra &, 217

Paella, 215

Pepper Conch &, 212

Pork Fried, 213

Pumpkin &, 217

Rum Raisin, 214

Seafood Baked with, 208

Seasoned, 216

Shrimp Fried, 213

Tamarind, 216

Wild Rice Cakes, 219

Wild Rice Stuffing, 235

❋ **Rissoles**

Chicken in Mushroom Sauce, 188

Conch, 170

Conch in Shrimp Sauce, 171

Fried, 62

Savoury Chicken, 188

❋ **Roast(s)**

Jerk Beef & Jerk Pork, 193

Pork Calypso, 197

❋ **Rollups**

Banana in Blankets, 275

Crispy Sapodilla, 279

❋ **Rolls**

Clover Leaf, 97

Dillie Dinner, 97

Stuffed Cabbage, 242

❋ **Roly Poly(s)**

Coconut, Dillie, Guava, 339

Mango, Pineapple, 339

Rotisserie Jerk Chicken, 192

Roux, 265

❋ **Rum**

Balls, 63

Banana Bread Pudding, 331

Banana Sunset, 373

Barbecue Bananas, 325

Blue Dolphin, 374

Cappuccino Shakes, 373

Chick Charney Moca Cookies, 311

Cocoa Pie, 281

Coconut Raisin Ice Cream, 346

Divine Fudge, 354

Ginger Limeade, 45

Glaze, 316

Honey Baked Bananas, 324

Key Lime Pie, 290

Ole Nassau Cake, 301

Pineapple Custard Pie, 282

Pineapple Fizz, 375

Raisin

Ice-cream, 346

Nut Turnovers (Fried Pies), 275

Rice, 214

Scones, 89

Rickey, 371

Runner Brown Sugar Sauce, 315

Guinep Royale, 63

Soka Hard Sauce, 315

Solar Punch, 375

Tamarind Guava Ball, 63

Tropical Shakes, 373

Whipped Cream Frosting, 314

Zombie,373

❋ ❋ **SALADS & SALAD DRESSINGS, 67 - 82**

Salads

Avocado, 70

Avocado, Orange Grapefruit, 71

Beet, 71

Breadfruit, 75

Cabbage Slaw, 73

Dill Seed Cucumber in Sour Cream, 71

Goombay Fruit, 70

Macaroni, 74

Mashed Potato, 74

Savoury Potato, 73

Meat Salads

Caribbean Chicken, 78

Chicken, 77

Corned Beef, 79

Egg, 79

Holiday Turkey, 79

Seafood Salads

Crab Meat, 77

Crawfish, 76

Quick Sliced Conch, 76

Shrimp, 77

Sir Clifford's Conch, 75

Spicy Tuna, 78

Salad Dressings

Avocado, 80

Cucumber, 81

Hot Benné Seed, 81

Mint, 80

Piña Colada Fruit, 80

Slaw, 81

❋ **Salmon**

Cakes, 167

Oven Fried Steaks, 166

Stuffed Tomatoes, 167

Samana Baked Red Snapper, 156

Salsa See Mango Salsa

❋ **Sandwiches**

Banana Peanut Butter Spread, 140

Chicken Salad, 141

Corned Beef, 141

Egg Salad, 140

Avocado Eggs & Ham, 140

Holiday Turkey, 141

Spicy Tuna, 141

Zippy Cheese, 141

San Juan Colada, 379

❋ **Sapodilla** *See also Dillie*

Bundt Cake, 304

Crispy Rollups, 279

Filling, 335

Fox Hill Cheesecake, 342

Fritters, 326

How to prepare, 27

Illustration & Description, 96

No Bake Cheesecake, 343

Pancakes, 133

Pie, 285

Pudding, 333

Stuffed Baked, 328

Syrup, 318

Tart, 277

Turnovers (Fried Pies), 275

Waffles, 133

❋ **Sardine**

Canapés, 58

& Grits, 130

Stuffed Eggs, 61

❋ **Sauce(s)**

Dessert

Coconut Cream, 317

Lemon, 317

Rum Runner Brown Sugar, 315

Soka Hard Rum, 315

Meat Sauces

Avocado, 257

Barbecue Poultry, 261

Cheese, 257

Cocktail, 260

Créole, 259

Curry, 257

Deluxe Curry, 258

Guanahani Tomato, 259

Kahlúa Barbecue, 261

Mint, 258

Nut, 258

Pizza, 260

Tarter, 258

White, 257

Seafood

Conch, 263

Fish Roe, 262

Ginger Fish,

Ginger Fish, 261

Seafood, 260

Seafood Tamarind Butter, 263

Sauté Macaroni Bake, 228

Sautéed Ginger Tofu, 146

❋ **Savoury**

Chicken Rissoles, 188

Macaroni & Cheese, 228

Potato Salad, 73

Sawyer's Guava Jelly Roll, 330

Scallops See Oven Fried

Scampi See Quick Currie

❋ **Scarlet Plum**

Jelly, 359

Juice, 28

Punch, 51

Scones – See Rum Raisin Scones

❋ **Sea Grape**

Jam, 362

Jelly, 359

Juice, 28

Punch, 50

❋ **Seafood**

Sauté Macaroni Bake, **228**

Avocado Seafood Sauce, **257**

Baked Avocado, 142

Casserole, 179

Ginger Seafood Sauce, 262

Oven Fried Scallops, 160

Quick Curried Shrimp, 176

Sauce, 260

Smoked Oyster Stuffed Potato, **144**

Stuffed Pasta Shells, **229**

Tamarind Butter, 263

❋ **Seasoned**

Crust for Meat Pies, 273

Grits, 221

Rice, 216

Seeds See Roasted Guinep

❋ **Sesame (Benné) Seed**

Benné Cakes, 357

Bread Sticks, 97

Hot Benné Seed Dressing, 81

❋ **Shakes**

Banana, 47

Cappuccino Rum, 373

Mango, 47

Tropical Rum, 373

❋ **Sherry**

Beef Bites, 61

Bananas with Cream, 325

❋ **Short Cakes**

Mango, 323

❋ **Shrimp(s)**

& Avocado Cânapés, 56

Beer Battered, 176

Carib Fried Shrimp, 174

Curry in a Hurry, 175

Fried Rice, 213

Salad, 77

Quick Curried, 176

Spiced Ginger Scampi, 177

Spice Bag, 367

❁❁ **DINNER SIDE DISHES, 203 - 236**

Casseroles & Pasta Dishes

Breadfruit Cheese, 230

Cassava, 230

Conch & Beer, 231

Crab Soufflé, 223

Potato Au Gratin, 232

Sauté Macaroni Bake, 228

Savoury Macaroni & Cheese, 228

Seafood Stuffed Pasta Shells, 229

Grits

Bahamian Pigeon Peas &, 206

Barefoot, 206

Black-eyed Peas &, 208

Cat Island Corn & Crab, 222

Croquettes, 222

Island Corn, 220

Seasoned, 221

Polenta

Grilled Squares, 226

Polenta (Plain), 226

Slices, 226

Spicy Corn Cups, 227

Squares, 226

Squares with Mushroom, 226

With Cheese Sauce, 227

Plantain & Banana

Green Banana Sauté, 245

Green Plantain Sauté, 245

Santa Maria, 225

See also Rice Dishes

Stuffings & Dressings

Corn Bread & Oyster Stuffing, 235

Island Corn Grits Stuffing, 233

Mashed Potato Dressing, 233

Rice Dressing, 234

Stuffing for Fish, 234

Wild Rice Stuffing, 235

❁ **Slaw**

Cabbage, 73

Dressing, 81

Skillet with Bacon Top, 243

Slice & Bake Guava Cookies, 308

Sliced Breadfruit with Bacon, 249

Slushie See Frozen Fruit

❁ **Smoked**

Fish Roe Canapés, 58

Oyster Stuffed Potatoes, 144

Soka Hard Rum Sauce, 315

Solar Rum Punch, 375

Soufflé see Crab Soufflé

❁❁ **SOUPS, STEWS & CURRIED DISHES, 101 - 124**

Curried Dishes

Chicken, 121

Conch, 121

Goat, 121

Grouper, 121

Soups & Chowders

Avocado Soup, 104

Bahamian Conch Chowder, 108

Beer Cheese Soup, 105

Charline Cabbage Soup, 110

Clam Chowder, 108

Cream of Potato, 109

Creamy Cassava Soup, 106

Okra Soup, 113

Onion Mushroom Soup, 105

Pumpkin Soup, 104

Vegetable, 124

Hearty Soups & Stews

African Beef Stew, 119

African Chicken Stew, 119

Conch Au Vin, 116

George's Chicken & Dumplin', 116

Green Pigeon Peas, 112

Guyana Pepperpot, 115

Holiday Turkey Soup, 110

Hurricane Ham Stew, 118

Mutton Stew, 120

Pigeon Peas Soup & Dumpling, 111

Stewed Conch, 121

Stewed Fish, 120

Tej's Guyanese Metagee, 114

Turtle Soup, 117

Souses

Chicken, 122

Turkey, 122

Conch, 122

Smudder (Steamed) Dishes

Chicken, 123

Chops, 123

Conch, 123

Fish, 123

Mutton, 123

❁ **Soursop**

Coconut, 375

Daiquiri, 49

How to prepare, 27

Ice Cream, 349

Illustration & History, 284

Filling, 335

Pie, 285

Punch, 51

South Beach Mango Cheesecake, 341

South Eleuthera Pineapple
Cheesecake, 342

❀ **Souse(s)**

Chicken, 122

Conch, 122

Turkey, 122

Spanish rice See Paella

Spiced Ginger Scampi, 177

❀ **Spicy**

Conch, 169

Conch in Shrimp Sauce, 171

Harvard Beets, 240

Tuna Salad, 78

Squares See Grilled Polenta

Stars See Tomato Stars

Steak & Kidney Pie See English

*Smudder (Steamed) Dishes See
Soups & Stews*

Stewed Dishes See Soups & Stews

❀ **Stir Fry**

Chicken Vegetable, 186

Pork in Garlic Sauce, 196

Stove Top Baked Cornish Hens, 189

Strudel See Mango & Pineapple

❀ **Stuffed**

Baked Sapodilla, 328

Breadfruit, 249

Cabbage Rolls, 242

Green Peppers, 243

Tomatoes, 241

❀ **Stuffing**

Corn Bread & Oyster, 235

Baked Grouper, 160

For Fish, 234

Island Corn Grits, 233

Mashed Potato, 233

Wild Rice, 235

❀ **Sugar Apple**

Daiquiri, 49

How to prepare, 27

Illustration & History, 287

Filling, 335

Pie, 286

Summer Fruit Kabobs, 55

❀ **Sugar Cane**

How to prepare, 28

Illustration & History, 303

Surprise See Guava Surprise

❀ **Sweet Potato**

Caribbean Pie, 282

Fu Fu, 251

In Orange Shells, 250

Pineapple Drops, 250

With Orange Peel, 251

Swirls See Guava Swirls

Switcher, Bahamian Limeade, 43

Sword Fish See Oven Fried

❀ **Syrup(s)**

Lemon for Lemonade, 318

Mango, 318

Sapodilla, 318

❀ **Tamarind**

& Rice, 216

Baked Banana In Sauce, 325

Chutney, 363

Cooler, 45

Grilled Guava Chicken, 185

Guava Grouper Fingers, 164

Guava Paste, 366

Guava Rum Balls, 63

Honey Glaze, 264

Mango Chutney, 364

Paste, 366

Punch, 52

Puree, 26

Seafood Butter, 263

Tarter Sauce, 258

❀ **Tarts (9x12-inch)**

Coconut, Dillie, Pineapple,

Green Mango, 277

See also Turnovers

❀ **Tartlets**

Dried Fruits & Tropical Fillings, 278

❀ **Tia Maria**

Cheese Straws, 57

Jamaican Bread, 94

Tia Shake, 378

❀ **Tofu**

Chili, 146

Fried, 145

Sautéed Ginger with Pork, Beef,
Chicken, Shrimp or Crabmeat 146

❀ **Tomato**

Crumb Bake, 241

Curry Fried Green, 240

Salmon Stuffed, 167

Star, 240

Stuffed, 241

Stuffed with Eggs, 131

Tortilla Sandwich Cookie, 310

❀ **Tropical**

Banana Split, 349

Cake & Ice Cream Roll, 349

Fruit

Drops, 327

Fillings, 332 - 335

Punch, 50

Sherbet, 344

Plum Punch, 50

Rum Shakes, 373

Solar Iced Tea, 43

❀ **Tuna**

In Avocado Half, 141

Pinwheels, 59

Quick Stove Top Casserole, 141

Spicy Salad, 78

Tomato Star, 141

Bread Cup, 141

❀ **Turkey**

Barbecue Pineapple Roll, 188

Bread Cup, 141

Holiday Salad, 79

Holiday Soup, 110

In Avocado Half, 141

Souse, 122

Tomato Star, 141

❀ **Turnovers (Fried Pies)**

Apple, 275

Apricot, 275

Mince Meat, 275

Peach, 274

Rum Raisin Nut, 275

❀ **Turnovers (Fried Pies) with Tropical Fillings,** 275

Coconut, Sapodilla, Green

Mango, Pineapple,

❀ **Turtle**

Pie, 178

Grilled Steaks, 177

Soup, 117

Upside Down Cake See Guava

Vanilla Ice Cream & Mango Syrup, 345

❀❀ **VEGETABLES, 237 - 254**

Akara (African Bean), 252

Cabbage

Chinese, 242

Skillet Slaw with Bacon Top, 243

Stuffed Rolls, 242

Plantain

Baked, 246

Cakes, 244

Drops, 245

Fried, 244

Ginger Fried, 244

Potato

Carrot Mash, 246

Croquettes, 247

Ginger Mashed, 246

Potato (Sweet)

in Orange Shells, 250

with Orange Peel, 251

Pineapple Drops, 250

Fu Fu, 251

Tomato

Curry Fried Green, 240

Crumb Bake, 241

Stuffed, 241

Star, 240

Sliced Breadfruit with Bacon, 249

Spicy Harvard Beets, 240

Stuffed Green Peppers, 243

Vegetable Soup, 124

Waffles See Sapodilla Waffles

Whipped Cream Frosting, 314

Whiskey Sour, 381

White Sauce, 257

❀ **Wild Rice**

Cakes, 219

Stuffing, 235

❀ **Whole Wheat**

Banana Muffins, 87

Bread, 95

406

Yamacraw Guava Cheesecake, 342

❀ **Yogurt**

Fruity Pie, 289

Fruity Cups, 345

❀ **Zippy Cheese**

Cânapés, 57

Pinwheels, 58

Sandwiches, 140

Zesty Boiled Crabs, 200

Zombie, 373

Bibliography

The Archives, Public Records Office, Nassau Bahamas

The Nassau Public Library, Nassau Bahamas

The Life of Admiral Christopher Columbus, Ferdinand Columbus

The Life and Times of Columbus, Paul Hamlyn

Christopher Columbus, his gastronomic persona, Lucio Sorre

Seeds of Change, Herman J. Viola and Carolyn Margolis

Fifty Tropical Fruits of Nassau, Kendal and Jula Morton

Fruits and Vegetables of the Caribbean, M. T. Bourne and G. W. Lennox

Fruits of warm climates, Julia F. Morton

The Aboriginal Inhabitants of the Islands of the Bahamas, Starks History & Guide to the Bahamas

The Story of the Arawaks, Desmond V. Nicholson

Photographs by Derek Smith include: pineapple p. 360; plantain p. 29; cassava p. 30; almond p. 368.

Photograph of Their Excellencies by Franklyn Ferguson